DIRT DON'T BURN

DIRT DON'T BURN

A BLACK COMMUNITY'S STRUGGLE FOR EDUCATIONAL EQUALITY UNDER SEGREGATION

Larry Roeder and Barry Harrelson

Contributing Authors: Anthony Arciero, Nathan Bailey, Emily Branch, Gert Evans, Mallika Lakshminarayan, and Dave Prebich, with the help of many volunteers.

GEORGETOWN UNIVERSITY PRESS / WASHINGTON, DC

The publisher is not responsible for third-party websites or their content. URL links were active at time of publication.

Library of Congress Cataloging-in-Publication Data

Names: Roeder, Larry W., author. | Harrelson, Barry, author.
Title: Dirt don't burn : a Black community's struggle for educational equality under segregation / Larry Roeder and Barry Harrelson.
Description: Washington, DC : Georgetown University Press, 2023. | Includes bibliographical references and index.
Identifiers: LCCN 2022051077 (print) | LCCN 2022051078 (ebook) | ISBN 9781647123635 (hardcover) | ISBN 9781647123642 (ebook)
Subjects: LCSH: African Americans—Education—Virginia—Loudoun County. | Segregation in education—Virginia—Loudoun County. | Education—Virginia— Loudoun County. | African Americans—Virginia—Loudoun County—Social conditions.
Classification: LCC LC2802.V8 R64 2023 (print) | LCC LC2802.V8 (ebook) | DDC 379.2/630975528—dc23/eng/20230221
LC record available at https://lccn.loc.gov/2022051077
LC ebook record available at https://lccn.loc.gov/2022051078

♾ This paper meets the requirements of ANSI/NISO Z39.48-1992 (Permanence of Paper).

24 23   9 8 7 6 5 4 3 2 First printing

Printed in the United States of America

Cover design by Faceout Studio, Tim Green
Interior design by Classic City Composition

CONTENTS

PREFACE
A Historical Perspective

When you see something that is not right, you must say something. You must do something. Democracy is not a state. It is an act, and each generation must do its part to help build what we called the Beloved Community, a nation and world society at peace with itself.

—John Lewis, "Together You Can Redeem The Soul
of Our Nation," *New York Times*, July 30, 2020

This is the story of a brave people forced to become a part of the American scene, more often than not treated unjustly, generally discriminated against, and frequently persecuted; yet, despite these handicaps, a people who have contributed generously to American culture.

—Preface to *Cavalcade of the American
Negro*, The Black World's Fair, 1940

When I started at Loudoun Valley High, some students would still call Blacks, "Niggers." In fact, I passed up tryouts for the football and base-ball teams because I would have been the only Black on those teams. I wouldn't have lasted a week being called "Nigger" before they would have had to throw me off the team. I did join the wrestling team, partly be-cause I was not the only Black on this team. We would take a school bus to "away" meets at places like Front Royal, Winchester, and Manassas. Athletic events like this were one of the few instances where Blacks and whites would ride the same school bus.

—Louis Jett, speaking of the early days of integration,
September 15, 2020, interview with Nathan Bailey

This is the story of how the Black community in Loudoun County, Virginia, heroically struggled before integration for an education and equality. Described in the context of events going on elsewhere in Virginia and the nation, *Dirt Don't Burn* tells many stories of courage and perseverance, such as when hand-written petitions were sent to the superintendent of public schools by parents and teachers to convince the white government to install toilets, conduct urgent repairs, keep schools open, hire better teachers, or provide equal transportation and salaries.[1] These wonderful documents were discovered wrapped in butcher paper in a decayed former schoolhouse. In the days of segregation, petitions had been lovingly passed around at church sessions or door-to-door and are now living monuments to democracy because they not only document the past, they also remind us that the struggle for equal, quality education continues for all "minorities." Leaping hurdles for Black residents of the Northern Virginia county was constant. Following the "slave revolt of 1831," until 1865, it was very hard and sometimes illegal in Virginia to teach African Americans to read. That said, there were slave owners who defied the law out of necessity at times because a modestly literate enslaved person could be valuable to his enslaver.[2]

It is important to note that today's Loudoun County is politically and demographically quite different in racial relations from the periods of enslavement and segregation, although problems still exist. The school population is very diverse. For example, in the 2021–22 academic year, 42.7 percent of students were white, 25.4 percent Asian, 18.3 percent Hispanic/Latino, 7.1 percent Black / African American, 5.7 percent multiracial, 0.6 percent Native American, and 0.1 percent Pacific Islander. Loudoun is also regularly listed among the wealthiest counties in the United States, with a median income of over $140,000 (twice the national average) and an expanding population of over four hundred thousand as well as an economy dominated by technology firms. It has one of Virginia's largest school systems, with a student population of more than eighty-one thousand. Over the roughly one hundred years of this story, the county was rural, with an agriculture-based economy and a stable population of around twenty thousand. As of the printing of this book, problems of equity remain and must be addressed, but—in fairness— today's Loudoun is not the one described in the following pages.

Edwin Washington

The struggle's heart might best be understood through the narrative of one extraordinary sixteen-year-old Black waiter named Edwin Washington, who won his right to schooling during Reconstruction when the embers of the Civil War were still hot. At that point in history, race relations were awful. While African Americans could finally study legally, there were no free public schools to attend until 1870. Knowing that education was a foundation for advancement, African Americans of all ages (parents and children) flocked to every opportunity. By September 1866 the Freedmen's Bureau had supported nine schools and benevolent societies, including one founded by an "intelligent, educated Colored man," undoubtedly William Obediah Robey.[3] Reflecting racial tensions, some white Quaker teachers were chased out of Leesburg, the county seat, for being too friendly with the Black community. Opportunities existed, but Edwin had a special problem. He was a hotel waiter where the Circuit Court of Loudoun now sits, earning five dollars a month and board. This was a great job, not backbreaking like the one held by his elder brother Joseph, a farm laborer. Edwin's dilemma was

This charcoal rendering of Edwin Washington by Larry Roeder was the result of a community discussion with the Black History Committee of the Friends of the Balch Library in which members imagined what the youth looked like and how he dressed and walked. He is depicted walking up a hill to commemorate the struggle for equal, quality education.
Larry Roeder

that he could keep the job and support his mother and siblings, or he could go to school instead of working and try to pay the fee without an income and possibly end up poor and with an uncertain future. The potential economic risks were huge. His mother, Nellie, was illiterate and kept house; his father was absent. Edwin's eleven-year-old brother was in school, not earning money, and there was brother William, age three. Mouths had to be fed and clothes purchased. Edwin bravely decided to ask to keep his job while also attending school, and the hotel agreed, although only between errands and not on court days. The stories of the struggle for education are countless, but Edwin is the earliest-known example of a teenager accomplishing such a bargain, so he stands out for his courage and dedication.

When young girls and boys and their parents rushed to school to learn to read and write, they also learned of their rights as new citizens. We do not have access to all their stories, so once again Edwin represents all those people yearning for equality while also demanding quality education. It is a legacy not to be forgotten. In fact, in June 1867, as if writing for future generations, Washington said:

> I think it is a very good thing to go to school and learn to read and write. It is the first opportunity we ever had, and we ought to make good use of it. I think it will be a great improvement to us. We ought to love our teacher, and mind her and respect her; and if we love her, she will love us, and we ought to love and respect everybody.[4]

Unfortunately, despite many efforts, we don't know anything about Edwin's later years. His Quaker teacher, Caroline Thomas, wrote, "I almost tremble for his future." However, the disappearance is not surprising. White historians were not interested in publishing biographies of Black members of the laboring class. There were famous Black individuals who rose from bondage in Loudoun, such as William H. Ash, one of Virginia's most famous educators, but it is in the success of historically minor figures—frequently quiet heroes who rise above seemingly insurmountable hurdles—that we often find the soul of a society. That was Edwin, the project's namesake. Despite his disappearance into history's shadows, he continues to inspire.

"Dirt Don't Burn" was the name of the project's countywide conference in 2018 inspired by memos written by a modern hero of Black education, Ethel Ray Stewart Smith. During the winter of 1955, her one-room schoolhouse ran out of coal. She wrote a letter to the superintendent saying they were "down to dirt, which doesn't quite burn." The Edwin Washington Project (EWP) team was so inspired by this modern young Black teacher's courage to confront the school system leadership that, after consulting Ethel, a version of her words led to the conference title. Her complaint was symbolic of a lack of proper attention to resources needed to provide an equal education for Black students through much of the public school era in Loudoun County. The present book is published during the Black Lives Matter movement, which has parallels to the civil rights movement of the 1950s and 1960s. We believe that Black *history* also matters.

The Value of Conversation

America is an increasingly diverse society, yet still full of prejudice. But the EWP team believes a careful study of history can contribute to a healthy, sustainable future without systemic racism. Society must learn from past mistakes, from heroes like Edwin and his teachers and many others. This study is not about assigning guilt to the contemporary generation, but these lessons will help locate the formula for a necessary conversation enabling society to map new paths. Put another way, one lesson from the research has also been that laws and court cases alone will not derail prejudice, nor will they by themselves change philosophy. That requires dialogue and understanding, a healing effort that the federal government failed to achieve during Reconstruction. Understanding that concept, in 2000 a biracial committee of Loudoun residents formed the Black History Committee of the Friends of the Balch Library. Its goal is "to preserve, collect, promote, and share the history of African Americans who contributed to the emergence and development of Loudoun County, Virginia," which it does through research, interviews, oral histories, and events.[5] Debates within its discussions have proven invaluable in clearing up historical misunderstandings and giving the

Pastor Carlos Lawson
of the Prosperity
Baptist Church.
*Photo courtesy of
Larry Roeder, 2014*

Black community a vibrant voice for truth. Over the years, the committee has also become one of the most respected history-oriented bodies in the county as well as an essential partner to the Edwin Washington Project (EWP).

The EWP has its origins in Prosperity Baptist Church in the tiny village of Conklin in southeast Loudoun County. The church was founded by formerly enslaved Americans who initially prayed in each other's homes, much like the earliest Christians, having no formal religious structure of their own. Later, evangelist Jennie Dean, herself a formerly enslaved person and a cousin of one of the community members, helped fund the construction of Prosperity Baptist Church. Prosperity was also associated with the Conklin Colored School, built a short distance away in 1872, only two years after the beginning of public education in Virginia. Descendants of the original parishioners still pray in the church. Freed from bondage, Black citizens wanted an education to better their economic prospects as well as the social and moral stability brought by organized religion. Those twin desires were seen in Black educational efforts from emancipation through Reconstruction to court-mandated integration in Loudoun in 1968, and even beyond.

In 2014 Prosperity's pastor and his congregation asked Larry Roeder to uncover the church's history. They shared their records, deeds, old tax receipts, memorabilia, and school files. Roeder also needed to know who attended or instructed at the school, what was taught, and how the Black educational experience compared to that of white counterparts. Loudoun's school system had lost most of its records from 1870 to 1968 as well as pre–public school files on educating the indigent back to the 1830s. Fortunately, not long before the Prosperity research began, Loudoun County Public Schools (LCPS) found the files in the 1880s era "colored" Training Center in Leesburg.

Saving History

The Edwin Washington Project might not have happened at all if not for a true hero to history—Donna Kroiz, then head of the LCPS Records Office. The state's education system wanted the old records to be destroyed—they would possibly scan them first, but they did not want to store them. Donna strongly objected, feeling that the many thousands of fragile files in the Training Center were historically important. Donna's action, and that of the superintendents we worked with, were important civil rights decisions that preserved Black history and that were strongly supported by the entire Virginia House and Senate in a joint resolution in March 2016, thanks to the intervention of then-delegate John

Bell.[6] Following the study of the Conklin Colored School, the EWP was officially born with the support of superintendents of LCPS Dr. Edgar Hatrick III and Dr. Eric Williams, who felt Loudoun's Black population had an absolute right to know what happened during segregation. The EWP team also suggested expanding the mandate, feeling that all Americans should be aware of this history, to include recent residents of Loudoun as well as those born in lands still suffering from repression. Dr. Hatrick agreed that Black history was relevant to the entire world because so many "minority" groups have suffered in the past and continue to do so.

The volunteers of the EWP and its parent 501(c)3, the Edwin Washington Society, are dedicated to the proposition that the lessons of Loudoun's past can help us all navigate the challenges of the present and the future. We also believe that to tell that story, we must authentically represent the voices of Loudoun's Black community.

Key Observations

The research detailed in this book has led the team to important observations. The first is that the core rationale for denying proper education, health care, political and economic power, and other aspects of life for Black students, such as school bus transportation, was appalling.[7] It was based on a belief in a hierarchical relationship, which argued that white people were somehow more human, more deserving of respect, and more fully citizens than Black people.

Productive change requires historical study, mature reflection, and conversation. The team interviewed some people who opined that it is unfair to criticize past leaders, saying this "rewrites" history, that those people lived in a time with different ethics. They also did not think it was fair to criticize the school system for being slow to provide racial equality. However, while the team acknowledges that the politics of the segregated era made progress difficult to achieve and even dangerous, the team also believes that recognizing past deliberate choices is responsible history telling, not "cancel culture," as is often alleged. We attempt in these pages to present that history in an accurate, objective way, believing it is important to honestly preserve both good and bad, to contribute to the record of Loudoun County's and America's past. The book also provides context but leaves to the reader to judge the past or whether progress has been sufficient.

For perspective, consider that the first to die for the American Revolution was a Black stevedore named Crispus Attucks. Described as a leader, Attucks was killed during the Boston Massacre of March 5, 1770, with "his breast leaning on a stout cordwood stick."[8] In Loudoun, John Chubb, James Morton, Charles Pierpoint, Joseph Proctor, Samuel Russell, and Abraham Warren also enlisted in the cause.[9] African Americans, including those in Loudoun County, have taught Americans about honor and bravery in every conflict, dying or being maimed for a country that did not provide equality. The monument in Leesburg for World War I veterans until recently separated the names of Black veterans from whites. The surgical experiments in Alabama by J. Marion Sims on innocent enslaved women—all without anesthesia—and the supporters of the Tuskegee "syphilis" study who perpetrated a life of pain and suffering on many young Black men in Loudoun and elsewhere, were unquestionably unethical.[10] The decisions that led to unequal medical care cannot be explained away by saying they happened in some distant, forgettable past. In other words, as Loudoun County Public Schools acknowledged in 2020, it is altogether fair to complain about segregation and its components as demonstrably unethical and a stain on the souls of the white leadership of that era, whether moderates (as some were) or violent segregationists like Senator Harry Flood Byrd Sr., who created the "massive resistance" policies. Their actions caused future generations of students to suffer, even after integration.

In the records researched by the EWP, we found stories of true heroes. These were real people who demonstrated grace and quiet courage under extraordinarily difficult circumstances. We focus on education, but the larger context of American society must also be kept in mind. The system of apartheid that existed from the end of the Civil War until the 1954 Supreme Court decision in *Brown v. Board of Education* (and beyond) affected every aspect of life for Black American citizens. Despite the dangers, these brave citizens of Loudoun County organized, petitioned, and even brought legal action to propel change and secure the blessings of liberty for themselves and their children.

Again, Black History Matters.

Signed,

The Directors and Officers of the Edwin Washington Society, which owns the Edwin Washington Project on behalf of its volunteers

Larry Roeder, founder, Chairman of the Board and CEO of the Edwin Washington Society

Neil Steinberg, Vice President, the Edwin Washington Society

Nathan Bailey, Secretary, Chief Historian on Transportation

Randy Ihara, Treasurer

Hari Sharma, Chief Financial Officer

Anthony Arciero, PhD, Director of the Edwin Washington Project

Julie Goforth, Chief Technology Officer

Carlos Lawson, Pastor of the Edwin Washington Society

Gert Evans, Board Adviser, Research Docent, and Volunteer

Sherri Jones Simmons, Board Adviser

Dave Prebich, Chief Historian on Petitions

Larry Roeder and Barry Harrelson, coauthors

Significant contributions are also made by Anthony Arciero, Nathan Bailey, Emily Branch, Christopher Brown, Gert Evans, Lori Kimball, Mallika Lakshminarayan, Carlos Lawson, Dave Prebich, Stephen Price, Eugene Scheel, Wynne Saffer, Claude Saffer, Edward Spannaus, members of the Black History Committee, and many volunteers.

Notes

1. Although often called county superintendent, the formal name in Virginia is division superintendent. Whites also effectively used petitions. The difference is that Black people had to overcome the class struggle of being kept behind whites.

2. Eugene Scheel, "Timeline of Important Events in African American History in Loudoun County, Virginia," *The History of Loudon County, Virginia,*

accessed September 29, 2020, http://www.loudounhistory.org/history/african
-american-chronology.

3. The formal name for the Freedmen's Bureau was the US Bureau of Refugees, Freedmen, and Abandoned Lands.

4. Caroline Thomas, "Going to School," *Friends Among the Freedmen*, no. 9, June 27, 1867, in *Friends' Intelligencer*, Vol. 24, by JME (Philadelphia: Friends Intelligencer Association, 1868), 332.

5. See Friends of Thomas Balch Library, *The Essence of a People: Portraits of African Americans Who Made a Difference in Loudoun County, Virginia* (Leesburg, VA: Black History Committee of the Friends of the Thomas Balch Library, 2001); and Kendra Y. Hamilton, ed., *The Essence of a People II, African American Who Made Their Worlds Anew in Loudoun County and Beyond* (Leesburg, VA: Black History Committee of the Friends of the Thomas Balch Library, 2002).

6. Virginia House of Delegates Joint Resolution No. 527, agreed to by the Virginia House of Delegates, March 9, 2016, and by the Virginia Senate, March 10, 2016. Bell is now a state senator.

7. Many interviews of former Black and white school bus drivers and passengers were conducted for this study. They are all reproduced in full on the project website at edwinwashingtonproject.org. The Edwin Washington Society also holds many videos on transportation and maintains a YouTube channel and a Facebook site.

8. Frederic Kidder, *History of the Boston Massacre, March 5, 1770: Consisting of the Narrative of the Town, the Trial of the Soldiers and a Historical Introduction* (Albany, NY: Joel Munsell, 1870), 6.

9. Paul Heinegg, "List of Free African Americans in the Revolution: Virginia, North Carolina, South Carolina, Maryland and Delaware (followed by French and Indian Wars and colonial militias)," *Free African Americans*, accessed October 26, 2020, www.freeafricanamericans.com/revolution.htm.

10. Meagan Flynn, "Statue of 'Father of Gynecology,' Who Experimented on Enslaved Women, Removed from Central Park," *Washington Post*, April 18, 2018; and Brynn Holland, "The 'Father of Modern Gynecology' Performed Shocking Experiments on Enslaved Women," History.com, August 29, 2017.

A NOTE ON ARCHIVAL CITATIONS

Many of the documents and photographs cited in the book are fragile artifacts discovered in a cache of thousands of items in a largely abandoned nineteenth-century school for African Americans in Leesburg, Virginia. These are being studied by a nonprofit called the Edwin Washington Society, and most have not yet been placed on the internet, so when cited in the book, the catalog number, which begins with EWP, is provided to facilitate email retrieval. Readers wanting access can write to the Project Docent (edwinwashingtonprojects@gmail.com) for copies, or request permission to visit the Edwin Washington Research Center in Leesburg, which opened in the spring of 2023. Keep in mind that some documents can only be handled with gloves and while wearing a face mask. Summary descriptions of the materials and related research efforts can also be found at edwinwashingtonproject.org, which will be undergoing significant enhancements in 2023, including adding access to a database and digital map.

INTRODUCTION

I am not one of those who believe that it is well to educate the mass of Negroes with academic or university education. On the contrary, I am firmly convinced that the hope of the Negro is in industrial education throughout the south and in teaching him to be a better farmer ... and to make more blacksmiths and more good farmers than there are now amongst the Negroes.

> —President William Howard Taft, letter read at
> the forty-fifth commencement, Fisk University,
> Nashville, Tennessee, June 14, 1911

Common school education should be free for all American children and compulsory. High school training should be adequately provided for all, and college training should be the monopoly of no class or race in any section of our common country.

> —W. E. B. Du Bois, "The Niagara Movement,
> Declaration of Principles," written for the annual
> meeting at Buffalo, New York, July 1905

No one desires litigation. But if the Negro citizens are forced to court for the protection of their constitutional rights, I hope the officials and white population of the county will recognize that we are fighting to preserve democratic rights in a free country, and that democracy is as democracy does.

> —Charles Hamilton Houston, dean of Howard
> University's Law Department, May 1940

Genocide does not happen by accident; it is deliberate, with warning signs and precursors. Often it is the culmination of years of exclusion, denial of human rights and other wrongs. Since genocide can take place in times of war and in times of peace, we must be ever-vigilant.

—Miguel de Serpa Soares, Undersecretary-General for Legal Affairs and United Nations Legal Counsel, December 6, 2017

We lived in tenant housing. My brothers and sisters and I rode O. Ray Stewart's bus (#34) to Carver. The buses were older with worn, uncomfortable seats and torn or missing rubber floor mats. It wasn't hard to notice the buses carrying white students were generally newer. The bus would pick up Black students living on other farms and along rural routes in the area. The route to Carver was a mixture of paved and dirt roads until we reached Purcellville. Those dirt roads were bumpy, narrow, and very twisty in places. If we met oncoming traffic, we would have to slow down and pull over onto the grass to allow the vehicles to pass one another. When the roads were dry, it would make for a dusty ride. If the weather was warm enough, we'd have the bus windows down and the dust would flow throughout the interior of the bus. I noticed that some of the roads in front of white homes would have been sprayed with oil. That would keep the dust down from passing vehicles. Which probably also protected any laundry that was hung out to dry from the dust. I used to wonder where they got the oil.

—Howard Timbers

The Beginnings of Anger

From the beginning of transatlantic slave trade, from the slave markets of Africa to the wretched sea voyages across the Atlantic to North America itself, enslaved persons such as Nat Turner in Virginia (1831) and others manifested their anger with rebellions. African Americans were justifiably angry over disproportionate deaths and injuries to their people, and over their treatment as inferior creatures who were incapable—other than by the exceptional—of attaining white accomplishments. For all his zeal about all people being created equal, Thomas Jefferson and many of his contemporaries agreed that Black people were not and should not be equal. Jefferson's 1784 statements on the inferiority of the Black race in *Notes on the State of Virginia* would be used well into the twentieth century to justify suppression of African Americans. Even many abolitionists did not support integration of the races. This attitude of Jefferson's, while not universal, was common in the elite white populace and thus enabled efforts that buried Black history and accomplishments.

A lack of preservation efforts in current society can still hinder understanding Black history, even when suppression is not the aim. This consistent attempt to bury or minimize Black history and accomplishments derives from the notion that Black Americans were not worthy of full citizenship. Even the graveyards of the formerly enslaved in Loudoun County, Virginia, have often been neglected for decades until local churches, the NAACP, or other friendly groups take direct action. At the largely white Harmony church in Hamilton, all gravestones—a form of record—of Black individuals were removed in the past and shifted to a corner of the cemetery and then embedded like dominoes in cement. That direct act went beyond neglect, so to their great credit, the church in 2021 and 2022 decided to use ground-penetrating radar to document the area occupied by the graves and the location of a Reconstruction-era school. While the identity of individual graves will be lost, the space they occupied will be known.

Also, in Loudoun County, thousands of segregation era school records lay forgotten in the 1882 wooden "colored" schoolhouse known as the Leesburg Training Center until the staff of the Records Office of Loudoun County Public Schools (LCPS) discovered them. The structure had no electricity, heating, or cooling and was infested with rodents and insects when the EWP team visited the building in 2016. The lower floors were sometimes covered in the spoor of wildlife, and holes existed on the top floor. In fact, during a photo shoot with some team members in 2019, bits of the exterior walls blew off in a mild breeze. The building was a disaster zone. On a third trip in the spring of 2022, a few additional files were found covered in dust on a shelf.

What LCPS staff found buried under layers of dirt accumulated over nearly a half century was a true treasure trove of historical documents. Maps, pictures, and handwritten ledgers dating back to the middle of the nineteenth century were among the many thousands of pages. LCPS

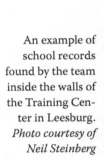

An example of school records found by the team inside the walls of the Training Center in Leesburg. *Photo courtesy of Neil Steinberg*

had considered destroying the records, upon advice from the Virginia Department of Education, due to their age. Fortunately, Donna Kroiz, then head of the Records Office, resisted, fearing the erasure of an entire community's educational history. Later in 2016 Larry Roeder, Dave Prebich, and Anthony Arciero, along with LCPS staff, found additional records hidden away inside the very walls of the frame structure, found only by the chance flitting of a flashlight's beam on a glint of color peeking out of a loose joint of plank. After pulling the plank loose, a set of large ceiling tiles were removed. Each had been inscribed in the 1960s with information on classes, including from Douglass High School. No records have revealed why the tiles were stuck inside the wall.

The Leesburg Training Center records survived, including the tiles, and became the core of the Edwin Washington Project, along with interviews of survivors of segregation. Copies of other records from additional sources around Virginia; Washington, DC; and Atlanta, Georgia, have been added. The EWP has done this in the spirit of a broad level of belief across ethnic and political lines in Loudoun County that Black residents deserve to know a more complete history of the county, and this book seeks to support that belief by building an authoritative narrative.

What the records and interviews reveal is a tale of civil rights suppression in Loudoun before 1968 as well as brave resistance by African

Vandalized Ashburn Colored School.
Photo by Larry Roeder, 2017

Americans and some white individuals, especially in the field of education. The story is not isolated; rather, it is a part of a larger set of similar suppressions and resistance efforts in other Virginia counties and
throughout the South. For example, when segregation ended in neighboring Clark County, the local government literally buried Black school
records in the dirt. The only reason any survived to eventually be housed
in the Josephine School Museum in Berryville is that a Black teacher used
his bare hands to uncover them during the night. In 2016 in Ashburn,
Loudoun County, a private school for the gifted began reconstruction of
the segregated Ashburn Colored School, built between 1887 and 1892.
Teenage vandals then covered the school with obscenities. Fortunately,
public reaction was immediate, with citizens of various races, religions,
and political parties banding together to make repairs.[1] In Campbell
County in southern Virginia, which is where Loudoun's court records
and enslavement files were stored during the Civil War, the Black community recently used bake sales to fund their work and provided volunteers to restore one of the largest collections of Rosenwald schools
in America. The rationale for all these acts is that Black history matters and must not be suppressed. Unfortunately, suppression of ethnic

histories has been a plague of sorts around the world for thousands of years. This is something Larry Roeder came to see in Albania regarding the Romani people and in Egypt regarding Bedouins, in South Africa during the apartheid period. Therefore, the hope of the authors and volunteers of this effort is that the history our team is revealing will inspire other communities to preserve legacies, whether of Native American nations, of Black communities, or of any other suppressed people. The EWP team stands ready to help any wishing to do that.

Hurdles and Heroes

The first chapter of *Dirt Don't Burn* explores two race-based themes that developed during enslavement that haunted African Americans throughout the segregation era and to an extent are still troublesome. For example, the "inferior race" theory, which dominated slave-owning areas of the country, carried well into twenty-first century, where it fuels what has emerged as a violent "don't replace me" phenomenon in certain ultraconservative circles. The second example is "paternalism," which was found among many opponents of slavery, including abolitionists, Quakers and progressives who genuinely tried to help African Americans. Paternalism sometimes coalesced around deportation schemes to send free Black people "back" to Africa, even if they were born in the United States. The rationales behind the concept varied, and most Blacks were disinterested. Such schemes were paternalist in nature and presented an attitude of white government officials and leading citizens who saw themselves as doing "the right thing," despite racist implications. In their view, African Americans were not ready to manage their own destiny. This attitude of Black individuals and groups being unready prevailed throughout the segregated era in Virginia and certainly in Loudoun County. Put into a global context, similar "not ready" concepts delayed the advancement of Black populations in apartheid South Africa.

Regardless of the motivation of the founders of the various related movements, the efforts existed because the leaders could not envisage the possibility of equality and integration, a philosophy relevant to this story because it underpins an ongoing justification of unfair and unequal education and medical care. African Americans were often thought to be neither in need of an education nor capable of attaining one. Inequality in the health system also created mistrust, a legacy manifested today as caution in many Black communities over receiving vaccines during the COVID-19 crisis.[2]

Health inequity for Black Americans began with enslavement. Consider that before the Civil War, enslaved women were surgery test subjects for noted gynecologist James Marion Sims. He felt that Black women had a higher pain tolerance than white women, obviating the need for anesthesia. Such practices on anyone were declared crimes against humanity in the Nuremberg trials following World War II. Lower standards of health care for Black citizens continued during segregation, bringing health disparities across the region and in Loudoun County, including unequal access by Black students. Although separated widely by time, the attitudes of Sims and later physicians like Dr. Paul Brandon Barringer, professor of medicine at the University of Virginia, influenced people to agree to eugenics legislation.[3] The laws were described by some as progressive because of their stated use of science to "improve humanity." The concepts were embedded in Virginia's sterilization law in 1924 and a second eugenics law in 1927. Although marriage between African Americans and whites had been restricted in Virginia since colonial times, the 1927 Racial Integrity Act made it unlawful for Blacks or anyone with nonwhite blood to marry whites (the "one drop" theory). Some experts today agree that Virginia's coercive laws fit the United Nations' definition of genocide.[4] Unfortunately, Thomas Jefferson and Virginia's eugenicists provided a unifying scientific theory to justify suppression. Harvey Jordan, professor of genetics at the University of Virginia, proposed laws to preserve the white race as early as 1912, which raises a question about white-designed health and sanitation rules for schools. Students and teachers need to be healthy; otherwise, they cannot succeed. But why would Blacks submit to white health rules if past experiences led them to distrust white medical practices? This realization would eventually lead to Black leaders, through the Hampton (Virginia) Institute and the Tuskegee (Alabama) Institute, recommending their own health and sanitation guidance for Black schools throughout the South. It also underpinned health efforts by the Negro Organization Society (NOS), which we discuss later in the book.

In 1863 came Lincoln's Emancipation Proclamation, followed by the end of the Civil War in 1865 and Union control of the former Confederacy.[5] Prospects initially looked up for African Americans (at least regarding the law), but words on a paper during a terrible armed conflict fought over the right to enslave were not enough to mollify inbred hatred or mistrust of Blacks among both the South's former upper class and ordinary citizens, or to significantly modify long-held ignorance or behavior. In the great debacle of Reconstruction following Lincoln's assassination, the provision of schooling for Black students in Virginia was poorer than for whites, and that educational disparity in Loudoun and elsewhere continued for a century until 1968, when federal courts ordered integration. During that extremely difficult period, Black residents in Loudoun County stood tall and expressed themselves with rallies, written petitions, or speeches and pronouncements in churches; at teacher institutes, which were official gatherings of instructors; and Parent-Teacher Association meetings and with the help of attorneys in the twentieth century. Unfortunately—it needs to be said—systemic racism still exists.

As already noted, the atmosphere for change was rough just after the Civil War when Edwin Washington made his epic move. Race relations were frankly raw, and the smoke of the recent conflict still hung in the air. Consider an article in a Leesburg local paper in February 1866: "A teacher in a negro school in Farmville, named J. W. Davis, got nicely thrashed a day or two ago, by a sensible Federal soldier, named Allan, for uttering seditious speeches, telling the negroes they were as good as the whites, if not better. Served him right."[6]

During Reconstruction, Blacks were elected for the first time as delegates to the General Assembly of Virginia and took the momentous step of helping design the public school system. Also for the first time, Black Americans could obtain a free education. Black residents in Loudoun already saw the value of positive educational experiences with the Quaker schools and Freedmen's Bureau schools. Some public schools were set up by the community, such as the Bluemont Colored School, which started in 1878, or were held in buildings that were continuations of prewar Quaker efforts, such as in the village of Waterford. The Black

Odd Fellows Lodge in Hamilton, about 1935. School functions were on the first floor. The building was demolished in the 1960s to make way for a home. *Courtesy of Virginia State University*

Odd Fellows fraternity in Hamilton and the Black Willing Workers Club in Purcellville also shared their buildings for schooling purposes.

Rough school conditions in Loudoun provided uninviting environments for students and teachers, and the treatment of students could be brutal in the early decades of Loudoun's public education. In chapter 3, we follow the growing inequality in education in Loudoun County due to "Jim Crow" in the early post–Civil War era and the challenges faced by the Black community to obtain education for their children.[7] Many buildings for Black students consisted of one poorly ventilated and cramped room, usually led by a single teacher. Outhouses, which teachers and students shared, were often of poor quality, and as late as the 1920s, urine and liquefied waste could seep out and be tracked into the classroom. Many white one-room schoolhouses were as bad.

Despite these hardships, Black educators improved their professionalism and the quality of student learning experiences through attendance at segregated normal schools, the precursors of today's historically Black colleges and universities, or at teacher institutes, which were county-level committees of instructors.

Typical one-room school construction. Round Hill Colored, about 1940. The building was also used for Black teacher institutes. Outhouses are on the right and left.
Courtesy of EWP Archives

Another problem faced by Black teachers was prejudice in textbooks. *Jack, Jill, and Tot* (1883), used in Loudoun, is a good example.[8] In keeping with the attitudes expressed by Jefferson in his *Notes on the State of Virginia,* this book portrayed African Americans as indigent, dirty, and lazy in the protection of their infants.[9] Indeed, even into the 1970s, the official Virginia history textbook taught Black students a perverted story of their forebearers' legacy, saying that "negroes grew to love the work and play on the plantation" and that "they worked hard in Africa, and so work on the Virginia plantations wasn't too hard on them."[10] The true tragedy and immorality of slavery—that families could be split apart at an owner's whim, like warm bread—was played down by the curriculum. The textbook also bolstered the myth of a race incapable of responsibility or social advancement.

How, then, did Loudoun's Black community react and make its case for equal education? Every state, city, village, and county has stories, some based on a mix of philosophies by two hugely prominent Black in-

From Emma E.
Brown, *Jack, Jill
and Tot* (1883).
*Courtesy of Jim
Roberts, private
collection of former
Loudoun textbooks*

tellectuals, Booker T. Washington, and W.E.B Du Bois.[11] Those stories
were at work in Loudoun even before the two giants articulated their
own ideas. In a speech on September 18, 1895, at the Cotton States Exposition, Washington proposed that the "Negro problem" would be solved
through gradualism and accommodation. That certainly described some
actions in Loudoun because the reality was that segregation was entrenched in the power structure, at least in part based on bad science.
Consider how racialized the health policy impacted all Black Americans,
including in Loudoun County. Some of this was based on a major study
by Prudential Insurance of Chicago, "Race Traits and Tendencies of the
American Negro," which proposed that African Americans were not
worth insuring because they were becoming extinct.[12] Extinction would
not come from the terrible conditions imposed on Blacks by whites; instead, racial decline was a result of inherited and inferior "race traits,"
according to Frederick Hoffman in 1896. If the Black race was destined
to extinction due to inherent weaknesses, why insure them—why even
provide other basic services?

Just four years after the Prudential study, Dr. Barringer gave a speech
on February 20, 1900, that was distributed to all medical societies in the
southern states.[13] Barringer said that the Black population should have
benefited from slavery, but centuries of servitude had not wrung out of
them a biological tendency toward savagery: "Not being able to resist

his impulses, he has no fixed purpose, no resolve, and the result, no pertinacity. The outcome of this moral deformity is a creature which . . . had made the ideal slave."[14] These are the narratives that helped sustain a legacy of white supremacy.

Between Washington's speech at the Cotton States Exposition in 1895 and Du Bois's seminal work *The Souls of Black Folk: Essays and Sketches*, published in 1903, was the 1902 Virginia Constitution, a great stain on the state's legislative reputation; it put into law the revocation of true democracy, making it essentially impossible for Blacks to vote, run for office, or have any meaningful say in political development or education. National racial issues in the first decades of the twentieth century were also marked by an expansion of Jim Crow laws and anti-Black violence. The white supremacist Ku Klux Klan (KKK) gained political strength and received support directly from the White House as President Woodrow Wilson screened the racist film *Birth of a Nation* in 1916 and segregated the federal work force in Washington, DC. In response, Black leaders and communities organized to challenge these forces and improve the health and education of African Americans. Chapters 4 and 5 (covering 1902–30) focus on the impact of these trends on Loudoun's schools and explain how Blacks and their supporters carried out their fight against the growing education and health disparities that threatened their lives and their futures.

In 1903, perhaps as a reaction to Barringer, Du Bois challenged Washington's theories in *The Souls of Black Folk* when he asked for direct, public action, and there were many direct acts of public bravery in Loudoun. In fact, the story of Black educational courage in Loudoun County is a legacy of people who collectively built a strategy for equality and stood their ground. Over time, teacher and parent actions, personal petitions, legal briefs, and collective action in Virginia knocked down segregation's walls like Gabriel's trumpet bringing down the walls of Jericho. Most important, the descendants of segregation have insisted to the EWP team, was the personal resolve of their ancestors working together, from the search for doctors and nurses needed to prevent and treat illnesses without prejudice to the political struggle for an accredited high school and modern school buildings. It is important to emphasize that equality did not arise from the labors of individual action alone.

It was sometimes inspired by leaders across the state and the nation, which is the way of all great civil rights movements. There were also dedicated teachers, who often served as both educators and social workers, who created alliances with parents and their fellow teachers to challenge the impact of segregation. And there were white residents who actively made common cause with Black community members in this fight.

One lesson of education learned by Edwin Washington and his contemporaries in the Reconstruction era was the constitutional right to assemble, to associate for common cause. In the early twentieth century this was done through the NOS, founded in 1912 at the Hampton Institute. The NOS had grown out of conferences held at Hampton and gave Black citizens a public voice through talented leaders like Booker T. Washington and Robert Russa Moton. Initially, it was simply about the social, civic, intellectual, industrial, and moral betterment of the Black man as expressed in various essays in the "Report of the Hampton Negro Conference" in 1907.[15] It set about recommending new health practices for African Americans and professionalizing teachers. Eventually this objective evolved into fostering local networks, such as the County-Wide League of Black PTAs, one of which formed in Loudoun in 1938 and would help Black residents lobby for better quality education. The NOS would also play a central role improving Black health. In addition, civic-minded white individuals ran supportive philanthropies to enhance Black education, like the Peabody Education Fund (commonly known as the Peabody Fund); the Slater Fund; and the Jeanes Fund, which supported Black teachers, and to build schools and provide library books, like the Julius Rosenwald Fund (also known as the Rosenwald Fund).[16]

Once again showing that Black Americans were unwilling to sit back and let fate take its course, Du Bois and Washington led the push to address health inequity. In 1906 Du Bois made the case to end the health disparity with the white population caused by a maldistribution of resources and poverty, by segregation and prejudice. In 1914 Washington appealed for a practical health movement that became the National Negro Health Week, which lasted thirty-five years. Hunger is also a health disparity problem. Hungry students cannot study or learn well, so at the white teacher institute on October 11–12, 1917, participants discussed food conservation in the home and the provision of hot lunches, although there is no evidence that hot lunches were provided to "colored" students until the 1930s.[17]

Then the infamous Chicago race riot took place between July 27 and August 3, 1919, one of approximately twenty-five such events that year. The riots were bad enough; more important was the impact of Hoffman's "research" brought into focus by the lens of the study—the Chicago riot—by the Chicago Commission on Race Relations. Hoffman's legacy was an attitude that presented a clear and present danger to Black people across the nation. To avoid repeating the violence, the Chicago Commission required an understanding of what white people perceived as the problem and its solutions. The most shocking revelation was the "hope for a solution through the dying out of the negro race";[18] Hoffman's research had influenced white views and was fuel for attacks on African Americans. The spark for the riot itself was the Great Migration and the competition for jobs and housing, which was also why there was such an emphasis in the public school system to keep Black people on the farm. This fear of competition is an early link to the origins of the contemporary replacement theory.

The real tragedy of the "extinction theory" and other so-called solutions like mass deportation to Liberia, which were rejected by the commission, is that social leaders in a country founded on the promotion of liberty were seriously advocating ideas deleterious to the health and civil rights of its own citizens. If people really believed in genetic failure or that assimilation was impossible, why would the government feel compelled to provide equal health care to Black residents in Loudoun County or anywhere else in the former Confederate States—indeed, or equality of any sort? This convinced the NOS and other Black rights–oriented groups, including in Loudoun, to take charge of their own health prospects by generating policies that educated Black citizens on basic hygiene. This was essential because despite improvements in laws and procedures over the decades, Black students suffered from lower life expectancies and quality of life.

Apart from racism impeding health care in the schools or society, there was also a financial philosophy prevalent in Virginia that providing proper medical care for any student was not a taxpayer responsibility. Medical care was seen as the responsibility of parents, regardless of their economic standing, or of churches and philanthropists. This regressive policy inevitably and disproportionately affected both disadvantaged Black people and poor white farmers. Ironically, while the policy aimed to save money, it also reduced tax revenue by depressing economic activity. This would begin to change in the fall of 1914 when Loudoun citizens privately hired a county school nurse, the first in Virginia. In addition to providing medical support to the schools, the nurse made house calls, offering shots, inoculations, and basic medical care for ear infections and worms, especially hookworm.[19] At the time Loudoun County had a large population of poor farmers and, thus, the tax base could not support quality medical care for all.

The 1920s was a time of extreme civil rights stress. Race riots and mass killings of Black Americans like the Tulsa riot and increased political repression brought great challenges, but there were also important accomplishments for Loudoun's Black communities. Early in the decade, both Black and white teachers and parents began to vigorously exercise their rights as citizens by writing petitions to the government. Black residents asked to keep schools open, improve the quality of teachers, increase teachers' salaries, conduct repairs on school buildings, and even install toilets. By 1938 petitions also effectively demanded an accredited high school and adequate school transportation, yet by 1939 there were twenty-two white bus routes and only one Black bus route.

Until 1920 the closest Black students got to high school training in Loudoun (often called upper branch) was an occasional lecture in a one-room schoolhouse, often about physiology, unless they traveled to another county or to Washington, DC.[20] By 1910, however, whites gained Lincoln Public High School, which was accredited in the village of Lincoln.[21] In the 1920s John C. Walker took the first organized step toward a formal Black high school at the Leesburg Training Center. Already a leader in the teacher institutes, Walker began a limited program on the second floor of the Training Center, which would continue until a formal high school program was started in 1930 on the same floor under Edythe Harris.[22]

Also for the first time in 1920, Superintendent Oscar Emerick, who had been hired in 1917 after being principal of Round Hill High School and serving as a teacher and surveyor for the US Army in the Philippines,

Members and the mascot of the Edwin Washington Project at the back of the Training Center building in Leesburg. The volunteers are positioned on a line of buried "sanitary outhouse" vaults. *Courtesy of Neil Steinberg, 2019*

hired supervisory teachers in Loudoun. The supervisors were trained professionals who managed the rest of the teachers. Emerick included a Jeanes Fund teacher, Mary E. Peniston, to supervise Black teachers. Philanthropist Anna Jeanes created the Jeanes Fund in 1907 to train Black teachers and supervisors. Social work and advocating for fresh approaches in education and in health were typical of Jeanes teachers who by 1938 became a crucial part of improving Black schools. Through the efforts of the County-Wide League of Black PTAs and working with Black education leaders from Richmond and legal scholars from Howard University in Washington, DC, Jeanes teachers convinced Loudoun's white government to approve building the modern Douglass High School in Leesburg on land purchased by Black residents. The government, however, did not furnish it; that was left to the Black community.[23]

The need for leaders such as John Walker, Edyth Harris, and Mary Peniston who also were tied to the NOS was apparent. Economic and educational prospects for Black people in Virginia remained bleak, as noted in a Virginia government survey from the late 1920s: "Many of the negro schoolhouses and environs are extremely unsanitary, unsightly, and ill-adapted to the efficient training of negro children. There are many children who are not in school at all, either because they are too remote from a schoolhouse or because the compulsory school law is not

enforced with them.[24] This is regarded as a serious defect in the education of the negro in Virginia."25 The survey staff could have used their
observations to pivot toward true equality, but instead the report once
again proposed paternalism: "The survey staff believe that the best interests of the negro population and of the State are not promoted by imposing upon negroes the same type of education that is provided for the
white population. The negro population must continue to be engaged
principally in agricultural pursuits."26

This was certainly a reaction to the Great Migration of Black citizens
from the South to the industrial North, Midwest, and West, which began about 1915, a movement that continued into the 1970s. Six million
Black people left the South, left sharecropping, and left agriculture in
general.27 In addition, the Virginia government's policy provides a general context to all policies in Loudoun County and across the Commonwealth of Virginia during segregation, a tone across the spectrum of
Black education, to improve "negro" education through the paternalist
lens of helping an "inferior race." In other words, although Black people
had emerged from legal bondage, the state law did not recognize their
political right to true equality. They were once again considered lesser
souls—back to square one in the eyes of some—but most African Americans remained undaunted.

The 1930s and 1940s were dominated by the Depression and World
War II. In chapter 6 we discuss how Black residents of Loudoun County
continued their struggle to improve schools and student health care
during economic hardships of the 1930s. In the 1940s, with the assistance
of the growing national civil rights movement, Black residents achieved,
among other goals, the long-sought high school building dedicated for
Black students, Douglass High School. They also finally achieved equal
salaries for Black teachers.

Building on John Walker's efforts, Edythe Harris improved the high
school program on the second floor of the Training Center, but it was
difficult to implement because of a paucity of resources. Families had to
donate bottles and pans for chemistry classes and staff was limited. Still,
the program grew and included French as a foreign language for the first
time as well as lectures that caused Black students to consider the origins
of their social and political standing.28 What Harris accomplished in the

1930s affirmed what should have been obvious—that Black students were ready for a true high school. In 1941, thanks to the efforts of Jeanes Fund supervisor Gertrude Alexander, the County-Wide League, and Howard Law School dean Charles Houston, Douglass High School was the first high school building dedicated for Blacks in Loudoun. Part of the rationale for moving the Harris program to the new building was that the old Training Center was a true fire trap, with poor fire escapes and with outhouses instead of toilets. The irony is that the elementary program stayed at the Training Center for many years, despite the safety risks.

The 1930s were a dark time for the nation, beset by financial turmoil. In rural counties, Black and white Americans suffered tremendous hardships. Emerick had to fight for every dollar from any source for the school system. It was the beginning of national welfare. For example, a Roosevelt program sent a teacher around the county in her Model T to deliver hot lunches to Black and white schoolhouses. She also instructed parents in the safe preparation and preservation of foods to support better health and nutrition. While there were advancements in that area, African Americans nevertheless suffered from an infamous medical program that continues to throw a shadow over today's medical system, the Tuskegee Study of Untreated Syphilis in the Negro Male. The study was one of the health programs that caused mistrust among many in the Black community toward government-provided medical care.

Early measures at consolidation began with the white schools in Loudoun, starting with Hillsboro and the closing of Edge Grove and at Round Hill in 1910 when the Cherry Grove school closed. The notion was to combine white-student one-room schools into multiroom graded schools to enhance student educational experiences, and some transportation was made available, but not for Black schools. Consolidation of Black schools did not begin until 1945, thanks to efforts by the County-Wide League of Black PTAs and an instructor named Janie Redwood.

Legalized Segregation Fades Away

The 1950s and 1960s continued to bring hope as well as brutal suppression. When considering tools used to end the inequities embedded in

Loudoun's social order, one would be expected to cite the wisdom of the US Supreme Court's *Brown v. Board of Education of Topeka, Kansas* (1954). This decision refuted the theory behind segregation: that Black and white students should learn separately, due to the inferiority of Black students. It was also a repudiation of the false biology proposed by Frederick Hoffman. However, when reflecting on *Brown*, we are also drawn to John Marshall Harlan, Supreme Court associate justice from 1877 to 1911. He was the lone dissenter to the odious *Plessy v. Ferguson* decision, which *Brown* overturned. He wrote, "Our Constitution is color-blind and neither knows nor tolerates classes among citizens."[29]

The 1950s also marked the end of an era in Loudoun County. Oscar Emerick, the superintendent for public instruction in Loudoun, retired in 1957 after forty years in the position. At the time of retirement, partly due to losing much of his eyesight, he was considered by many to be the most influential man in Loudoun County, a reputation gained in no small measure by his struggle to keep the schools open during "massive

Undated early photo of Oscar Emerick.
EWP: 4.5 White Teacher Cards

resistance" and his support of advances in teaching and administration techniques. Emerick is an important and complex figure in the history of Loudoun public education. He led the consolidation and professionalization of the school system, speaking against inequality but also officially supporting segregation.

The 1960s were the stage for the last gasp of segregation. Whereas in the 1950s the power structure put up walls against all integration, destruction of those walls came through judicial decisions. The state pursued delaying actions and rules like the Freedom of Choice Plan, allowing students to choose their school so that white students need not study with Blacks. But a few Black students, under both the "choice plan" and court pressure, began attending Loudoun County high schools as early as 1962. Some had good experiences, but as will be seen later in this book, not all experiences went well. In 1967 the US District Court for the Eastern District of Virginia ordered Loudoun to comply with *Brown* and to fully integrate in the 1968–1969 school year.

After examining over a century of records from various archives, the Edwin Washington Society stands as a witness to the courageous and persistent but calm protest of Black individuals and communities against segregation's injustice. To paraphrase Roman emperor Justinian, with whom white high school students would have been familiar, justice is the "set and constant purpose which gives to every man his due."[30] To achieve justice for their people, the Black community had a fervent demand for education, using protests, discussion, petitions, collaboration with allied programs and networks, and the effective threat of lawsuits as steel threads in a fabric of heroism that deserves to be honored and remembered.

Notes

1. Danielle Nadler, "Teens Get Extensive Homework in Colored School Vandalism Case," *Loudoun Now* (blog), February 1, 2017.
2. US Department of Health and Human Services, Centers for Disease Control and Prevention, "Increasing COVID-19 Vaccine Uptake among Members of

Racial and Ethnic Minority Communities: A Guide for Developing, Implement-
ing, and Monitoring Community-Driven Strategies," January 28, 2021.

3. P. Preston Reynolds, "UVA and the History of Race: Eugenics, the Racial
Integrity Act, Health Disparities," paper in an occasional series about the findings of the President's Commissions on Slavery and on the University in the Age
of Segregation, *UVAToday*, January 9, 2020.

4. The Convention on the Prevention and Punishment of the Crime of Genocide was passed in 1948. It defines genocide as "acts committed with the intent
to destroy, in whole or in part, a national, ethnic, racial or religious group."

5. Emancipation was celebrated across the United States; in Loudoun, Black
citizens took a unique approach in the village of Hamilton in 1890 by creating the Loudoun County Emancipation Association, which continued until
1971. The source of information on this body is *In the Watchfires* by Elaine E.
Thompson, The Friends of the Thomas Balch Library, Leesburg, 2005. The term
"watchfires" is derived from the "Battle Hymn of the Republic," sung by Union
soldiers and ever since on Emancipation Day.

6. *Democratic Mirror*, February 7, 1866, p. 2, col. 1.

7. Jim Crow was a period between 1870 and the 1960s, when laws were passed
in the southern states to disenfranchise Blacks.

8. Emma Elizabeth Brown, *Jack, Jill and Tot* (Boston: D. Lothrop, 1883).

9. Thomas Jefferson, *Notes on the State of Virginia* (1785), ed. by Frank Shuffelton (New York: Penguin, 1999). A response to question by Francois Barbe-
Marbois, secretary of the French Legation to the United States.

10. "'Happy Slaves' Described In 7th Grade Virginia Textbook Used for
20 Yrs," Black History Collection, Civil Rights Heritage Museum Online, accessed August 8, 2020, https://Blackhistorycollection.org/2019/10/03/happy
-slaves-described-in-7th-grade-virginia-textbook-used-for-20-yrs/. The textbook is Francis B. Simkins, Spotswood H. Jones, and Sidman P. Poole, *Virginia:
History, Government, Geography* (New York: Scribner, 1957).

11. Du Bois was the first fellow of the Southern Education Foundation and a
founder of the NAACP in 1909.

12. Frederick L. Hoffman, "Race Traits and Tendencies of the American Negro," *American Economic Association* 11, no. 1–3 (1896): 1–329. See also Chicago
Commission on Race Relations, *The Negro in Chicago: A Study of Race Relations
and a Race Riot* (Chicago: University of Chicago Press, 1922), xxiii.

13. Hoffman, *Race Traits and Tendencies*. See also Chicago Commission on
Race Relations, *The Negro in Chicago*, xxiii.

14. Paul Brandon Barrington, *The American Negro: His Past and Future*
(Raleigh, NC: Edwards and Broughton, 1900), 9–21.

15. "Report of the Hampton Negro Conference," *Hampton Bulletin* 3, no. 3
(1907).

16. The Peabody Education Fund was created February 7, 1867, by George Peabody with a grant of $1 million, about $17 million in 2020 dollars. It was folded into the John F. Slater Fund in 1914.

17. EWP 4.2.A: Yr. October 11–12, 1917, White Teacher Institute.

18. Chicago Commission on Race Relations, *The Negro in Chicago*, xxiii.

19. Jim Rogers, interview by Larry Roeder, August 6, 2020.

20. Joel Dorman Steele's *Hygienic Physiology: Fourteen Weeks in Human Physiology* (New York: American Book, 1889) was the textbook used by Blacks in nineteenth-century Loudoun.

21. Lincoln was called Goose Creek until July 1865, when it was renamed for President Abraham Lincoln.

22. Teacher institutes are not normal schools, although both foster "normal," standard methods of learning. Normals were actual schools educating non-teachers to be educators. Teacher institutes were committees of licensed teachers that aimed to reach a common understanding of the proper educational goals for the term, as set by the local school board and the Virginia Department of Public Instruction.

23. On April 8, 1941, the board decided that "the colored high school be named Douglass High School in memory of Frederick Douglass."

24. This was important in the context of rural Virginia because early compulsory attendance laws did not apply to students living two miles from a school.

25. "Public Education in Virginia," report to the Educational Commission of Virginia (Richmond: Superintendent of Public Printing, 1928), 32.

26. "Public Education in Virginia," 32.

27. Isabel Wilkerson, *The Warmth of Other Suns* (New York: Vintage Books, 2011).

28. German was also taught to two students at the Willing Worker Colored School in Purcellville, during the academic year 1937–1938. EWP 6.1.2: Yr. 1937–1938, Register for Willing Worker School. Lead teacher Rosalie McWashington.

29. Charles Thompson, "Plessy v. Ferguson: Harlan's Great Dissent," originally published in *Kentucky Humanities*, no. 1 (1996), reprinted at https://louisville.edu/law/library/special-collections/the-john-marshall-harlan-collection/harlans-great-dissent.

30. John Baron Moyle, *The Institutes of Justinian* (Oxford: Clarendon, 1937).

1

THE AGE OF ENSLAVEMENT

In contrast to deprivations by other of our nation's founders against Blacks and their right to education, George Washington was different. He was the only founding father to manumit his enslaved people and provide for their education so that they might be productive free people.[1]

> In the name of God amen I George Washington of Mount Vernon—a citizen of the United States and lately President of the same, do make, ordain and declare this Instrument; which is written with my own hand and every page thereof subscribed with my name, to be my last Will and Testament, revoking all others. . . .
> Upon the decease of my wife, it is my Will & desire that all the Slaves which I hold in *my own right*, shall receive their freedom.
> —Last Will and Testament of George Washington, July 9, 1799

Understanding the story of school segregation requires a short dive into the foundations of white supremacy, including the attitudes of elites about funding public schools in the colony and the Commonwealth of Virginia, for poor white people or any Black person. For example, "of all the states in the Union, Virginia was perhaps the least disposed up to this date [1860] to adopt the common school system of the northern states of the Union."[2] Further, between the secession in 1861 until the Underwood Constitutional Convention, 1867–1868, the idea of free schools was essentially dead. Black delegates and others in favor of Reconstruction held the majority of seats in the convention. This provided the opportunity to enact reforms such as giving every male citizen, including Blacks, twenty-one years or older the right to vote and establishing a free public school system. (The 1870 Underwood Constitution will be discussed in more detail in chapter 2.)

So why did the elites tolerate—even extol—the inhumanity of enslavement that befell Black people before Lincoln's Emancipation Proclamation speech and how did that policy of white subjugation intersect with schooling? These issues, born in the age of enslavement, formed the dark philosophical foundations of Virginia education after 1865 until integration in 1968. Common threads include a lack of a schooling tradition, continuing negative attitudes toward Black citizens, control by white elites, and a reluctance to spend tax dollars on Black education.

This initial era was a time of great pain for America's Black population, whose stories often began with their journey as cargo in unlit lower decks of slave ships and whose lives then were managed by a system grounded in a belief in white superiority. It was also a time of great hesitancy by policymakers when they considered a free school system for either Black or poor white students.

Because of the actions of Washington, Jefferson, and other Virginian founders of the American Revolution, it is easy to think of colonial Virginia as a cradle of democracy; yet their culture was more about serving the upper classes. The founders did believe in the betterment of man, which led to the gift of a new kind of republic that allowed for societal evolution in the field of civil rights, but the founding of the colony had less to do with protecting residents from prejudices or religious persecution than with benefiting English investors who wanted to exploit the region's resources. The House of Burgesses, created in 1642, was the elected arm of the Virginia General Assembly, created in 1619, so some form of democracy had been the tradition. Yet, this was not a true democracy. Only white, land-owning males could participate. Any law could also be vetoed by the governor or the Virginia Company of London.

> I thank God there are no free schools or printing presses and I hope we shall not have them these hundred years: for learning has brought disobedience and heresy, and sects into the world and printing has divulged them and libels against the best of government. God keep us from both.
>
> —Governor Sir William Berkeley, 1671

To put Berkeley into context, despite the trappings of democracy, Virginia's governance tradition of "rule by aristocrats" dominated, although immigrant Scots and Irish felt that even the landless had a right to education and the vote.[3] Life followed seventeenth-century English political philosophy, meaning obedience by the commoners. The social status of the unborn was also frozen—there was no upward mobility.[4] The rigid caste system under Berkeley led to Bacon's Rebellion in 1676, a failed attempt by Nathaniel Bacon and a coalition of recent immigrants, farmers, indentured servants, and enslaved Black people to overthrow the government. The unfortunate result was the institutionalization of race-based, hereditary slavery intended to divide white servants and Black slaves.

This highly static class structure became a barrier to free public education and influenced public perceptions into the nineteenth century. When public schools were eventually proposed in 1869–70 in Virginia, many Loudoun aristocrats were still opposed, not being sympathetic to paying for educating the lower classes and Black people. That said, beginning in the seventeenth century, some settlers were willing to invest in education for all, even efforts to school the "infidels," meaning Indians.[5] In fact, Virginia's first free school was for Native Americans called Henrico College, but that ended with the uprising of 1622, which resulted in the deaths of nearly a third of Virginia's settlers.[6] There were also efforts to minimally educate orphans, but little serious interest in the poor or their children existed except to enable them to fulfill their role of serving the elite. Educating might be to convert them to Christianity or engage in what would later be called industrial education.[7] However, not all elites were opposed. After independence Jefferson argued for a university and a common school program, but apathy on the part of national leadership stood in the way of common schools. He wrote to George Washington in 1786: "It is an axiom in my mind that our liberty can never be safe except in the hands of the people themselves and that too with the people of a certain degree of instruction. This is the business of the state to effect and on a general plan."[8] In 1779 Jefferson had already caused a law to be passed in Virginia to raise taxes in every county for various school categories, including elementary schools, but it failed due to opposition by the courts, who were led by the wealthy, and by the general population, which was not empathetic to the cause. The latter worried the program would make the poor the charges of the government, and they had not been taught the value of common education either to themselves or to society as a whole.[9] Also in 1779, permission was given to build a schoolhouse on the southwest corner of the courthouse lot in Leesburg, roughly forty feet square, although it was never built.[10] This reluctance is a bit surprising given the religious fervor in the colonies and the commonwealth. After, all educating children was an important part of the Proverbs.

Dark Cargo—Black Anger

Some who helped with this book are the descendants of German, Scots, and Irish immigrants who went to America for economic advancement and, in one case, to escape being hung by the Kaiser's secret police. But many are also descendants of enslaved Africans. The search for their ancestors' stories is a difficult, painful journey. Black people did not first arrive as migrants of any kind. That would imply freedom of choice. They also were not escaping political or religious persecution, nor were they here for booty or conquest. Those were white stories and European dreams.

Black Africans came to American shores as unwilling, often malnourished, tortured cargo on white-managed ships destined as cheap labor to further the original purpose of many of the colonies. They were chained to the point of immobility in ship holds, sitting in their own excrement, and were sometimes dumped screaming into the ocean, chains on. Entire families were drowned when an unfriendly foreign sail approached from across the horizon. Sometimes, the weak and injured were simply tossed to roving sharks because they could not be sold. The most infamous example was the British slave ship *Zong*. In 1781 the crew massacred 130 slaves when drinking water went low, and then the slavers filed for insurance coverage for their losses, like any lost cargo.[11] Enslaved individuals, however, were not passive; they frequently fought back, sometimes killing their torturers and even blowing up ships. They were angry, having been ripped from the arms of their loved ones and suffering from beatings, rapes, and dismemberment at the hands of the slavers.

The *Zong* slaughter inspired many to support the growing anti–slave trade movement. Britain outlawed international slave trading in 1807; however, slavery itself would not be banned in the British Empire until 1833. The dehumanization of Black people had made British ports like Liverpool international centers of commerce where, today, stone busts of the enslaved still adorn some buildings. The investors in this industry justified their actions by saying that the enslaved who survived the fetid cargo holds were ignorant savages. The enslaved only required religious education, or to learn a new trade like handling tobacco, or to be exploited for their native knowledge of rice farming. Investors also opined that slavery was not unique, that Africans also engaged in the same trade. While it is certainly true that in West Africa, slavery was sometimes the only form of private property, the people who survived the disease and cruelty of the Atlantic slave ships were not savages.[12] Many Africans were literate in their local languages or Arabic. Cooks arrived who would inspire the cuisines of the American South. Musicians came whose descendants would invent jazz. Phillis Wheatley, captured in Gambia, would become America's first female African American poet.[13] There were also master fishermen and farmers. Some were skilled in extracting iron, gold, and diamonds. Some were explorers or sophisticated artisans. There were also religious leaders, scientists, astronomers, and teachers. In short, they were representatives of cultures, equal in many ways to those of the West.

A few basic statistics help describe the enslavement tragedy. It is estimated that by 1867 approximately 12.5 million Africans had started their journey to the Americas; fewer than 11 million survived.[14] About 5 percent arrived in the British colonies of North America, often going directly to Virginia.[15] By 1810 approximately 40 percent of Virginia's population of 95,000 was Black, and most were enslaved.[16] The international slave trade had also been formally banned by the United States in 1807–8.[17] Ironically, the ban found support in Virginia—but because of economics, not a rejection of inhumanity. Black births in Virginia were outstripping the number of incoming enslaved people, so banning competition from the international slave markets meant the domestic market became more lucrative. The enslaved were a commodity, like cattle.[18]

While it was not uncommon early on to educate the enslaved in some manner, two events changed the landscape. The failed Denmark Vesey revolt of 1822 in Charleston, South Carolina, inspired by the Haiti slave revolt in the 1790s, was arguably the most extensive revolt in the United States to that time, involving about nine thousand enslaved individuals. Vesey had been born about 1767 into slavery in the Danish colony of St. Thomas. He served as a special assistant to a Bermudian sea captain and slave merchant and was known to be fluent in French, Spanish, and English. A self-educated carpenter, he purchased his freedom after winning a lottery in 1799. He had also read a great deal of literature on abolition. Considered the originator of the insurrection, his idea was modeled after the Haiti rebellion against French colonial rule (1791–1804) that ended with Haiti's independence. Vesey wanted not simply to overthrow the government, he supposedly also wanted to seize the arms of the guardhouses, kill all the white residents, and burn down the city.[19]

There also was the 1831 Nat Turner rebellion in Virginia. Turner, an enslaved educated preacher, led a revolt in Southampton County that resulted in the deaths of more than fifty white people and approximately two hundred Black people. Both Vesey and Turner were literate, so their violent rebellions led to repressive laws limiting the education of the enslaved. Harkening back to the statement by Governor Sir William Berkeley in 1671, the government in 1831 believed that educated slaves would be able to read abolitionist literature, which might lead to more trouble. The southern governments opined that the only way to successfully subjugate Blacks was to prevent their education. Additionally, the insurrection prompted the Virginia legislature to pass acts forbidding enslaved and free Blacks from assembling for the purpose of reading, writing, or listening to a Black preacher. However, religious education, but not literacy, by white ministers was acceptable under Virginia law as part of the commonwealth's attempt at post-Turner rebellion control of Black religious life.

Despite the prohibitions, Quakers and others from the North continued educating Southern enslaved and freed Black individuals. Jane DeVeaux secretly operated a school in Savannah, Georgia, for thirty years until Union troops occupied the city.[20] Loudoun County Quakers in the villages of Goose Creek (called Lincoln after the Civil War) and Waterford educated both the enslaved and the freed. Also, as already noted, some slave owners taught their enslaved to read and write, in part to enhance Christian morality and in part to increase the economic value of their property.[21] However, real progress in Black education would not come until Quakers like the Janneys of Loudoun and northern missionaries began efforts in territories reclaimed from the Southern rebellion by the Union army. This is a story with echoes into the twenty-first century. Although the laws and regulations of Virginia and the other Southern states were not always a total ban, they were essentially a Great Barrier Reef of rules and practices that effectively stymied Black residents from obtaining secondary schooling and college, often limiting them to only what was needed for labor professions. What is also true is that ever since these rules were implemented, systemic racist policies of the past have harmed the growth of this important segment of American culture, thus hindering true equality.

Jefferson considered the color of Blacks as similar to bile. In his mind skin color and other physical features were proof of racial inferiority.[22] Modern science has proven that once the visual attributes Jefferson ascribed to Blacks are discarded, genetic differentiation between "races" is irrelevant. The politics of subjugation that enabled slavery and the segregation of free Black people had been "justified" by those misperceptions. The same kind of racialized science was used in European and other American colonies, and later included Virginia and other Southern states because it was easy to morally justify the oppression of an "inferior race" when "science" supported the concept of natural inferiority.

Health inequity is also an important part of the story of education because sick children cannot learn. Under slavery, the health care of the enslaved was primarily the responsibility of owners. The women were both breeding stock and labor but not considered fully human. Consider that between 1845 and 1849, enslaved women were surgery test subjects for gynecologist James Marion Sims. Although Sims did ask the women for permission to operate, informed consent was impossible because they were enslaved. To deny the will of owners was dangerous, especially given their condition. Similar medical experimentations were declared crimes against humanity in the Nuremberg trials following World War II. Lower standards of health care for African American people continued into the segregation era, resulting in health disparities across the region and in Loudoun County, affecting both the community and the schools.[23]

Deporting Black Peoples to Africa

In 1816 the American Society for Colonizing the Free People of Color of the United States (later the American Colonization Society, or ACS) was supported by Charles Fenton Mercer of Loudoun and others to advocate moving former slaves from the United States to what became Liberia as well as to Sierra Leone and Haiti. The society met at the Oakdale school in the village of Goose Creek, now Lincoln, Loudoun's oldest brick schoolhouse, which educated both Black and white students.

By the 1830s ACS leaders and prominent supporters included many leading slave-owning politicians such as Henry Clay of Kentucky and former presidents from Virginia (James Madison and James Monroe); however, abolitionists such as William Lloyd Garrison strongly opposed the ACS, correctly viewing its key goal as less about eliminating slavery than simply about removing Blacks from America. The ACS's general membership was mostly made up of Quakers and Methodists.

Oakdale in Old Lincoln.
Photo by Larry Roeder, 2019

Charles Fenton Mercer (1778–1858): Mercer graduated from Princeton in 1797 and was admitted to the Bar in 1802, practicing in Aldie, a village he founded in Loudoun County. He was also a member of the Virginia House of Delegates from 1810 to 1817 and a lieutenant colonel in the War of 1812, rising to the rank of brigadier general in command of the 2nd Virginia Brigade. Elected in 1816, he served as a US congressman until 1839. In 1817 Mercer also drafted an unsuccessful bill providing for a board of public instruction with a permanent secretary, free schooling for white children, wards, or apprentices, and a system of academies. It did not have Jefferson's support, who wanted to focus on a university, "not petty academies and colleges."[1] The bill was then amended and passed in 1818 to include a college and a system for primary schools. From 1828 to 1833 Mercer was president of the Chesapeake and Ohio Canal Company. He was also a delegate to the Virginia Constitutional Convention of 1829–30. Mercer was not a true friend of the Black community, instead seeing the ACS as a tool to eliminate a perceived burden to society that was easily radicalized and could inspire slaves to be free. Needless to say, he did not believe in assimilation.

1. Buck, *Development of Public Schools in Virginia*, 46.

Repatriation, as it was called, was considered progressive by many who wanted an end to slavery, but leaders like Mercer participated because deportation reduced labor competition with whites; thus, the ACS was a potentially effective method of removing a "problem" group. Approximately fifteen thousand Blacks were transported to Africa under this and similar schemes, but most freed Blacks had little interest in going to Africa, instead wanting to stay in their adopted country, even though that same nation resisted equality.

Regardless of the personal motivations of advocates, the repatriation movement's logic was inherently racist and paternalistic, although the concept was revived in the late 1870s and early 1880s under Rev. Henry McNeal Turner, a Black nationalist and former Union army chaplain. Wanting to save his people from the violence of post-Reconstruction segregationists and disillusioned about the prospects of practical integration, he reenergized the movement and transported settlers until

1904. In the 1920s the idea resurfaced again with Marcus Garvey's plan for an evacuation of a vulnerable people, but his views were at variance with mainstream Black leaders who advocated integration.

The Liberia plans were also inherently inhumane to indigenous Africans because they imposed an artificial "political elite" of US-born Black individuals on the local population. This was a classic white European colonial model or scheme that caused major inequities and established economies dependent on white investment, ripe for abuse by large industries, well into the twentieth century. In other words, this was at best paternalism, an attitude of white government officials and leading citizens who saw themselves as doing "the right thing." At worst, it was a case of naked racism and control over the lives and bodies of people subject to their rules. The efforts to remove Black citizens existed because most white leaders could not envisage the possibility of equality between the races or integration in the United States.

Prewar Education Disparities

Early white schooling in Loudoun County consisted primarily of tutoring at home or sending young ladies to a school maintained by Miss Margaret Mercer, cousin of Charles F. Mercer, at Belmont.[24] Very wealthy citizens might also have sent their children to a local academy or even to England. For those who could not attend an "academy" or hire expensive tutors, classes were frequently held in outdoor spaces or a log cabin built by a farmer but managed by an itinerant teacher. The most common method of education in Loudoun and elsewhere in Virginia were these field or community schools, located on any spot convenient to the students.[25] Itinerant teachers brought their own textbooks and materials and canvassed for students, including among the poor, since the Literary Fund, financed by the commonwealth, paid teachers a tuition for each indigent pupil and an extra stipend for school supplies. The poor were seen as a market, but the program's impact was not widespread. According to Dorsey Ford in his 1935 study of Loudoun schools, by the time of the Civil War, "only one half of the white children were reached by education, and they composed only one third of the school age population, the other two thirds being colored children."[26] Since the "colored children" spoken of were not supposed to be educated under Virginia law, this statistic is not surprising.

Records don't describe many details, but schools were not uniform in curriculum or physical structure. As already noted, some schools convened in rooms, others under a tree or in a field. A close examination of the records that still exist also shows no direct support of Black students, free or enslaved, by the commonwealth. It is obvious that children of many freed Black adults would have qualified for a free education on economic grounds alone, but the legislature only allocated fund monies to be distributed annually for the education of indigent white children.[27] One school that did support Black students was Oakdale. John Jay Janney remarked that "two mulatto boys and one negro boy" attended in what was one of the first "integrated" schools in Virginia.[28]

Despite the initial opposition of most white elites to funding education for poor citizens, the concept of publicly funded common schools did have support among some leading elected politicians. Loudoun's own Charles Mercer supported the concept. As early as 1801 Gov. James Monroe asked the legislature to support such schools, as did Gov. George Cabell in 1806, but with little effect; then in 1809 Gov. John Tyler criticized the General Assembly for its general apathy, which he felt was disgraceful.[29] In reaction, in 1810 the General Assembly passed a bill that established the Literary Fund, the commonwealth's first true public effort to provide any meaningful financial support to education. It was originally managed by trustees led by the governor, lieutenant governor, treasurer, president of the Court of Appeals, and attorney general.[30] However, the schoolhouses being supported were private before 1870. The target indigent white children were an oft-ignored population that could be very numerous in Loudoun, over five hundred in 1826, nearly one thousand by 1830, and more than that in 1856.[31]

The law stated: "Be it enacted; That all escheats, confiscations, fines, penalties and forfeitures, and all rights in personal property accruing to the Commonwealth, as derelict, and having no rightful proprietor, be, and the same are hereby appropriated to the encouragement of learning. That the aforesaid fund shall be appropriated to the sole benefit of a school or schools, to be kept in each and every county within this Commonwealth."[32]

The Literary Fund expanded in 1816 after a loan to help finance the War of 1812 was paid off by the federal government. Then, in 1818, a bill set up a board of commissioners to establish the University of Virginia, which was a Jefferson priority. In 1829 the General Assembly authorized that the fund could be used for school construction if local patrons raised three-fifths of the cost.[33]

The 1818 School Act required each county court to appoint five to fifteen commissioners to establish or administer schools for indigent children.[34] Prior to 1818 counties were given the option of whether to appoint a board of school commissioners. Loudoun does not appear to have taken up that idea until 1818, and then commissioners looked after affairs in small districts, up to twenty-three in 1846.[35] In 1870 the small-district concept of the commissioner era would be replaced by a public school system managed through a leaner network of districts identical to magisterial districts, a county subdivision used to conduct elections. Enslavement-era records mainly focus on the appointment of school commissioners, although they also show that many indigent children needed assistance. There were many schools in Loudoun, between seventy and eighty in 1832, likely because of the difficulties associated with travel at the time.[36] In 1825, of the sixty-eight schools of all types then in existence, forty-seven partly supported the indigent.[37]

Records don't show exactly how many schools existed in Loudoun year by year, nor many of their names, but they do illustrate the basic problems of educating in a sparsely populated rural county that continued after 1870. Poverty was one issue as well as the "peculiar circumstances of parents," perhaps referring to many children being pulled out of school during harvest time as farm labor, a concern David Campbell, governor of Virginia, expressed as early as 1838.[38] As a result, the number of months of education varied widely, with some students attending for six months, three months, even one month or less. However, the commissioners cared deeply about their mission, as seen in this quote from 1826. "It is much to be regretted that the benevolent intentions of the Legislature in regard to the education of poor children cannot be carried to full effect by the children being kept at school, but various causes exist to prevent this, over which we have no control."[39]

In summary, the Literary Fund did much good in Loudoun County. Certainly, the commissioners were intent on excellence, even complaining about fund rules, when seen as artificial limitations. For example, the fund's support beyond tuition in the pre-public-school era was limited to books, pens, and paper. This could be very restraining, as in 1820, when commissioners realized that some children did not attend class because their parents could only afford rags against the cold or inclement weather.[40] Practical clothing was needed to avoid low attendance, but the fund didn't allow for that contingency.[41] It should also be noted that 1861 marked the end of the fund as a tool focusing on the education of the indigent.[42] Fund appropriations were then diverted to the Civil War effort, not reverting to education again until 1870.

William Henry Ruffner and the Transition to Reconstruction

One ally of limited Black education before the Civil War who would become a leader during Reconstruction and beyond was William Henry Ruffner, whose father was a former president of Washington College, Presbyterian minister, and farmer in Rockingham County. Ruffner was deeply religious and in 1845 established a Sunday class for "negroes" at the Presbyterian church in Lexington. The program continued off and on until the Civil War and counted among its supervisors then-reverend Thomas (Stonewall) Jackson.[43] With the support of Washington College president Robert E. Lee, the House of Delegates elected Ruffner as the first Virginia superintendent of public instruction in 1870.

Like many so-called moderate whites, Ruffner's attitude on the Black population was complicated. His father, Henry, a supporter of a separate state of West Virginia, believed slaves in western Virginia should be manumitted. William felt instead that the institution was neither dishonorable nor sinful. Further, he leased slaves as servants. His point of view on educating Black individuals was therefore about practicality, not ethics, relating it to Virginia's economic prosperity.[44] Unlike Berkeley, Ruffner also believed that the government could not hope to effectively govern a large uneducated population, but that was not advocacy for equality. It was advocacy for a tool to advance economics. In other words, Ruffner was less about civil rights, than he was about making people effective production units. In 1874, after he became superintendent for public instruction, Ruffner would write an essay titled "The Co-education of the White and Colored Races," which is an argument against integrated schools. He said, "the Africans are lowest in the scale of races, while the white Americans rank with the highest."[45] This philosophy would also lead him to say in response to the Civil Rights Bill of 1875, which called for integrated schools, "unless there is a due recognition of caste in public education at the South, the common school education in fifteen states will be a failure."[46]

Notes

1. Henry Wiencek, *An Imperfect God: George Washington, His Slaves and the Creation Of America* (New York: Farrar, Straus and Giroux, 2003), 4. The entire text of the will, including instructions on the treatment of freed slaves, is on the official website of Mount Vernon as a primary source for students and teachers: https://www.mountvernon.org/.

2. J. L. Blair Buck, *Development of Public Schools in Virginia, 1607–1952* (Richmond: State Board of Education, 1952), 46. The term "common school" was also used to refer to primary schooling (30).

3. Buck, 7.

4. Buck, 4.

5. Buck, 8.

6. Cornelius J. Heatwole, *A History of Education in Virginia* (New York: Macmillan, 1916), 41–42.

7. This link between extolling basic education and Christian values was a constant theme in Virginia education for many decades, despite the fact that the enslaved had their own faiths and despite the fact that practices under "Christian values" permitted enslavement, racial prejudice, and segregation. As an example, in 1938 Emerick said "no teacher can do wrong in modeling her teaching after that greatest of all teachers Jesus, the Nazarene." See EWP 3.1 Yr. 1938 Purpose of Education Including Jesus. Little doubt that those teachers are of great values; but what if the student was of a different faith, an agnostic or atheist. Those options were pushed aside.

8. Letter from Thomas Jefferson to George Washington while in Paris, January 4, 1786, *The Papers of Thomas Jefferson*, vol. 9, *1 November 1785–22 June 1786*, ed. Julian P. Boyd (Princeton, NJ: Princeton University Press, 1954), 150–52.

9. Buck, *Development of Public Schools*, 27; and Heatwole, *A History of Education*, 101.

10. Dorsey Ford, "History of Education in Loudoun County" (Honors thesis, the University of Richmond, 1937), 4–5. The author had direct access to the files of Superintendent Oscar Emerick and conducted interviews of local educators who guided the school system through World War I and the Great Depression.

11. James Walvin, *The Zong: A Massacre, the Law & the End of Slavery* (New Haven, CT: Yale University Press, 2011).

12. Hugh Thomas, *The Slave Trade: The Story of the Atlantic Slave Trade, 1440–1870* (New York: Simon and Shuster, 1997), 47.

13. David Eltis and David Richardson, *Atlas of the Transatlantic Slave Trade* (New Haven, CT: Yale, 2010), 214. See also *Letter of Phillis Wheatley: The Negro Slave Poet of Boston* (Boston: Private printing, 1864), and Phillis Wheatley, *The Poems of Phillis Wheatley: As They Were Originally Published in London, 1773* (Philadelphia, 1909), ed. Richard R. Wright and Charlotte Crogman Wright (repr., Whitefish, MT: Kessinger, 2007).

14. Eltis and Richardson, *Atlas of the Transatlantic Slave Trade*, 10.

15. Walvin, *The Zong*, 28.

16. V. T. Thayer, *Formative Ideas in American Education: From the Colonial Period to the Present* (New York: Dodd, Mead & Company, 1965), 24.

17. Act Prohibiting Importation of Slaves, March 2, 1807, effective January 1, 1808.

18. "The Transatlantic Slave Trade," *Encyclopedia Virginia*, https://encyclopediavirginia.org. Source of statistics: https://faculty.weber.edu/kmackay/statistics_on_slavery.htm.

19. "Denmark Vesey," *Encyclopedia Britannica* (online article).

20. Jenel Few, "Massie Opens Exhibit on Local African American Education History," *Savannah Morning News* (blog), February 18, 2017, https://www.savannahnow.com/story/news/2017/02/18/massie-opens-exhibit-local-african-american-education-history/13895860007/.

21. Gene Scheel, "Timeline of Important Events in African American History in Loudoun County, Virginia," *The History of Loudon County, Virginia* (blog), n.d., accessed September 29, 2020, http://www.loudounhistory.org/history/african-american-chronology. Scheel is considered one of the top historians in Loudoun County.

22. Thomas Jefferson, *Notes on the State of Virginia* (1785), ed. by Frank Shuffelton (New York: Penguin, 1999), 149–52, 155.

23. During an 1857 lecture, Sims said that he never used anesthesia for fistula surgery "because they are not painful enough to justify the trouble and risk," an attitude of dismissing the pain of women that was common at the time and has continued today in some parts of the medical community. https://www.washingtonpost.com/wellness/interactive/2022/women-pain-gender-bias-doctors/

24. Harrison Williams, *Legends of Loudoun: An Account of the History and Homes of a Border County of Virginia's Northern Neck* (Richmond, VA: Garret and Massie, 1938), 171.

25. Foney G. Mullins, "A History of the Literary Fund" (PhD dissertation, Virginia Polytechnic Institute and State University, 2001), 14.

26. Ford, "History of Education in Loudoun County," 4.

27. Heatwole, *A History of Education in Virginia*, 105.

28. Werner L. Janney and Asa Moore Janney, eds., *John Jay Janney's Virginia: An American Farm Lad's Life in the Early 19th Century* (McLean, VA: EPM Publications, 1978), 56.

29. William Arthur Maddox, *The Free School Idea in Virginia Before the Civil War* (New York: Teacher's College, Columbia University, 1918), 47.

30. EWP: 2.9 Literary Fund.

31. Reports of the Commissioners, School Box 1, Folder 1826, Loudoun County Circuit Court Archives (LCCCA); Reports of the Commissioners, School Box 1, Folder 1830, LCCCA; and Reports of the Commissioners, School Box 1, Folder 1856, LCCCA.

32. *House Journal*, February 2, 1810, 15.

33. Heatwole, *A History of Education*, 106.

34. Eventually in Loudoun the Board of Commissioners was led by a president and a superintendent.

35. Reports of the Commissioners, School Box 1, Folder 1846, LCCCA.

36. Reports of the Commissioners, School Box 1, Folder 1832, LCCCA.

37. Reports of the Commissioners, School Box 1, Folder 1825, LCCCA.

38. Reports of the Commissioners, School Box 1, Folder 1826, LCCCA.

39. Reports of the Commissioners, School Box 1, Folder 1826, LCCCA.

40. EWP: 2.9 Yr. 1820 Literary Fund and the Poor.

41. EWP: 2.9 Yr. 1820 Literary Fund and the Poor.

42. Mullins, "A History of the Literary Fund," 31.

43. David Walton Coffey, *William Henry Ruffner: Race and Public Education in Post-Reconstruction Virginia* (Chapel Hill: University of North Carolina, Department of History, 1972); and Charles Chilton Pearson, "William Henry Ruffner: Reconstruction Statesman of Virginia," reprint from the *South Atlantic Quarterly* (1921), 6.

44. Staff Writer, "The Public School System," *Richmond Times*, September 7, 1901, 4.

45. William Henry Ruffner, "The Co-education of the White and Colored Races," *Scribner's Monthly*, May 1874, 87.

46. Pearson, "William Henry Ruffner," 19.

2

1865-70

Resistance and Evolution

The black man is free, the black man is a citizen, the black man is enfranchised, and this by organic law of the land. . . . Never was revolution more complete.

—Frederick Douglass after the ratification
of the Fifteenth Amendment

There was one thing that the white South feared more than Negro dishonesty, ignorance, and incompetency, and that was Negro honesty, knowledge, and efficiency.

—W. E. B. Du Bois

For purposes of this book, Reconstruction in Loudoun was between 1865 and 1870, when Virginia ratified the Fourteenth Amendment and rejoined the Union under a constitution that established formal public schooling for Black and white learners. However, for much of the South, Reconstruction ran from 1865 to 1877. It should have created a rebirth and healing time, similar to the Marshall Plan in Europe after World War II, fostering national economic, cultural, and political consolidation. However, Reconstruction was a failure because the assassination of President Abraham Lincoln in 1865 by extremist John Wilkes Booth eliminated the program's heart, leaving it in the hands of President Andrew Johnson's corrupt administration, led by a man who believed in states' rights and rural America, not the awakening promised by new agricultural technology and the railroads. Johnson first declared all of the leaders of the Confederacy public enemies, worth trial and confiscation of their property, but then provided amnesty for the average rebel soldiers.[1] There was no support for Black suffrage and little interest in reconciliation.[2] In fact, Johnson eventually set the stage for southern politicians to reassert the evils of white supremacy through Black Codes. At the same time, America's bloodiest war had ended, or at least the soldiers had stopped killing each other, and, thanks to Congress, massive changes in civil and human rights were thrust on a defeated South. Many southern leaders also began to better perceive the role of schools in poverty reduction and economic revival. However, resolving race relations was more problematic. Persuading the white South to change was slow because of embedded cultural racism and the view of many southern politicians and ordinary citizens that Black people were not ready for full rights, such as voting, especially because of their rate of illiteracy. Waves of discontent from those years over the perceived unfairness of Reconstruction still ripple into today's political currents, including in the debates over voting rights, mass incarceration, segregation in public education, and ongoing disparities in everything from health care to employment. Also, while publicly funded education in the twenty-first century is considered a normal, important social role that reduces inequality and helps the class structure evolve, this was not the goal of the southern white political class until at least the second half of the twentieth century. Quite the opposite was true. Archie Gibbs Richardson, one of Virginia's most important pioneer Black educators, made the following observations in 1976 about the tension during Reconstruction between the former social order and the desires of Black Americans to be educated and equal:

> It was in this time that the old antebellum idea of many white Virginians that any education for the Negro was questionable, gave way to the idea that the Negro might be educated even at nominal expense if his education remained under control of persons who would not let the system endanger white supremacy or allow the Negro to forget his place. . . .
>
> The idea of equality plagued the minds of many white persons who held to the dogma that giving the Negro the right to vote or go to school would be tantamount to the mongrelization of the white race.[3]

In other words, in the mind of whites, progress was possible for African Americans only if done on white terms. Reconstruction also marked a continuation of the epic tension between southern states wanting to retain some level of autonomy versus accepting their responsibility to the

United States as integral threads of a common fabric of shared duties, rights, and freedoms. That was the very political conflict that led to the rebellion called the Civil War. At the same time, northern citizens and many in the federal government wanted to punish the insurrectionists and reintegrate the former rebels into a reunified nation while also giving equality to the formerly enslaved.

Unfortunately, but not unexpectedly, while the former rebels understood they were defeated on the battlefield, they still felt their political causes were just. Former Confederate leaders, the white planter class, women-managed autonomous memorial societies who reburied the war dead and erected monuments, and others fomented a false narrative that slowed healing. Many members of the memorial societies melded into the incorporated United Daughters of the Confederacy in 1894, which was a major proponent of white supremacist theories.

> The South, during the dread reconstruction period, bore persecution, treachery, and misrepresentation from her enemies; but still lifting her noble countenance to the ever-living God, she to-day stands triumphantly erect and points with pride and veneration to her immortal heroes, "who fought for a cause, though lost, still just. . . . Time will yet vindicate our cause."
>
> —Mrs. P. M. Moody, president of the Mississippi Division
> of the United Daughters of the Confederacy, on the
> society's position on the lost cause and Reconstruction

There was also the emergence throughout the South of the Ku Klux Klan, the Knights of the White Camellia (1867–70), and other white supremacist organizations, which were often terrorist bodies. Some Confederate groups' efforts were benign, humanitarian, and needed, such as efforts to establish Confederate cemeteries and the Memorial to the Unknown in Middleburg, Loudoun County, in 1866 as well as to care for veterans. However, other Confederate groups' efforts led to the Jim Crow era that would last until the 1960s. In fact, this period was the proof of a theory offered by Carl von Clausewitz in 1832. In his view, winning battles was not a strategy, only a tool.[4] War was just one tactic of a strategy aimed at changing a political landscape. While changing southern minds would have been difficult enough, effecting this strategy required national political leadership. However, while the Republican Congress was willing to make seismic changes through legislation and constitutional amendments, the post-Lincoln White House of Andrew Johnson was unsympathetic to the Black population. The language of social change was often seen as more about punishment than conciliation and healing—which cemented resentment and white southern resistance. Reconciliation never had a chance, and the blame must be shared in part by the federal government.

Funding Common Education

As already noted, between the secession of Virginia from the Union in 1861 and the establishment of the public school system in 1870, the Literary Fund stopped being a source of income for education, with these monies diverted to support military operations. Following the war, the money allocated for education also helped repay war debts, amounting to $45 million by 1865.[5] Black communities had never benefited from the Literary Fund to begin with, so this meant the main victims of the loss of funding in Loudoun were impoverished white children, who mostly went without schooling. However, with Lincoln's 1863 emancipation order and the cessation of hostilities in 1865, Black students began to see more educational opportunities, thanks to the Quakers and the Freedmen's Bureau, America's first federal relief agency. Unfortunately, the latter closed its doors in 1872 due to lack of funds and hostility by white southerners.

While white indigent students could seek support from the Literary Fund before the public school system was established in 1870, Black students had to rely on white, religiously oriented groups like the Quakers, Baptists, Methodists, and others. In 1935 one of the few academic studies of early Loudoun schooling was drafted in cooperation with then-superintendent Oscar Emerick and others with a deep, personal knowledge of the county and its people. The study indicated that one reason for the county's modest educational infrastructure in the early nineteenth century, quite apart from reluctance of the wealthy to be taxed to support the poor of any race, was that most farmers depended on subsistence farming. Balancing schooling with the requirements of farm labor meant that by Reconstruction, poor whites were very ill-educated. They had also not been tutored as to the advantages of a common education and were reluctant to become charges of the state.[6] The study's author also posited that the War of 1812, the Mexican War, and then the Civil War had reduced the perception of education as a social priority. To the advantage of Black communities, however, once federal troops reasserted national authority in rebel territories during the Civil War, about eighty societies, starting with the American Missionary Association (AMA), a Congregationalist organization, began their own operations. The AMA and others started schools for "contraband" Black learners (escaped slaves). A mix of religious and secular associations in Boston, Chicago, Cincinnati, New York, and Philadelphia also collected money for their own efforts in support of Black education. In Loudoun, local and Northern Quakers led the main effort.

By 1870 most of these societies had stopped work, but the AMA continued employing teachers who instructed thousands of students across the former Confederacy. The AMA also fostered normal schools to train Black teachers and successfully partnered with the Freedmen's Bureau, in part because the bureau's commissioner, Gen. Oliver Otis Howard, and education superintendent, John Alvord, were both Congregationalists. Howard would also start Howard University, which would be enormously important to Loudoun's Black education.[7]

It was Alvord who led efforts to form the Freedmen's Bureau in 1865, which created or funded Atlanta University (1865), Fisk University (1866), Howard University (1867), and Hampton Institute (1868). Loudoun County indirectly benefited from these investments because each of these schools would eventually train some of Loudoun's Black teachers. One of those, the Hampton Institute, would also later play a major role in the twentieth century, advocating for equal health access through its Negro Organization Society.

One of Alvord's other innovations was to form the Freedman's Bank in 1865, which allowed for savings accounts for Black soldiers and veterans. At its peak, it had over seventy-two thousand Black depositors—people who had often been denied access to conventional banks—but by 1874 it almost collapsed due to mismanagement and fraud. To deal with the situation, famed Black leader Frederick Douglass became the bank's president and invested $10,000 of his own money. However, the rescue mission was too late, and Congress closed the bank that June. Depositors also lost their savings because Congress didn't guarantee them.

Resistance to White Supremacy

According to Harrison Williams's oft-cited history of Loudoun, during Reconstruction "there was little, or no racial animosity and the negroes appear to have been more content and appreciative, as well as dependable in their work, than in many of the other counties."[8] Evidence to the contrary was seen in the treatment of Quakers, like Caroline Thomas, who came from the North to educate Black students. There was also disdain in Loudoun, seeing that white southern voters in March 1865 had been disenfranchised while former slaves and Virginian Unionists were enfranchised.

Now Black communities had fresh legal tools at hand. For example, the Thirteenth Amendment, enacted in December 1865, outlawed slavery and involuntary servitude. Following this—but only after overriding a veto by President Andrew Johnson—the US Congress passed the Civil Rights Bill of 1866. This was the nation's first civil rights law and the first time Congress had overridden a veto. The law said that "all persons born in the United States" except for American Indians were "hereby declared to be citizens of the United States." The legislation granted all citizens the "full and equal benefit of all laws and proceedings for the security of person and property." It also marked, along with the Thirteenth Amendment, the beginning of the legal struggle for civil rights in the former Confederacy as well as a federal government willing to assertively protect citizens' rights. Black people in Virginia also voted for the first time in the fall of 1867 for delegates to the Constitutional Convention. The Fourteenth Amendment, passed in 1868, provided equal protection of the laws to any person within its jurisdiction. States could not pass or enforce any laws "which shall abridge the privileges or immunities of citizens of the United States; nor shall any State deprive any person of life, liberty, or property, without due process of law; nor deny to any person within its jurisdiction the equal protection of the laws."

The amendment also strengthened elements of the 1866 law, which could have otherwise been erased by later Congresses or administrations, by embedding into the Constitution the definition of citizens as anyone born in the United States. The Fourteenth Amendment would prove essential to dismantling segregation in the twentieth century. Finally, in February 1870, just before the beginning of the public schools in Virginia, the Fifteenth Amendment passed, prohibiting the denial of the right to vote based on a citizen's "race, color or previous condition of servitude." Black communities in Loudoun were eager to exercise that right.

Whites pushed back. The KKK, with their white robes imitating the spirits of dead Confederate rebels and with the support of many white politicians, worked hard to undermine Black civil rights through mob violence and lynchings. The KKK is still attempting to foment racial tensions in Loudoun in the twenty-first century, although its influence is now negligible.[9] Although the Constitution made it illegal to discriminate, serious federal penalties would not come about until the twentieth century under President Lyndon Johnson. Instead, Black Americans had to rely on examples set by those who came before, such as the personal efforts of Edwin Washington of Loudoun who negotiated "the privilege" of going to a Quaker school while keeping his job. Even after 1870 Black communities continued to rely on the efforts of parents, teachers, and school patrons who would subsidize their schools when they were underfunded and would petition the county government for needed improvements. Later they would turn to the courts and attorneys like Charles Hamilton Houston of Howard University, Edwin Cicero Brown Sr., and James H. Raby of Alexandria, all of whom emerge later in the book as legal giants supporting Loudoun's Black communities.

In the latter part of 1865 or early 1866, Black residents in the Loudoun County town of Leesburg established the Colored Man's Aid Society to assist their infirm and indigent citizens. However, in a patronizing tone, and harkening to the points made by Archie Richardson, the *Democratic Mirror* of Leesburg said that, "The negroes of this community, are as a general thing, polite and well behaved."[10] Editor Benjamin Sheetz commented a year later that without such a group, many of the formerly enslaved would "go supperless to miserable beds."

Reconstruction Era Schools for Black Students

Despite racial tensions, with the bans on educating Black students relegated to the dustbin of history, the Freedmen's Bureau began erecting schools for Black students in Loudoun, as did the Quakers. In addition, the curriculum went beyond the basics. Caroline Thomas, Edwin Washington's teacher, remarked in 1867, "I have one class in Short Division, one in Multiplication, one in Subtraction and three in Addition. With a very few exceptions, most of these children could not make a figure when they first came to school. I have one class in definitions; have some very good readers and spellers and think my first class is now

Caroline Thomas (1833–96): Caroline Thomas was born in Philadelphia to a family with ties to the Quakers, although it is unclear if her immediate family were members until the 1870s. Little is known about Thomas's life prior to being hired in 1867 by Philadelphia Quakers to teach Black students at the Freedmen's School in Leesburg. In 1868 threats of violence from whites resulting from her boarding with a Black family and poor working conditions led her to leave for Lincoln, the home of her close friends the Janney family, prominent Quakers. Funded by the Friends of Long Island, New York, she then left for Nebraska in 1871 to teach the Winnebago Indians with Samuel M. Janney of Loudoun, who was superintendent of Indian Affairs in Nebraska. She instructed the Winnebagos there until 1880.

Thomas and her Quaker friends in Loudoun genuinely wished to educate, clothe, and generally help Black residents in Loudoun County, and they did much good, although it is unclear that they saw either the Black or the Winnebago communities with whom they worked as truly equal. Despite what was likely a bit of paternalism, most who instructed Blacks were on a moral quest to correct the ills borne of slavery, like illiteracy, which certainly inhibited the potential of freed people to materially advance. A lack of literacy also set up the recently freed for abuse if they could not read their contracts. Interestingly, Quaker schools were not free, and Thomas opposed free schools, an irony for one who fought hard to educate nearly penniless people.

prepared to take some other studies—either Grammar or Philosophy, or both."[11] Philosophy was an upper branch (high school) course.

The Freedmen's Bureau set up offices in Middleburg and Leesburg in March 1865 and by 1869 created or supported at least nine Black schools, including in Aldie, Brownsville (Swampoodle), Hamilton, Hillsboro, Leesburg, Lincoln, Middleburg, Waterford, and Willisville.[12] Some of the more notable schools include the following:

- **1815:** The Quaker Janney family established Oakdale in Goose Creek (later Lincoln); it was converted in 1866 to a Freedmen's School with funding for teachers from the Charity Society of Jericho Long Island Friends. The school had been teaching Black students since the 1850s.[13]
- **1866–67:** Caroline Thomas led the first Freedmen's School in Leesburg, which Edwin Washington attended.
- **1866:** William Obediah Robey, a Black man, established a Black school in Leesburg at his home on the corner of Church and North Streets.[14]
- **1866:** Richard Bailey established a school on his Leesburg property that was used for both worship and education.
- **1867:** Waterford's school, formerly the Colored School "A," was set up with the help of the Freedmen's Bureau, Waterford and Philadelphia Quakers, and the local Black trustees. The first teacher, Sarah Steer, did not wait for construction and began teaching Black students in her home and backyard. The schoolhouse, colloquially known as the Second Street School, is still standing today and is part of the Waterford National Historic Landmark.[15]
- **1868:** Willisville land was obtained from Black farmers for the benefit of local "colored youth" to be educated during the week and to pray during the weekend. The Freedmen's Bureau paid for construction of the schoolhouse.[16] Similar to the first school in Saint Louis, and the Yellow School House on Snickersville Turnpike, the building was a pale yellow, which was an unusual color.[17]

Virginia Constitutions and Black Rights

The story of how Virginia's constitutions changed during this period has broader boundaries than the narrative on education but does shed light on the reasons for the decades of white suppression of African Americans after the Civil War, on the emergence of the federal government as a sometimes-inept guarantor of civil rights, and on how a public school system emerged from the turmoil.

From the start of the Civil War, the status of Black rights was confusing, even after the Unionist Restored Government's declaration of a revised constitution in April 1864. It recognized the secession of West Virginia and outlawed slavery but did not define Black rights well, other than to legalize marriages of the former enslaved. That document also restored voting rights to most Confederates, so long as they took an amnesty oath or were pardoned by the president. In addition, the war was still going on, so it only applied to liberated lands. However, once the war was over in 1865, it became the authority for all of Virginia, until the Underwood Constitution of 1869. The methodology of the convention, which took place under martial law, was also controversial, opaque, and even undemocratic. Press coverage was limited to reporters who took an oath of allegiance to the United States, and formal proceedings were not published, just a few media reports. All white males who had lived in the state for at least a year, including many who moved in from the North, could vote, but only if they had not been associated with the rebellion since January 1, 1864. Further, the new constitution was never submitted to the people for a vote; it was simply proclaimed and put into force.

It should be noted that in 1864 most of the area covered by the Restored Government was under martial law, which could account for the restrictions on the convention. The key point is that once the Constitution applied to all Virginia (at the end of the Civil War), it was not presented to the people for a vote and disenfranchised most of the white population with its oath requirement. Although this disenfranchisement was a logical punishment for treason, the scope gave pause to Gen. John M. Schofield, the military governor.[18] It also caused much political resentment by the very people who, in the long term, were needed for meaningful political reconciliation.

Archie Gibbs Richardson, EdD (1904–79): The grandson of enslaved people, Dr. Richardson was a pioneer in Black education who began as principal of Mecklenburg County Training School, South Hill, Virginia, in 1927 and then in 1936 was elevated to the position of assistant state supervisor of negro education, which was the first appointment of an African American to the Virginia Department of Education. In 1966 he was again promoted to be associate director of the Division of Secondary Education, making him the most senior Black educational administrator in Virginia. Before he retired in 1969, Richardson played a major role helping Black communities around the state and in Loudoun County, including advising on the design of the Douglass High School building in Leesburg. Despite his high office but indicative of segregation, he was required to use a toilet in the basement. He also could not use the office kitchen but instead was restricted to eating alone in his office or venturing to a local diner.

To advance compliance with the requirement on Virginia to endorse the Fourteenth Amendment and other Reconstruction acts before being allowed to rejoin the Union, General Schofield called for another state constitutional convention, which met in Richmond from December 3, 1867, to April 17, 1868. Led by Judge John C. Underwood, the result became known as the Underwood Constitution, which voters approved by referendum in 1869. Part of the aim was to guarantee Black citizens equality under state law. Another was to set up a free public school system: "To provide by law, at its first session under this Constitution, a uniform system of public free schools and for its gradual equal and full introduction into all the counties of the state by the year 1876, and as much sooner as possible."[19]

Virginia's school system was influenced in part by the $2 million Peabody Fund, designed to support southern elementary education. Observers to the Constitutional Convention believed that this portion of the Constitution was drafted in part by Barnas Sears, general agent of the fund. According to Richardson, much of the credit should also go to the Black delegates to the convention.[20] Other than costs, the major debate was over school integration. This caused significant argument and eventually led to a compromise that omitted race, leaving the system to be segregated without mandating it. Some Black individuals did not object, feeling the deal might minimize white opposition. The Peabody Fund also accepted that segregated schools would be inevitable.[21]

It is clear that the federal government was ineffective at healing the nation's racial divide. James Lawrence Blair Buck noted in his history of Virginia education that the 1869 Virginia Constitution was hated because as contemporaries put it, "the Legislature was made up of a motley group of scallywags, carpet baggers and negro allies who met under the protection of military authorities and assumed to speak for the people of Virginia."[22] One goal of the Edwin Washington Project is to understand how African Americans were depicted in the public school textbooks, so it is interesting to see how the hatred discussed by Buck was taught in high schools. As late as 1952, Dr. James Southhall Wilson of the University of Virginia described the period as one of humiliation for white people, with nearly all whites disenfranchised, whereas "the Negroes under the leadership of violent radicals, the worst was feared. Especially in the country districts, with many roving 'displaced' Negroes who were unwilling to work and full of lawless ideas, the women lived in constant fear."[23]

During the October 1867 election for delegates to the Underwood Convention, many of Virginia's conservative whites refused to vote, which meant that so-called Radical Republicans, those who had favored the abolition of slavery and believed that freed slaves should have complete equality with white citizens, took control. Twenty-four of the delegates were also Black. Fearing a new political structure that "threatened complete overthrow of white supremacy," the Conservative Party was then formed in December 1867, made up of former Whigs and Democrats.[24] Branches formed and debates were held throughout Virginia to thwart enactment. In Loudoun, northern whites and Black leaders spoke in favor of the Republican Party.[25] The Loudoun branch of the conservatives had leaders in Aldie, Blakeley's Grove, Goresville, Guilford, Gumspring, Hillsboro, Leesburg, Lovettsville, Middleburg, Mt. Gilead, Purcellville, Snickersville (now Bluemont), Union, and Waterford.[26] This new group was described as an anticonstitutional party and was opposed to a common free school system. Black citizens were then about

30 percent of the state's population, and Virginia was in deep debt due to the war. Most elite whites felt educating liberated slaves was a much lower priority than debt servicing.[27]

The draft constitution was sent to the citizens of Virginia and agreed upon by a vote of 210,585 in favor to 9,136 opposed. This happened after two of the provisions were put to a separate vote, thanks to a compromise accepted by President Ulysses Grant and authorized by Congress. Underwood and others wanted to disenfranchise former Confederate officials, but this was defeated. A loyalty oath was also recommended, but that too was voted down. With those decisions, the Underwood document was authorized by Congress on January 26, 1870, replaced the 1864 Constitution, and enabled Virginia to rejoin the Union. This Constitution would remain in effect until 1902, when white supremacists replaced it with one that disenfranchised most Black people and poor whites.

The persistence of white resistance continued as described in a 1919 study, which suggested that "most of the friction between the races in the South since the War of Secession has grown out of the work and teachings of political agitators who have sought to use the untutored negro to further their selfish aims."[28] Reflecting the attitude of many former Confederates during Reconstruction, the study reinforced the myth that the Underwood Constitution meant "disenfranchisement of the whites and negro rule, and the continuance of military rule, which is degrading to a people who are accustomed to govern themselves."[29] However, the study ignored the fact that the white Conservative/Democrat Party had dominated the state's government and legislature for most of the years since the Constitution's approval.

Judge Underwood had proposed expanding the right to vote to both Black citizens and white women; however, the concept of women's suffrage did not survive. Ultimately, Virginia's conservative whites who voted to ratify the new Virginia Constitution, with its provision of Black suffrage, felt they did so under duress. Conservative whites' acceptance of Black voting was part of a bargain in 1869 that allowed Virginia's members of Congress to take their seats in January 1870, thus ending Reconstruction. Also removed were restrictions on voting from former Confederates whose rights had been abridged since the end of the Civil War. However, because their point of view on the righteousness of their cause was unabated, Black citizens would have to fight every day to keep or expand their new rights. Another way many whites looked at it was expressed by C. Chilton Pearson of Wake Forest College in 1921 who described the new constitution as a treaty with the Union.[30] Treaties are made between legal equals, but the Confederacy was a rebel regime. His view was also that the school system was to provide "democracy for the whites and opportunity for the Blacks through the agency of an increasingly socialized state" or, as he imagined the contemporary white feelings, schools were not to be built by choice. They were of "a system of common schools which has been thrust upon us."[31]

A Plan for Schools Emerges

Although most whites resisted funding a public school system for Black students, the reality was that poor whites were also largely illiterate. As Dr. Jabez Lamar Monroe Curry, agent for the Peabody Fund, said in 1898, referring to the entire South after the Civil War, "the illiteracy of the inhabitants was appalling, and by no means confined to the freedmen, but embraced a large percent of the white population."[32] Buck reported that in Virginia in 1870 there were over two hundred thousand illiterate freedmen and nearly seventy thousand illiterate whites.[33]

After William Ruffner was elected superintendent for Virginia, he spent years building public support and searching for funds, the latter a special burden because of the massive war debt and the loss of income from West Virginia, which had become a separate state. The burden would not be paid before 1937.[34] Meanwhile, the Underwood Constitution said that funding for schools was to come from interest on the Literary Fund, the poll tax, and a state property tax to be divided based on the number of school-age children in the various districts. Local taxes were not required, but counties were authorized to levy their own property capitation taxes.

The plan Ruffner developed was adopted by the assembly, then signed by the governor on July 11, 1870, and quickly became a model for southern school laws, especially in its insistence that white and "colored persons" receive a separate education. To some extent, it was built on the experiences in the North as well as a local management architecture used by the Literary Fund. "The public free schools shall be free to all persons between the ages of five and twenty-one years, residing within the school district; and in special cases to be regulated by the board of education, those residing in other districts may be admitted; provided that white and colored persons shall not be taught in the same schools; but in separate schools."[35]

County superintendents and school district trustees who were under the overall direction of the State Board of Education headed by the superintendent of public instruction were to supervise day-to-day school operations. To Ruffner's great credit, his accomplishments were huge, setting up a system to attract appropriate teachers and superintendents, establishing the curriculum, but especially building public support for what certainly was a revolutionary and controversial idea. The problems were also immense, growing so fast in the first years that qualified teachers would be hard to find.[36] Ruffner was also prescient in his understanding that the South was never going to economically develop without improving education for all the masses, including African Americans. By 1876 every county and city had public schools. They were unequal in quality, but they existed.[37]

Notes

1. Hans L. Trefousse, *Andrew Johnson: A Biography* (New York: Norton, 1997), 216–17.

2. Frank Moore, *Speeches of Andrew Johnson, President of the United States* (Boston: Little, Brown, 1866), vlv.

3. Archie Gibbs Richardson, *The Development of Negro Education in Virginia, 1831–1970* (Richmond: Richmond Virginia Chapter Phi Delta Kappa, 1976), 3.

4. Carl von Clausewitz, "War Is Merely the Continuation of Policy by Other Means," in *On War*, ed. and trans. Michael Howard and Peter Paret (Princeton, NJ: Princeton University Press, 1984), 87.

5. Foney G. Mullins, "A History of the Literary Fund" (PhD dissertation, Virginia Polytechnic Institute and State University, 2001), 49.

6. Dorsey Ford, *History of Education in Loudoun County* (Richmond, VA: University of Richmond, 1935); Edgar Wallace Knight, *A Documentary History*

of Education in the South before 1860, 5 vols. (Chapel Hill: University of North Carolina Press, 1949–1953); and Cornelius J. Heatwole, *A History of Education in Virginia* (New York: Macmillan, 1916), 210.

7. It is interesting to note that probably one reason the AMA was so supportive of Black education was their caution over giving Blacks citizenship following the Civil War since the large percentage of formerly enslaved were illiterate. They saw potential danger in such people having the power of the vote. A. P. Foster, "Work Among the Freedmen" in *The 13th Annual Report of the American Missionary Association* (New York: American Missionary Association, 1876).

8. Harrison Williams, *Legends of Loudoun: An Account of the History and Homes of a Border County of Virginia's Northern Neck* (Richmond, VA: Garret and Massie, 1938), 225.

9. "KKK Propaganda Distributed on MLK Weekend," *LoudounNow*, January 16, 2021, https://www.loudounnow.com/news/kkk-propaganda-distributed -on-mlk-weekend/article_4de06504-a6b9-5c9b-8e31-d186ee5c5cff.html.

10. *Democratic Mirror*, February 7, 1866.

11. Caroline Thomas, "Friends among the Freedmen," #7, April 24, 1867, *Friends Intelligencer* vol. 24 (Philadelphia: Friends Intelligencer Association, 1868), 137.

12. A Freedmen's Bureau office was located on the corner of Marshall and North Jay Streets in Middleburg, which became known as Bureau Corner, anchored by the Grant School, named after nineteenth-century Black instructor Oliver L. Grant (1847–1908). Bureau of Refugees, Freedmen, and Abandoned Lands, 1865–1869, Roll 45, pp. 489–90; and Roll 1865–1870, p. 303, Balch Library, Leesburg, Virginia.

13. "Earliest Black School in Virginia?," *Nest of Abolitionist* (blog), June 22, 2020, https://lincolnquakers.com/2020/06/22/earliest-black-school-in-virginia/.

14. The school closed in 1869. Betty Morefield and Elaine Thompson, "William Obediah Robey," in *The Essence of a People: Portraits of African Americans Who Made a Difference in Loudoun County, Virginia*, vol. 2 (Leesburg, VA: Black History Committee of the Friends of Thomas Balch Library, 2001).

15. "Waterford's Second Street School," n.d., *The History of Waterford Virginia*, https://www.waterfordhistory.org/history/second-street-school/.

16. This Reconstruction era Willisville School House is not the current structure, which was built in 1921 as a replacement after the first burned in 1917.

17. Ethel Smith, interview by Larry Roeder and Maddy Gold, August 5, 2017.

18. The Reconstruction Acts of March 1867 transferred civilian authority to the military.

19. Sec. 3, Constitution of Virginia. In Letter of the Secretary of War Communicating a corrected copy of the Constitution framed by the Virginia Convention, as furnished by Brevet Major General J. M. Schofield, the First Military District. 40th Congress, 2nd sess., Senate Ex Doc No. 54, May 9, 1868, p. 20.

20. Richardson, *Development of Negro Education*, 4.

21. Richard Lowe, *Republicans and Reconstruction in Virginia, 1856–70* (Charlottesville, University Press of Virginia, 1991), 138–39.

22. J. L. Blair Buck, *Development of Public Schools in Virginia, 1607–1952* (Richmond: State Board of Education, 1952), 65.

23. James Southhall Wilson, "History HS-22," in *The Commonwealth of Virginia: From 1776 to the Present* Charlottesville, VA: Home Study Program, University of Virginia, Extension Division, 1952), 44.

24. Williams, *Legends of Loudoun*, 226.

25. Wynne C. Saffer, *Loudoun Votes 1867–1966: A Civil War Legacy* (Westminster, MD: Willow Bend Book, 2002), 6.

26. *The Washingtonian*, February 21, 1868.

27. Buck, *Development of Public Schools in Virginia*, 67.

28. Richard Morton, *The Negro in Virginia Politics, 1865–1902* (Charlottesville: University of Virginia Press, 1919), 6.

29. Morton, 61.

30. Charles Chilton Pearson, "William Henry Ruffner: Reconstruction Statesman of Virginia," *South Atlantic Quarterly* 20, no. 1–2 (January and April 1921).

31. Pearson, 7.

32. J.L.M. Curry, *A Brief Sketch of George Peabody and a History of the Peabody Education Fund* (Cambridge: University Press, 1898), 116.

33. Buck, *Development of Public Schools in Virginia*, 68.

34. Brent Tarter, "The Virginia Debt Controversy," in *Encyclopedia Virginia*, July 25, 2022, https://encyclopediavirginia.org/entries/debt-controversy -the-virginia.

35. "Public Free Schools," *Reconstructing Virginia: The Richmond Daily Dispatch, 1866–1871*, June 9, 1870, accessed June 26, 2021, https://reconstructing virginia.richmond.edu/items/show/1709.

36. Edgar W. Knight, *Reconstruction and Education in Virginia*, reprinted from the *South Atlantic Quarterly* 15, no. 1–2 (January and April 1916): 19.

37. Park S. Rouse, "Virginia Public Education Owes Much to William Ruffner," *Daily Press* (Newport News, Virginia), March 24, 1982, 4.

3

1870–1901
From Hope to Jim Crow

Discrimination against Negroes yields super-profits to employers and landlords and commercial enterprises—at the expense not only of Negroes, who suffer most, but also of the masses of white people. Indeed, this is the fundamental purpose of the Jim Crow system. . . . It severely restricts the educational opportunities of Negro children; but it also reduces the educational opportunities of southern white children by imposing the burden of two parallel sets of schools on state and local budgets which are hardly adequate to finance even one decent system of schools.
—Doxey A. Wilkerson, former research associate, President
Roosevelt's Advisory Committee on Education

Hope and Jim Crow

The period after Reconstruction in Virginia was both vulgar and brave. In October 1871 in Loudoun County, the papers were full of attacks on the new constitution that

> provided for a Common School System, and the white people of the State (under the gentle impulse of the bayonet, it is true) accepted that constitution. . . . [They] not only had to provide schools for their own children, but also for the colored children, whose parents were banded against them politically, and did all in their power to wrest the control of the State and of the school system from them. It was not believed by the colored people that they would execute in good faith this provision of the Constitution.[1]

Thus began the political case, against Blacks and public education.

For their part, Blacks, although free and citizens, had little educational equality despite being an intimate part of creating a free public

Table 3.1
Loudoun County Public School Superintendents

Loudoun County Public School Superintendents, 1870–2021	
Date	Name
1870–80	John William Wildman
1881	Louis Murphy Shumate
1882–86	Col. William M. Giddings
1886–91	Louis Murphy Shumate
1892–93	John S. Simpson
1894–1907	Louis Murphy Shumate
1907–16	William G. Edmondson
1917–57	Oscar L. Emerick
1957–68	Clarence M. Bussinger
1968–88	Robert E. Butt
1988–91	Dr. David N. Thomas
1991–2014	Dr. Edgar B. Hatrick III,
2014–21	Dr. Eric Williams
2021–Present	Dr. Scott A. Ziegler

school system. Yet the period was also brave because Blacks were determined to learn and grow, not just survive. In 1872 Loudoun's first school superintendent, John William Wildman, was asked by State Superintendent William Henry Ruffner, "Have the colored people continued to manifest a great desire for education?" In response, Wildman lauded Loudoun's Blacks. "They are much more liberal in proportion to their means than the whites, and willing to submit to sacrifices to accomplish their object."[2] Indeed, this self-sacrifice would prove to be the norm throughout segregation. Although Black parents did invest in their children out of proportion to whites, Black children were exposed to books that depicted their race in cruel, demeaning ways. The 1883 *Jack, Jill and Tot* book discussed in the introduction is a good example.[3]

With the end of Reconstruction in Virginia (1870), the Conservatives (former Confederates) reasserted political power. In 1871 the Virginia government agreed to fully pay back the war debt at the prior agreed interest as a "matter of honor." However, given Virginia's poor tax base, paying the debt and investing in critical infrastructure and public education proved impossible. That led to the rise of a new party promising to "readjust" the state debt. The Readjuster Party came into power in 1879 offering a "time of hope" to Blacks as a key part of the Readjuster movement. The party was a biracial alliance of white and Black farmers, and others, led by a former Confederate general and railroad executive named William Mahone. Mahone wanted to reduce the influence of the traditional elites and, at the same time, proposed reducing the principal and interest of the war debt to protect internal development projects and the public schools. By 1882 the party managed to pass the Riddleberger Act, named after one of the party's cofounders, Harrison H. Riddleberger. Fifty-year bonds reduced the principal of the debt and the interest owed from 6 percent to 3 percent. The Readjusters also abolished the poll tax and the public whipping post.

However, the Conservatives feared rising Black authority in state government and situations like Danville, where Blacks (Readjuster Party) ran the local government and the police force was integrated. The Conservatives (now part of the white Democratic Party) successfully ran on anti-miscegenation platforms, finally causing the Readjusters to lose their legislative majority in 1883 after a race riot in Danville. Following that riot, white gangs prevented Blacks from voting. The Democrats took over, and by 1885, state-wide opposition to the Readjusters caused them to cease operations. However, before their demise, investments were made in Black schools for higher education and training, and in 1882 the Virginia Normal and Collegiate Institute (today Virginia State University) near Petersburg was established as a Black counterpart to Virginia Tech. Immediately after the end of the Readjuster Party, a series of anti-Black policies began the steady march to the Jim Crow constitution of 1902. Theories of Black inferiority became more accepted in white society and violence against Blacks more common, as was the danger of lynching if one violated the Black Codes.

Despite the growth of Jim Crow policies, the era was also a time of educational advancement because early superintendents in Virginia and Loudoun, as well as teachers and parents, were determined to build a viable system, even if it was racially split and unequal. The need for public education was critical because there was poverty and illiteracy across the South following the Civil War, which could only be cured with schooling. According to the 1870 US Census, 20 percent of the American population was illiterate (defined as anyone over ten years of age who could not write in any language). The growing illiteracy scourge had been obvious since the 1840 census and would continue until it become a national security issue during World War I when large numbers of soldiers were discovered to be illiterate.[4] In the census of 1870, the combined former Confederate states of Virginia, North Carolina, South Carolina, Georgia, and Florida had an illiteracy rate of 50 percent.[5] As for Virginia, in 1870 Ruffner reported that 32 percent of Virginia's population was illiterate, and in 1880 it was still significantly high, at 24 percent. By 1890, twenty years after the start of the public school system, probably reflecting the relative investments in education between the races, 75.2 percent of Blacks remained illiterate, compared to 14.3 percent of whites.[6]

Ruffner was a staunch missionary for education, which was especially important as he was the first superintendent of a system that was politically controversial from the start. To push back against those not wanting to school Blacks, he pointed out in his first annual report of 1871 "that every reason for educating whites applied equally to educating blacks; and that whilst it was necessary to educate the races in separate schools there should be no discrimination in respect to their schools."[7] However, the Edwin Washington team does not believe that Ruffner was being literal when saying "no discrimination." It was a system that provided services based on the relative contributions (taxes) of the two races, thus seeing discrimination through a commodity, not civil rights, lens. This same relativism continued into the next administrations, in both overt statements and an imbalance of provided resources.

In his 1872 annual report, Ruffner said "there are some counties in which many of the landowners have yet strangely failed to recognize the advantages of popular education to the owners of the soil."[8] In the same report, Wildman said about Loudoun County, "The present system of public instruction, on its introduction in this county, encountered the most determined opposition by the educated and refined portion of the community, who regarded it as an organization to promote the interests and elevate the conditions of the negroes and lower classes of whites at the expense of the property holders."[9] This led to low local revenues that could not support the salaries or accommodations needed by the best instructors. To mitigate this, Wildman directly supported the village of

Waterford with supplementary funding of $550 and $450 for Lovetts-ville;[10] however, the records do not show if any of the funds went to Black schools.

The overall political-economic system in Virginia did not offer equal opportunities for Blacks to acquire middle-class jobs, so they tended to earn less than whites on average; thus, they paid fewer taxes. However, ignoring the systemic inequality, the State Department of Education eventually argued that equitable sharing of resources between the races was unfair. Former lieutenant governor John E. Massey, serving in 1893 as state superintendent of public instruction, felt that since 90 percent of the taxes were borne by whites, they deserved better, an opinion shared by the local press in Alexandria, which covered Loudoun.[11] Massey did support the idea of summer teacher institutes at the Hampton Normal and Agricultural Institute to enhance the professionalization of Black faculties, but he also proposed limiting investments in Black schools.[12] Massey's transactional argument that the amount of taxes paid by one race relative to another should determine the level of government investment in schools will come up again. Massey, a former member of the Readjusters movement, which supported Black enfranchisement at the beginning of the public school system, broke with that party in 1882 to join the Democrats, who would disenfranchise Blacks and poor whites.

There was also a continual heated debate over whether Blacks should be schooled at all. Ruffner won that argument and did much good for Black education. That benefit should not be ignored; however, his argument focused on the economic growth potential for Virginia if Blacks were educated—and losses if they were not. This was admittedly clever, given the political environment, and it created an incentive to school Blacks, but it was ironic that in a post-enslavement era Blacks were still treated mainly as a commodity instead of as citizens with an inherent right to the best education. To be fair, Horace Mann, who was a strong believer in civil rights, including emancipation, made a case for the economic benefit of educating poor (white) people through public education, but he had a broader goal in mind. However, Ruffner was not making Mann's humanitarian argument. In America, the idea was that a child, regardless of economic origin, could advance. But the man in charge of designing and managing a system for educating both Blacks and whites believed Blacks were inferior and had to be taught in segregated schools or not at all. Why? An answer might be found in his 1874 annual report where he said he understood "Negroes," having grown up with slaves, having gotten to know them around the state, and "hav[ing] all my life been considered their special friend . . . the southern negroes are polite, amiable, quiet, orderly, and religious; and hence it is hard to believe that as a class they are without moral character. And yet such is the unhappy fact."[13]

Also consider the official statement in 1880 about Black teachers in the context of recommending for them access to normal schools. "Because of the superior culture of the white race, to say nothing of race pride, our theories would incline us to prefer white teachers for colored . . . and a strong and varied argument can be made on this side of the question. But the world's experience seems to have demonstrated that a people are best taught, that is most acceptably and successfully taught, by members of their own race." Ruffner went on to say, "colored schools need as good teachers as white schools,—indeed better, because colored children have more to unlearn than white [students]."[14] Interviews of survivors of segregation explained to the team that their ancestors would also have wanted Black instructors. They agreed with Ruffner's conclusions but not his rationale. Considering the times, Blacks felt whites had much to unlearn about Black stereotypes. Blacks wanted to avoid the embedded prejudices brought by whites of the time, which is a different argument than used today when it is felt a good idea is use a multicultural teaching staff to instill role modeling and cultural familiarity. Ruffner just felt white teachers were better, only proposing Black teachers for efficiency reasons.

At the same time, Ruffner did push Black education hard, noting that 512,841 Blacks lived in the state and that every consideration should be given them.[15] However, even that level of qualified support gained him opponents, the most influential being Robert Lewis Dabney, professor at Hampden-Sydney College, who wrote in 1876 that Blacks did not need education to exercise suffrage, a right that he believed they would lose anyway. In fact, Dabney believed that education would make Blacks idle, inefficient, and immoral and would lead to race amalgamation, which Dabney felt was a curse.[16] Despite Ruffner winning in the sense that the project of educating all children would move forward, the dark gong of Dabney's bell and that of fellow travelers continued to be heard by ready ears of the KKK and others, continuing into the 1950s, when the "massive resistance" strategy to school integration roared forward under the leadership of white supremacists.

Lack of equality meant that white teachers made more than Black teachers, but male teachers also made more than females, regardless of race. This discrepancy was debated in meetings of superintendents and the segregated teacher institutes throughout the era. However, between 1881 and 1904 white male teachers averaged $38 a month, versus $27 a month for Black males. In the same period, white females earned $30 a month, versus $24 for Black females.[17] This system of racial and gender discrimination clearly violated the Fourteenth Amendment's equal opportunity clause, but it would not be fully addressed until the 1940s.

Organization of the School System

The initial Virginia Public School structure was rooted in Ruffner's experiences, suggestions by northern advisers, and the fertile soil of the Literary Fund, the latter which had local superintendents, trustees, school boards, and districts.[18] Previously, the fund had only managed a relatively small system when compared to the quickly expanding network of public schools. As a result, the early structure would prove to be administratively burdensome yet would not seriously change until the 1920s. The Literary Fund originally operated as a supplement to private rural schools, often run out of small log cabins within walking distance of farm communities.

While the fund's commissioners funded supplies for indigent education, they did not set up or manage schools in the direct manner that public schools were by their district public school boards after 1870. The Literary Fund school districts were also of varying size, loosely managed, and in Loudoun were named after the commissioner covering the area. Once public schools were formed in 1870, school districts became the same as magisterial districts, had the same name, and were run by their own school boards. School trustees (a.k.a. patrons) also reported to the local boards. Funds for public schools came from a variety of sources, including patrons, local taxes, and special funds. This meant that in this inherently regressive system, a public school in the relatively prosperous village of Lincoln could afford to buy excellent supplies and supplement instructors salaries. Other public schools in poorer communities did not have that option.

Public school boards owned the schools and directly managed operations, which could vary widely in a single county and throughout the state. Boards also reported to an administratively weak county-level official called a division superintendent (or county superintendent), who then prepared statistical reports for Richmond. The superintendent, hired by Richmond, was also an ambassador for the public school concept. Unfortunately, this lack of uniformity between the districts plus their sheer numbers meant it was hard for Richmond to effectively manage local conditions.

Similarly, superintendents could not effectively manage teacher discipline. In his plan, Ruffner included a "teachers supervisory" system that, although segregated, was a progressive innovation in education with the potential for improving teacher professionalism. However, the decision to implement was left to the individual counties. Loudoun would not see teacher supervisors until the 1920s with the arrival of Superintendent Oscar Emerick.

The Literary Fund's sole focus was supporting indigents, which was only a fragment of the total school-age population. In addition to accepting indigent students, the public school system also opened its doors to anyone between the age of five and twenty-one, a vast expansion.[19] As during the prewar Literary Fund era, indigents were provided free books; between 1888 and 1901, an annual average in Loudoun of fifty-two white indigent and thirty Black indigent students received textbooks. The cost of indigent books was quite small, less than 1 percent of the budget (e.g., 0.14 percent in 1888). The other students had to pay a fee. Adult students over twenty-one were also required to pay tuition.

Credit for designing the public school system had many claimants for parentage. William Henry Ruffner is mentioned most often because when he was appointed as Virginia's first Superintendent for Public Instruction, he was required to prepare within thirty days a formal plan for a public school system. However, there were also others that surely

William Henry Ruffner
*Virginia Historical
Society*

influenced the completed blueprint. Archie Richardson suggests that Samuel F. Kelso, the Black Constitutional Convention delegate from Campbell County who in 1867 called for "all classes of people to partic- ipate," was one such influence.[20] Another Black Constitutional Conven- tion delegate and member of the 1870 House of Delegates, William H. Andrews of Surry County, may have suggested that the new state su- perintendent present a plan within thirty days and reportedly recom- mended a state board of education, county boards of education, and county superintendents appointed by the state superintendent. He also proposed additional state normal schools for Blacks to which eventually was added the Virginia Normal and Collegiate Institute at Petersburg in 1882, which trained many of Loudoun's Black teachers.[21] Andrews also recommended that the Literary Fund be inviolate, no doubt to avoid diversions to noneducational purposes such as occurred during the Civil War and Reconstruction. Therefore, while Ruffner was absolutely a leader in the growth and development of the public school system, some of the Black representatives also provided important leadership.

The Peabody Fund, which, according to some experts, may have largely written the language in the Constitution articulating the nature of a future state system, worked closely with Ruffner in development of the plan.[22]

The first Virginia Black normal school, Hampton Normal and Agricultural Institute, was created during Reconstruction by the Freedmen's Bureau (1868). During the next two decades, additional Black teacher training schools and institutes were established. They included the Richmond Colored Normal School in 1876 and the Virginia Normal and Collegiate Institute at Petersburg in 1882. There were also summer institutes for both Black and white teachers in Farmville in the mid-1880s. These institutes and many others would be heavily supported by the Peabody Fund.[23]

Types of Schools

Schools were constructed of all manner of materials, from logs to stone, brick, and plank. Many did not even have outhouses, forcing students to toilet among the trees. Drinking water was typically done from a bucket, and the students used a shared cup. Heat was often provided by a coal stove in a poorly ventilated building. Loudoun's Superintendent Wildman immediately recognized that the building stock was insufficient and promised in his annual report of 1872 to improve and expand as rapidly as funds permitted.[24]

There were also white academies for the wealthy, but according to Loudoun superintendents, some were of short duration, either meaning wealthier whites were not in sufficient numbers to sustain them or perhaps some children attended public schools. That kind of analysis is not provided in the annual reports.

Most records from 1870 to 1884 are missing for Loudoun public schools, but the record is more complete after that. One thing our team noticed was the difference in whether a schoolhouse combined all grades in one class (one-room schools) or had classes organized around grades in multiroom structures. Between 1887 and 1901, whites in Loudoun could take advantage of an average of fifteen graded schools. However, Blacks were only provided five graded schools in 1888 and 1889, then three each year thereafter. The initial five Black graded schools were

Greggsville, Leesburg, Lincoln, Middleburg, and Waterford.[25] Only Leesburg, Lincoln, and Middleburg continued as graded schools after 1889.

Schools could be closed for low attendance, which would become
a major political problem for both white and Black communities. As
early as 1872, Wildman (with lower than needed funds at hand) was opposed to paying for teachers to instruct a school with an attendance below twenty, saying it was not cost-effective. But he was also opposed to
lowering salaries, as that would reduce Loudoun's ability to attract instructors.[26] Future superintendents would face similar problems. In July
1890, to enhance attendance, Loudoun County Superintendent Louis
Shumate recommended to the Virginia Department of Education that
the school trustees be required to visit the schools and be paid for services.[27] "Anything that would bring the people themselves into closer
sympathy with the officers and teachers, and that would induce them to
keep their children in regular attendance upon the schools would be of
great service."[28] However, closing a Black school "for want of attendance"
did occur at least once in academic year 1891–92, but it closed without
Shumate's input—a reminder that local districts controlled the buildings. Shumate appeared to have been miffed, though, noting that the
decision had been made before he had an opportunity to visit.[29] Records
of specific venues were often minimal or missing.[30]

The Five Black Graded Schools

- **Greggsville:** Built in the 1870s for the children of the former enslaved, this school continued until it was closed in 1929.[31] When it
  was shuttered, it had been providing only a one-room experience,
  which seems to have begun in 1889 when the graded school offering ended.
- **Leesburg:** Normally known as the Training Center, the two-story
  structure was built around 1880 as a graded school, a program
  it continued to support into the 1940s. By the 1920s, elementary
  education to the seventh grade was limited to the first floor. This
  was because an experimental high school program was started on
  the second floor, which was then expanded in 1930. By 1941, with
  the creation of Douglass High School, the entire Training Center
  building became known as Douglass Elementary School.

- **Lincoln:** Also known as Janney's school, this two-story stone and frame structure was built by Quakers in 1871, making it one of Loudoun's earliest Black schools. It replaced (for Blacks) the use of the Oakdale school. Lincoln then closed in 1947 when the entire program was moved to Carver, a modern consolidated school constructed in the village of Purcellville. However, although Lincoln was two stories, the graded school program was probably converted to a one-room program by 1919, when the staff was reduced from two teachers to one.[32] Today the old Lincoln school is a private home.
- **Middleburg:** Constructed in 1886 as a two-room frame building at a cost of $1,000, it was known as Grant School after a popular Black teacher named Oliver Grant. The structure continued as a graded school until it closed in 1947.[33] The student body then moved to Banneker graded school in Saint Louis. The Middleburg school building continues as a small multi-office building across the street from the old Freedmen's Bureau Middleburg headquarters.
- **Waterford (Second Street School):** Originally a Freedmen's school started by Quaker Sarah Steer in 1867 or 1868 (depending on the source), it stopped being listed as a graded school in 1889. However, research indicates classes continued to be organized around grades until the school closed in 1957 during the consolidation process then going on. The school was built on the corner of Fairfax and Second Streets on land donated to the Black community by Quaker Reuben Schooley (1826–1900). Support was provided by the Freedmen's Bureau as well as the Friends Association of Philadelphia and Waterford's local Quakers.

The last one-room Black school was the Second Street School in Waterford. The last one-room white school was Mountain Gap White on Route 15, near the town of Leesburg. It was sold in 1959 to an attorney who used it to demonstrate the value of a one-room education, a role also now served by the Second Street School museum.

One research goal has been to determine how many white versus Black students attended school annually on average versus how many were enrolled. Attaining maximum attendance was considered a serious matter for educators as early as the Underwood Constitution, which under article VIII, section 14, permitted the General Assembly to make laws requiring parents and guardians to not permit children to grow up in ignorance or vagrancy.[34] Compulsory attendance laws had existed in the north in places like Massachusetts Bay Colony as early as 1642, but none of the southern states enacted such laws before 1895, and Virginia did not pass such a law until 1908. This led to a lack of attendance and poor literacy rates, with Virginia in 1895 ranking forty-second in the nation, a likely reflection of a lack of attendance enforcement and a disparity in investments in white versus Black schools and teacher salaries.

Rural, agricultural counties like Loudoun faced a unique attendance problem. Children, especially boys, often worked on the farms as free labor. Especially in the first generation of public schools, some parents did not believe in the value of a formal education. Public school transportation was an additional issue. None was provided for any student of any race, so some students did not attend because the walking distance between a school and home was too far or unsafe due to weather or conditions of the path, or if a parent could not spare a horse or the time for wagoneering.

Another problem was the disparity in instructed hours. Table 10 in these annual reports indicated that the average number of months of instruction provided whites was more than for Blacks. In 1887–88, for example, the white schools averaged 7.17 months versus 6.37 months for Blacks. In 1900–1901, white schools averaged 7.17 months, and Black schools still averaged below that of whites, at 6.38. This meant Black children on average (even in the graded schools because of this disparity in learning hours) were exposed to an inferior experience, and this disparity remained a major issue for decades. For example, in 1935 schools for Blacks tended to offer two months less learning time than for whites.[35]

Funding Education

According to the laws of 1872, each county school board was to prepare by the first of December an annual estimate of the aggregate funds needed for the following academic year as well as an allowance for the county superintendent. Legislation passed by the General Assembly at its session of 1871–72 also stated that county boards of supervisors were required to take measures, including the raising of taxes and proper distribution of state revenues, to ensure the viability of the public schools. That estimate, having been laid before the county board of supervisors, was recommended to be funded by a property tax to fulfill the requirements. However, a board of supervisors did not have to fully honor the local school board's budget. For researchers interested in these statistics, the county treasurer was also required to keep in accessors' land and property books three separate school accounts—district, county, and state funds—and to make proper disbursements.[36]

Fully funding the public schools was always an issue throughout the segregated era, involving federal, state, local and philanthropic support including help by patrons and families associated with a specific schoolhouse. In addition, there was an inevitable tension between the budgets proposed by the school board and the superintendent versus the priorities set by the county supervisors. As a result, local superintendents had to be part administrator and part public advocate and politician. Being a public advocate meant building both public and staff support by attending teacher meetings in various parts of Loudoun and then reporting on the proceedings to the public. A good example of that occurred in Waterford on December 20, 1873, at the third teacher institute for whites in Loudoun. Presiding was Loudoun's superintendent, John William Wildman. He was a graduate of Virginia Military Institute, although had not served in the military, instead making a career as a dry goods merchant and as treasurer of the Loudoun Agricultural Association.[37] Particularly in the early period of public education, it was important to explain the value of the new system and how it worked. Perhaps reflecting the influence of religion in the community, helping Wildman in this endeavor was a local reverend who delivered a strong statement explaining the school structure and its value.

This tension over funding between the public school system and the commonwealth was evident as early as January 1871. Due to the lack of public school money in half of the counties of the commonwealth, schools were forced to open by means of private subscription, meaning donations and tuition fees.[38] According to Tax Commissioner records in the Circuit Court of Loudoun County for 1872–1901, Loudoun, as required, funded its public schools out of taxes drawn on formulas associated with the population of students. They were in the form of warrants specifically designed to support district and county schools.[39] School records in the Edwin Washington Archives show breakdowns for the years 1884 onward of how much state money was apportioned to the county by the state auditor. For example, in 1884, the combined student population (Black and white) was 8,679, which permitted an apportionment of $2,169.75; however, further division of funds to specific schools and for salaries was determined locally, not by Richmond.[40]

Support in Loudoun also came from the Peabody Fund, legislative efforts to recoup monies previously diverted from the Literary Fund (arrearages), and local sources such as a dog tax, which had originally been created to compensate sheep owners for losses due to dog attacks. Other sources included delinquent land taxes, interest on state bonds held in Loudoun's name, and tuitions from people over twenty-one years old.[41] Keeping in mind that school management was divided between districts and counties, between academic year 1887–88 and academic year 1900–1901 about 30 percent of support came from the state. Another 28 percent was raised locally to support the county system, especially salaries, and 28 percent was raised for the use of districts. About 1 percent came from tuition and 2 percent from other unnamed sources, likely patrons. However, there was still a funding gap every year. This was a problem across the commonwealth, especially in the beginning, although it was mitigated somewhat by the Peabody Fund, which focused on graded schools and teacher institutes.[42] Unfortunately for Loudoun, aid didn't come in 1872, and there was a disparity between the number of white and Black graded schools for later years. Wildman spoke directly in 1872 on the tension between budget priorities. Feeling that schools were not getting their fair share, Wildman posited that while the citizens were willing to be taxed to support all schools, the county school board was better placed than the county board of supervisors to determine the most judicious and equitable balance in funding, including the power to "curtail or cancel the proposed levy."[43] However, boards of supervisors in Virginia have never supported that concept.

Underfunding of all schools was a persistent problem, and it exacerbated racial inequality, especially regarding health care. The lack of funds led to poor health situations in both Black and white rural schools, with many schools having unsanitary outhouses or no outhouses at all. By the 1890s, epidemics of flu, tuberculosis, and smallpox led the school system to exclude students with contagious diseases and not admit students without a vaccination. Sanitation and cleanliness were regular health-related topics in Loudoun schools as early as academic year 1893–1894, which led to requirements that teachers be tested in physiology and hygiene.

Increasing Teacher Professionalism

From the beginning, there was agreement that teachers and superintendents needed to be as highly qualified as possible. Unfortunately, some state superintendents like John E. Massey also took a white supremacist tone and focused more on upgrading white teachers than Black. Professionalism was enhanced through gatherings across county lines. An example occurred on July 17, 1888, when teachers and superintendents gathered in Alexandria in a teacher institute sponsored by the Peabody Fund. Superintendent Shumate attended, along with superintendents from Fauquier County, Fairfax County, and the city of Alexandria and many teachers.[44] Teacher institutes in Loudoun County had begun in August 1872 and January 1873, featuring speakers from outside the county so that local teachers could share ideas on how to instruct the various grades, discuss health issues, and other matters important to the school system.[45] The records do not, however, show exactly when Black institutes began.

There were sometimes conflicts between state regulations and local needs. Although teacher institutes were held from the beginning, none were probably held in Loudoun between 1888 and 1891 because they were not supposed to take place during the school year, and enough teachers could not be gathered during the summer since many lived outside the county.[46] However, the rules apparently changed because several were held in the academic years 1891–92 for white teachers and

1893–94 for both Black and white teachers, probably on Saturdays. According to the superintendent, the institutes were well attended and interesting; unfortunately, no minutes were retained.[47]

In 1872 Wildman noted his desire to elevate standards with the start of each academic year.[48] According to Shumate, in later years "we are compelled to depend largely upon the employment of untrained youths who teach for a little while in order to obtain funds to use in preparation for other avocations." In July 1891 Shumate further observed that "most of the teachers are young and inexperienced, and there seems to be an increasing disposition on the part of parents to interfere with the discipline of the schools and to criticize the laws and regulations controlling the system." Later in the same report Shumate mentioned that "occasionally, other things exercise an influence in the selection [hiring of teachers]. The system of petitioning on the part of patrons is perhaps on the increase and the effect is not beneficial."[49] As already noted, whites were paid more than Blacks and men more than women, but none were paid well enough, a point Ruffner made many times, and Shumate agreed.

In addition, Shumate complained about a lack of standards, saying

> the Legislature in repealing what was known as the 'average requirement' and failing to give us something in its stead, struck a heavy blow at the efficiency of many of our country schools. . . . I try to select the best material for teachers and then by rigid examination and by all other available means strive to impress upon them the necessity of preparation for their work. In addition to this, I try to exercise a careful supervision over all the schools of the county.[50]

Shumate also suggested that there was a need for the age requirement for teachers to be raised from eighteen to twenty, and "inexperienced teachers should be required to have or to get some Normal Training."[51] This topic of professionalization was also something the superintendent often lectured on.

Similar complaints continued well into the twentieth century. There is no doubt the comments were valid descriptions of *some* instructors, white and Black, but having examined the personnel records of hundreds of Black educators across the expanse of segregation as well as their personal biographies, the EWP team came away feeling that the educators were mainly very dedicated professionals because, for the Black race to succeed, education was essential.[52] White teachers were also dedicated, and both races in the twentieth century used petitions to argue for improvements in salaries and work conditions. But, because of the social order of the day, whites had an easier hurdle to leap over than the challenges Blacks faced, which had to do more with less compensation and fewer resources. One example of a teacher who went beyond high school to learn his profession was John Waters, who graduated from Virginia Normal Institute in Petersburg.[53] Another example of an exemplary Black instructor was William H. Ash of Leesburg. He was born enslaved but graduated from the Hampton Institute and later represented Amelia and Nottoway Counties in the 1887–88 session of the General Assembly. He was also principal at the Training Center in Leesburg in 1891–1893, among many other accomplishments.[54]

Regular Curriculum

There was little textbook uniformity in the early years of Loudoun's system, although instructors could avail themselves of prescribed books.[55] However, the EWP team did discover the 1898 daily program for Round Hill Colored School, which is the only surviving hour-by-hour, grade-by-grade breakdown of classes offered at a one-room school for Blacks in nineteenth-century Loudoun (see table 3.2).[56]

Access to Upper-Branch "High School" Lectures

In 1875 the Virginia General Assembly approved formal secondary education, and by the mid-1880s some public schools in Loudoun County, primarily larger ones (those with two to four classrooms), began offering courses above the seventh grade.[57] Called the "higher branches," the courses were generally Latin, history, geography, higher arithmetic, mathematics, philosophy, grammar, and science (without lab work). Today we would call them high school courses. Books such as William Webster Wells's *Essentials of Algebra* and Joel Dorman Steele's *Hygienic Physiology* were commonly used.[58]

Table. 3.2
Daily Program to Be Made by Teacher

Time		Recitations		Seat Work				
Begin	Minutes	Grade	Subject	Grade I	Grade II	Grade III	Grade IV	Grade V
9:00	5			Opening Exercises				
9:05	15	I	Reading		Reading	Arithmetic	Arithmetic	Arithmetic
9:20	15	II	Reading	Slate Work	Slate Work	Arithmetic	Arithmetic	Arithmetic
9:35	20	III	Arithmetic	Slate Work	Slate Work		Arithmetic	Arithmetic
9:55	20	IV	Arithmetic	Slate Work	Slate Work	Arithmetic		Arithmetic
10:15	20	V	Arithmetic	Number Work	Slate Work	Study	Study	
10:35	15	I	Arithmetic	Number Work	Number Work	Reading		Study
10:50	10			Recess				
11:00	10	II	Arithmetic	Writing			Study	Study
11:10	10	III	Reading	Writing	Arithmetic		Grammar	Grammar
11:20	20	IV, V	Grammar	Slate Work	Language	Geography		
11:40	20	I, II	Language			Geography	Study	Study
Noon	50			Recess				
12:50	20	III	Language	Spelling	Spelling		Geography	Geography
1:10	20	III	Geography	Spelling	Spelling		Geography	Geography
1:30	10	I	Reading		Spelling	Spelling	Geography	Geography
1:40	20	IV	Geography	Reading	Reading	Spelling		Geography
2:00	15	V	History	Reading	Reading	Spelling	Spelling	
2:15	10	I	Spelling		Reading	Spelling	Spelling	
2:25	10	II, III	Spelling	Spelling			Spelling	
2:35	10	IV, V	Spelling	Spelling	Correcting S.W[a]	Correcting S.[b]		
2:45	15	V	Geography	Spelling	Correcting S.[b]	Correcting S.[b]	Spelling	
3:00	5			Recess				
3:05	10	II	Reading	Study			Study	Study
3:10	20	ALL	Writing					
3:30	20	IV	Reading	Study	Study	Study		Study
3:50	10	V	Reading	Study	Study	Study	Study	

[a]Could be spelling and writing.
[b]Could be spelling.

Until the 1920s, the course work for Black students was nearly always in one- or two-room schoolhouses and formed only a portion of the day's primary schooling—if permitted at all. In fact, limiting the allowable hours of higher-branch courses offered to anyone was normal in Virginia country schools in the nineteenth and early twentieth centuries. The district school board had the authority to offer both elementary and higher-branch courses but was prohibited by the State Board of Education from offering courses that would "interfere" with the "regular and efficient instruction in the elementary branches."[59] If a school had only one teacher, she or he was to devote five hours or more (but not less) to elementary branches.[60]

One of the mandates of the Edwin Washington Project is to document students who, like Edwin Washington, exemplified the determination to learn. One nineteenth-century public school era example is interesting in this light, even though the amount of schooling for this student was limited. Unusual for any Black, Annie Rivers gained some upper-branch training in 1892, perhaps because of her father's espionage exploits. From an examination of the 1892 register for Lovettsville Colored and other research on the Rivers family, we are left with the impression that Annie O. L. (or A. L.) Rivers was an early beneficiary of higher-branch coursework because she was the oldest student at age nineteen. But perhaps the local Black community recommended this to the local school board because Annie's father, Joseph Rivers, had risked his life as a spy for the Union army informing them about the operations of John Mobberly's band.[61] Annie continued at Lovettsville Colored in the November 28 to December 23 session. The table of statistics in the register doesn't show higher branches being offered to her again; what matters isn't the amount but that she (a Black female) was offered anything.[62] We know of some white students who gained such permission in that period but no examples of other Black students.

Conclusions

This first era of public education was one of "chalkboard" bravery by the Black community because while they had been at the forefront of the decision process to provide their race free public schooling, they had to struggle harder than whites to achieve their academic goals. This included providing partial financial support for their own schools despite their impoverishment relative to whites. The hope following emancipation and the advent of Black citizenship was for a broad opening of doors, but instead white supremacist philosophies predominated, with barriers to education like reduced instruction hours for Blacks versus whites, inadequate and unequal teacher salaries, heavier teacher workloads relative to that of white counterparts, and so on. Blacks even had to contend with powerful white religious leaders who felt education for Blacks was improper. Despite these barriers, Blacks stood their ground, which was good training because in the next period of history they would have to face even more hurdles, including losing many hard-won political rights. Nevertheless, their bravery would continue unabated.

Notes

1. "What the Conservative Party Has Done for Public Schools," *Mirror*, Leesburg, October 25, 1871, 2.

2. "Report by Superintendent John W. Wildman of Loudoun," in *Second Annual Report of the Superintendent of Public Instruction of Virginia for the Year Ending August 31, 1872* (Richmond, VA: 1872), 88.

3. Emma Elizabeth Brown, *Jack, Jill and Tot* (Boston: D. Lothrop, 1883).

4. Sanford Winston, "From 1870 to 1920," in *Illiteracy in the United States* (Chapel Hill: University of North Carolina Press, 1930), 8.

5. Winston, 14.

6. J. L. Blair Buck, *Development of Public Schools in Virginia, 1607–1952* (Richmond, VA: State Board of Education, 1952), 117.

7. Buck, 89.

8. *Second Annual Report of the Superintendent*, xiv.

9. "Report by Superintendent John W. Wildman of Loudoun," in *Second Annual Report of the Superintendent*, 88.

10. *Second Annual Report of the Superintendent*, 28.

11. *Alexandria Gazette*, August 19, 1893, 3.

12. The Hampton Normal and Agricultural Institute is also known simply as the Hampton Institute and, today, as Hampton University.

13. *Fourth Annual Report of the Superintendent of Public Instruction of Virginia for the Year Ending August 31, 1874* (Richmond, VA: 1874), 147–48.

14. "Colored Teachers for Colored Schools," *Educational Journal*, February 1880, pp. 56 and 58.

15. Archie G. Richardson, *The Development of Negro Education in Virginia, 1831–1970* (Richmond, VA: Phi Delta Kappa, 1976), 7.

16. Thomas Cary Johnson, *The Life and Letters of Robert Lewis Dabney* (Richmond, VA: Presbyterian Committee of Publication, 1903), 396.

17. EWP: 3.3.1 AYr. 1884–1901. *1884–1901*. Table 2 in *Loudoun County Superintendent Annual Reports*.

18. The Virginia legislature permitted free schools as early as 1846, if counties wanted them, but Loudoun demurred for fear of attendance by freed Blacks.

19. The ages were proposed by Black legislator Peter K. Jones.

20. Luther Porter Jackson, *Negro Office Holders in Virginia 1865–1895* (Norfolk: Guide Quality Press, 1946), 70.

21. Buck, *Development of Public School*, 113; see also L. M. Curry, *A Brief Sketch of George Peabody and a History of the Peabody Education Fund* (Cambridge: University Press, 1898).

22. Charles Chilton Pearson, "William Henry Ruffner: Reconstruction Statesman of Virginia," reprint from the *South Atlantic Quarterly* (1921), 7–9. See references to Kelso and Andrews in Jackson, *Negro Office Holders in Virginia*, 69–70.

23. Buck, *Development of Public Schools*, 113; see also Curry, *A Brief Sketch of George Peabody.*

24. *Second Annual Report of the Superintendent*, 98.

25. Waterford Colored was not multiroom.

26. *Second Annual Report of the Superintendent*, 59.

27. Shumate was a teacher before joining the Confederate Army as a private. He mustered out as a second lieutenant, 8th Virginia Infantry, Company C. See US Prisoner of War Records, 1861–1865. US National Park Service, Civil War Soldiers 1861–1865 [database], film no. M382, roll 50. See also US Historical Data Systems, Civil War Soldier Records and Profiles 1861–1865 [database], Provo, UT, Ancestry.com Operations Inc., 2009.

28. Opening questions in EWP: 3.3.1 AY 1889/90, Loudoun County Superintendent Annual Report.

29. Table 9 in EWP: 3.3.1 AY 1891–92, Loudoun County Superintendent Annual Report. The school in question has not been determined.

30. The Edwin Washington Project has been developing a chart to show for the first time all the public schools developed before 1968 and many private schools developed prior to 1870, when public schooling started. This is an especially difficult task because in the early days of public education, few street addresses existed. EWP: 9.2 Yr. 2019, School-Building-Map-Study.

31. EWP: 6.6 Black Student Enrollment Cards.

32. EWP: 6.6 Black Student Enrollment Cards.

33. EWP: 2.2 County School Board, Yr. 1918–1952, *Report of Survey Committee on Long Range Planning for Loudoun County*, January 1940.

34. Buck, *Development of Public Schools*, 69.

35. Edward E. Redcay, *County Training Schools and Public Secondary Education for Negroes in the South* (Washington, DC: The John F. Slater Fund, 1935).

36. *Acts and Joint Resolutions Passed by the General Assembly at Its Session of 1871–1872* (Richmond, VA: 1872), 444–45.

37. Letter to Larry Roeder from Mary Laura Kludy, VMI Archives and Records Management Specialist, May 5, 2021.

38. Edgar Wallace Knight, *Reconstruction and Education in Virginia*, reprinted from the *South Atlantic Quarterly* 15, no. 1–2 (January and April 1916): 19.

39. Warrants were authorizations to pay something after a claim for salary or some other purpose had been made to the treasurer. See records of the Tax Commissioners, Yr. 1870–1901, Archives of the Circuit Court of Loudoun County.

40. Circular No. 380 of September 4, 1882, in EWP: 2.4.2 Yr. 1882–1921, District and Census Reports.

41. Letter from Second Auditor's Office, Commonwealth of Virginia, to Mr. William Giddings, Superintendent for Loudoun County Schools, July 14, 1885.

42. *Second Annual Report of the Superintendent*, xi.

43. *Second Annual Report of the Superintendent*, 49.

44. "Alexandria Affairs," *Evening Star*, July 28, 1888, p. 5.

45. *Second Annual Report of the Superintendent*, 77.

46. EWP: 3.3.1. *Loudoun County Superintendent Annual Reports 1887/88–1890/91*.

47. EWP: 3.3.1. *Loudoun County Superintendent Annual Reports 1891/92–1893/94*.

48. *Second Annual Report of the Superintendent*, 66.

49. EWP: 3.3.1., *Loudoun County Superintendent Annual Report for the Year Ending July 31, 1889*.

50. Supplementary Report in EWP: 3.3.1 Yr. 1891. *Loudoun County Superintendent Annual Report*.

51. Supplementary Report in EWP: 3.3.1 Yr. 1891. *Loudoun County Superintendent Annual Report*.

52. EWP: 4.5 Lists and Teacher Cards.

53. Question 9 in Supplementary Report in EWP: 3.3.1. *Annual Report of the Superintendent for the Year Ending July 31, 1891*, in *Annual Reports for 1887–1918*.

54. Table 3 in EWP: 3.3.1 Yr. 1892–1893, *Loudoun County Superintendent Annual Reports*.

55. *Second Annual Report of the Superintendent*, 85.

56. EWP: 5.2 Yr. 1898, Curriculum, Round Hill Colored.

57. Act Approved March 31, 1875, chap. 354, p. 439, *Acts of the General Assembly of the State of Virginia, Passed at the Session of 1874–5* (Richmond, Superintendent of Public Print, 1875).

58. William Webster Wells, *The Essentials of Algebra for Secondary Schools* (Boston: Leach, Shewell and Sanborn, 1897); and Joel Dorman Steele, *Hygienic Physiology: Fourteen Weeks in Human Physiology* (New York: American Book, 1889).

59. *The Virginia Public School Register* (Richmond: J. W. Randolph Publishers and Booksellers, 1895), 7.

60. *Virginia Public School Register*, 7.

61. Claim of Joseph Rivers (37320), Lovettsville, Loudoun County, VA, SCC Approved, "Southern Claims Commission Approved Claims, 1871–1880:

Virginia," M2094, 45 rolls, Records of the Accounting Officers of the Department of the Treasury, RG 217, NARA, Washington, DC; and Scott Thompson, "Their Homes Were in the Enemy's Lines: Loyalty, Military Occupation, and Irregular Warfare in a Northern Virginia Border County, 1861–1865" (Master's dissertation, Texas Tech University, 2013), 61. John W. Mobberly, also known as John Mobley or Morbly, (ca. 1844–1865) was a Confederate guerrilla who operated in the Loudoun Valley and between the Hills region of Loudoun County, Virginia during the American Civil War.

62. *Virginia Public School Register*, 7.

4

1902-20
Battling Health and Education Disparity

"I know the Negro." Perhaps no single phrase has been more frequently used in discussing the race problem in America than that familiar declaration. It has been commonly employed to support opinions and sustain the convictions of large numbers of white men and women who are zealous to defend existing customs and practices which give to the Negro a different status in social and civic life from that occupied by his white neighbour.

—Robert Russa Moton, 1930

[The new Virginia Constitution will] forever remove the negro as a factor in our political affairs and give to the white people of this Commonwealth the conduct and control of the destinies which they have the right to shape and determine.

—Broadside, 1901

During the Wilson administration, 1913 to 1921, Virginia-born President Woodrow Wilson welcomed the racist film *Birth of a Nation* into the White House. Wilson saw himself as progressive, but he abandoned the Black community after his election. From his writings and actions it is also clear that he was not wedded to the structure set up by the Founding Fathers, and while he had once advocated parliamentary rule, he also had a commitment to the unitary theory or autocratic presidency as the efficient way of achieving goals. This is seen in his use of police and especially false information (propaganda) when he demonized Germans to build public support for war. This unitary executive approach undermined civil rights in general to the point that concerned citizens felt compelled to form the American Civil Liberties Union in 1920. His disdain for socialists would also lead to problems in Loudoun County

Robert Russa Moton
M. Miley & Son, Lexington, 1916

for Quakers who had voted for Eugene Debs and set the stage for a later generation of segregationists in the 1950s who equated support for Black integration with support for communism.[1] Virginia also suffered from a similar tension between a new focus on progressive efficiency by county and state educational leaders and a propensity to treat Black people in an unequal manner.

The point made by Robert Moton in the opening epigraph, although stated in 1930, could apply to this period of segregation, especially when examining statements by state superintendents like William Ruffner and Joseph Eggleston, regardless of their many estimable accomplishments, including those that helped Black Americans. The period began with a great civil rights tragedy in Virginia, the holding of the state's Constitutional Convention of 1901–2, which was a repudiation of the Underwood Constitution. The Constitution of 1902 restored white supremacy as law and the way of life and disenfranchised most Black

Americans and working-class whites, remaining in effect until July 12, 1971. The document reframed conservative politics, was a rebuttal to any effort to desegregate, and gave philosophical oxygen to another half century of white supremacists like Sen. Harry F. Byrd Sr., who led the massive resistance to integration in the 1950s. Although called "progressive," the constitution was largely a return to Confederate beliefs on race relations—which were autocratic and undemocratic, although without slavery—and advanced states' rights over shared national responsibility.

Covering the entire progressive movement is beyond the scope of this book. Nevertheless, progressive policies played an important role in Loudoun, Virginia, and the South. It was a time of national political reform aimed at improving society by ending corruption as well as inefficiencies through better science and engineering. The policies of Oscar Emerick fit that mold because he insisted on providing better accounting, reducing waste, and improving management. Schooling for both races improved, although unevenly. Similarly, many fresh public health policies on inspections, vaccinations, and sanitation were structured to reduce infectious diseases and other health problems in the schools, something that benefited all races, although there were significant failures like the Tuskegee program and unequal access to health professionals and facilities. The movement is also often described as an effort to improve democracy, but this was a bridge too far in the South where racial inequity was entrenched in the laws such as the Virginia Constitution of 1902.

Progressive Administrative Changes

The modern Department of Public Instruction was formed and Joseph Dupuy Eggleston Jr. became the first popularly elected state superintendent in 1906. He was a hard worker and quite impatient with politicians and demanding of practical change. Like Ruffner at the beginning of the public school era, Eggleston traveled widely to sell his perspective on learning. For example, he traveled to Loudoun in 1908, arguing for better school buildings at the Leesburg Courthouse and in the villages of Lincoln and Middleburg.[2] Eggleston continued to serve until 1912 and is credited with increasing the number of Virginia's high schools and salaries for teachers; he also worked for longer school terms. He helped create the County School Fairs experiment or movement, an agricultural demonstration effort in cooperation with the US Department of Agriculture. Those fairs were a major component of Loudoun educational life for many years, although they did not benefit Black citizens in that county until near the program's end.

When Eggleston began his term, there were only 75 high schools in Virginia, but there were 448 by the time he left six years later. His advocacy required heated debates in the House of Delegates, apparently to the point of personal exhaustion, causing him to retire to academia. Other progressive changes included allowing local school boards to borrow from the Literary Fund to finance salary increases or construction, essential tools in Loudoun. Eggleston also encouraged research on the effectiveness of rural schools, which led him to accept an invitation in 1912 by the US Commissioner of Education and Virginia's governor to travel to Switzerland for ten weeks. At the time, Swiss village schools were considered a model for rural education.[3]

In addition, Eggleston regularly attended education conferences and encouraged all teachers to do this as well, which Loudoun's school leadership regularly did before and after his time as state superintendent. In 1902 Loudoun's superintendent, Louis Shumate, presented a formal paper at a conference of county and city superintendents on "what constitutes" an efficient superintendent.[4] In 1919, following a conference in Richmond on public schools, Superintendent Oscar Emerick reported to the citizens of Loudoun many of its findings, including that reading efficiency in Virginia was ranked thirty-fifth to fortieth in the forty-eight states. He blamed short terms and limited professionalism in the educator ranks. Twelve out of eighty-six division (county) superintendents in Virginia had never taught, and fourteen had not completed high school. About 25 percent of all teachers had no experience, and teacher shortages were so severe that nearly anyone who wanted to teach could obtain a contract "regardless of personality, tact, common sense, and those other things . . . necessary to make a good teacher."[5] Physical conditions of schools had been a problem since 1870 and were still ruining health and morale. The conclusion was that faculty management and instructional practices needed a total revamping.

Despite all the good work he did, Eggleston neglected Black education. A *Los Angeles Times* study in 1909 boldly noted that southern states only expended 14 percent of their school funds on Black students, although the race made up 40 percent of the student population. The US Commissioner for Education asked Eggleston for a response, who then presented a transactional perspective. This was only a few years since passage of the new commonwealth's constitution, so perhaps it is not surprising that instead of agreeing that all citizens had a right to equal education regardless of their personal financial status, the quality of what a race was to receive in Virginia was based on the percentage of taxes paid by that race. In 1907 Virginia spent over $500,000 on Black schools, but Black citizens contributed only a fraction in taxes and fees. That, to Eggleston, justified a lower investment per capita for Black students than for white students.[6] The problem, of course, was that the prevailing sentiment among most whites of the time was that Black workers were not supposed to be in jobs that paid as well as whites, a concept that, if it persisted, would have doomed Blacks to indefinite underfunding of their schools and a bleak economic future.

In response to underinvestment in Black educational needs, Robert Russa Moton and other Virginian Black leaders formed the Negro Organization Society (NOS) at Hampton Institute in 1912. The Edwin Washington Project team discovered a handful of records in the project archives referencing the NOS. It was also known by various subtitles such as "State Organization in Virginia for Community Leagues."[7] That

Robert Russa Moton (1867–1940): Robert Moton was one of the most prominent Black educators in the United States in the first decades of the twentieth century. He authored *Finding a Way Out: An Autobiography* (1920) and *What the Negro Thinks* (1929) and was a trustee of the Anna T. Jeanes Fund and second principal of Tuskegee Institute, making significant contributions to teacher training and the conditions of Black soldiers during World War I. He was also a trustee of numerous Black colleges and several philanthropic funds and was the recipient of many honorary degrees and awards, notably the Spingarn Medal for service to African Americans.

subtitle captured the body's essence, facilitating supportive leagues and "self-improvement," which occurred in Loudoun. However, the NOS did not control local operations.

The NOS was also the parallel to the white Cooperative Education Association (CEA), founded in 1904; but unlike the CEA, which received government financial assistance, the NOS depended on its own fundraising and white philanthropies. The NOS grew out of conferences hosted by the Hampton Institute and gave African Americans a public voice through talented leaders like Booker T. Washington and Moton. The NOS also focused heavily on health, sanitation, and assisting local Black communities in negotiating better arrangements with local governments.

Oscar Emerick emerged as superintendent for public instruction in Loudoun in 1917, a position he held until 1957. His meticulous record-keeping is responsible for the bulk of the Edwin Washington Project archives. Emerick, like Eggleston, was a progressive as we have defined it, who introduced modern management innovations into the county's school system, yet he also took a public stand in favor of segregation during the massive resistance era. Despite the racial overtones of the times and his own prejudices, Emerick did introduce important measures helpful to Black citizens. For example, early in his career, with the support of the newly formed League of Women Voters in Loudoun County, he convinced the board of supervisors to fund school supervisors, including the first Black supervisor in Loudoun's history, Mary Peniston. He continued to make similar hires that significantly improved the lives of Black students and teachers.

Because of the disparity between white- and Black-directed investments, success improving Black schools also required philanthropies like the Peabody Fund, the Slater Fund, and the Jeanes Fund, which supported Black teachers, or the Rosenwald Foundation, known for building schools for Black students. George Peabody created the Peabody Fund on February 7, 1867, with a grant of $1 million (about $17 million in 2020). In 1914 the Peabody Fund was folded into the John F. Slater Fund, which had been created in 1882 by John F. Slater, a Connecticut textile manufacturer. The Jeanes Fund, also known as the Negro Rural School Fund and the Anna T. Jeanes Foundation, was created April 22, 1907, when Quaker Anna T. Jeanes donated $1 million to assist small schools for Blacks. President William H. Taft, Andrew Carnegie, Booker T. Washington, and George Peabody initially managed this fund. The Rosenwald Foundation, also known as the Julius Rosenwald Fund and the Julius Rosenwald Foundation, although active in other Virginia counties, did not build any schools in Loudon County and only funded some library collections there.

Another major player in the field of Black education was the General Education Board, a national nonprofit established in 1903 with a grant from John D. Rockefeller to promote education. At the state level, 1910 saw the hiring of Jackson Davis (a white man) as the first official Virginia supervisor of Negro Schools, initially financed by the Peabody Fund.[8] This decision was based on recommendations of the General Education Board. By 1940 the Peabody Fund had spent over $85 million dollars on southern education.[9] The annual reports of the various funds show a deep commitment to serious financial investments in broad categories of school activities such as teacher training, industrial schooling, country schools, science, and standardization of school equipment as well as a commitment to what they called Negro Education and strategic partnerships such as with the Jeanes Fund, which had been set up to help compensate Black supervisors in places like Loudoun.

In 1908 Dr. James Hardy Dillard, a nationally recognized educator and advocate of Black education, became president of the Jeanes Fund; to manage collaboration, he also was head of the John F. Slater Fund for the Education of Freedmen by 1910.[10] Dillard stood at or near the pinnacle of white educators dedicated to enhancing Black education. In 1913 Dillard returned to Virginia and for the remainder of his career resided in Charlottesville. In 1931 all the funds were merged into the Southern Education Foundation, which still exists to this day. Their archives are at the library of Atlanta University.

One of the most important of Dillard's negotiations caused the training centers for Blacks to emerge in Virginia. Progressive leaders like Dillard wanted Blacks to have true high schools but faced adamant opposition from the white educational establishment. Training centers were a 1911 compromise, which had its origins in Kentwood, Louisiana, Tangipahoa Parish, not far from Baton Rouge.[11] The centers came to be

a structural alternative to high schools, particularly in rural communities, intended to train brighter students to become teachers. This second
goal never fully took off, although some students did indeed become
teachers. The Peabody Fund also supported Dillard's work by providing
a supplement of $350,000 in 1914.[12]

In summary, during a resurgence of white supremacy that began with
the 1902 Constitution and included serious underinvestment in Black
education that eliminated the potential of equal social and economic
advancement, good things still happened to public schools. However,
most benefits accrued to white schools. In other words, overlaying the
positive developments was a thick, hard political structure that insisted
on treating Blacks as second-class citizens. Further, race relations in the
United States were turning very violent as the first wave of the Great Migration collided with the demobilization after World War I and a poor
economy and competition for jobs became a flash point. Anti-Black violence spread beyond the South leading to approximately twenty-five
"race riots" across the nation in 1919, including in Chicago. In addition,
groups such as the United Daughters of the Confederacy worked hard
to establish a romanticized version of the Confederacy and the myth of
the "Lost Cause" throughout the South.

Upper-Branch Education

Between the academic years 1886–87 and 1904–5, the average annual
number of whites taking upper-branch courses across the county was
220. For Blacks in the same period, the average was 2! Even accounting
for the larger white population, this is a significantly disproportionate
difference in enrollment. The rules on higher-branch access stated that
any who wanted to take such classes needed permission from the local
school board, which was all white in Loudoun. This restriction must
have been intimidating for a Black family wanting their child to tread a
path to higher learning or to seek access to employment requiring secondary schooling; yet Blacks did persist, despite many whites viewing
them as competitors.

In academic year 1917–18, there were only three accredited Black
public high schools in all of Virginia: Armstrong (Richmond), Booker T.

Washington (Norfolk City), and Mt. Hermon (Norfolk County). There were also several private boarding schools supported by churches, for the most part, such as Manassas Industrial, started by the evangelist Jennie Dean, who also started an education-centric chapel in the village of Conklin. This was a time when a high school diploma was for many what a bachelor's degree is today. It marked an achievement on the highway to prosperity, college, and possibly law and medical professions, jobs that could make a difference for an entire family. Whites had been using private academies for a long time when, in 1910, LCPS created Loudoun's first public high school in Lincoln. Before the 1920s, if a Black student wanted to attend high school in Loudoun (public or private), it was impossible, except for upper-branch-level courses occasionally offered in one-room schoolhouses.

The problem was not just prejudice. The Commonwealth of Virginia was still recovering from the Civil War at the start of public school segregation and had to service massive debt, so it initially did not budget funds for any public high schools, Black or white. Eventually, cities and counties were permitted to establish high schools that charged tuition, but not more than $2.50 a month per pupil. In Loudoun, the monthly tuition at Lincoln's white high school, established in 1910, was $1.50 to $2. This was more than a typical Black worker earned in two days, so if a Black high school had been built in Lincoln or Waterford, villages friendly to Blacks, few could have attended.[13] Commonwealth education budgets during and just following World War I also suffered.

The County School Fair Movement

One progressive effort by Eggleston that directly impacted Blacks and whites across Virginia, as well as the school system in Loudoun, was the County School Fair movement, which began in 1908 and continued to the mid-1920s.[14] During segregation, there were huge legal and social debates in America over what defined appropriate kinds of education for Blacks. Many white politicians like President Taft pushed industrial training over academics, with the goal of maintaining the traditional social order.[15] Their language often portrayed a disbelief that Blacks could attain an academic education. At the same time, Black leaders like

Larry Roeder and Delores Nash-Hicks, a member of the Campbell County Training School Complex Commission in Rustburg, discussing the 1908 County School Fair. *Nancy Catherine Watford, Rustburg, Virginia, September 6, 2019*

Booker T. Washington felt political power would emerge only after economic leverage was secured and, for different reasons, saw industrial education as the most practical lever to attain Black success. This idea was manifested in the County School Fair movement. The movement was essentially a social experiment rooted in the efforts of the Virginia Federation of Women's Clubs, Booker T. Washington, Seaman Knapp, and others to avoid potential of famine in the South by improving the production of Black and white farmers.[16] This was needed because agriculture across the nation was not keeping up with demand, and famine was a real risk.[17] Thus, county school fairs were a fresh tool to address a true national security problem, and states responded with their own fairs.

The fairs were mainly designed to attract large crowds to see demonstrations by Black and white students of modern farming methods considered more productive than traditional ones, and to encourage children in rural counties to stay on the farm. The hope was also that older farmers would be inspired by the students, who were trained by professionals, and then change their own methods. The events also featured sports, arts, and academic learning. These special fairs required enormous planning and logistical support, so the Department of Public Instruction in Richmond provided a detailed brochure on how to manage the fairs but no funding, only encouragement and partnering.[18] Counties were asked to volunteer to set up their own fairs and cover their own expenses.

Black- and white-oriented fairs took place in many locales, starting with Rustburg, Campbell County, in 1908, but Black fairs did not happen in Loudoun until 1921. Loudoun's fairs between 1910 and 1920 were for whites only. Its 1910 event was the largest annual social gathering in Loudoun and one of the most important in the commonwealth.

Eggleston worked hard on many progressive programs during his tenure, but the fair project was a good example, among many, where the superintendent could not rely on the state legislature for sufficient financial support. This was frequently the story across Virginia. For counties

Black County School Fair in Campbell County, 1908. No photographs have survived from the Black fairs in Loudoun.
Courtesy of Campbell County Historical Society

to advance progressive programs in health, hire supplementary faculty, buy extra school equipment, or invest in needed repairs or construction, there never seemed to be enough official funding.

Funding Local School Activities

Success for bold initiatives often depended on private donors. An excellent example was the hiring of a county school nurse for Loudoun in 1914, the first rural school nurse in Virginia. Her position came about not because of state or board of supervisors funds but thanks to private contributions by a federation of wealthy citizens. Without the federation's support and some charities outside Loudoun, her services and other similar ones probably would not have happened, a detriment to both races.[19]

By 1913–14 the American Red Cross and the Virginia State Board of Health endorsed the idea of federations of civic-minded citizens helping in health policy. Such federations had been tried in other communities, and one was established in Loudoun.[20] The "federation" in Loudoun first met in Hamilton to form the Public Health Association of Loudoun County, later called Loudoun Federated Society for Community Betterment.[21] In a meeting in Purcellville in 1914, the Federated Society also was made to consist of sustaining members and others who paid a nominal fee. All religious/social bodies in Loudoun were also invited to join, making the organization a federated charity body of sorts with a main goal of paying for a visiting rural nurse.

By August 24, 1915, Dr. Harvey W. Wiley, former chief of the Bureau of Chemistry of the Federal Department of Agriculture and known as the father of the Pure Food and Drug Act of 1906, was appointed as president of the Federated Society in Loudoun.[22] Wiley was a resident of Loudoun, owning Grasslands Farm.[23] By this point the Federated Society sessions were held in Purcellville "bush" meetings (annual temperance rallies).

Of course, events outside of Loudoun's control did impact the availability of funds for school operations, which were reduced due to World War I, but Emerick still doggedly asked for an enhanced budget.[24] He also wanted better supervision of money, especially on how teachers spent funds, which was of deep concern to the House of Delegates. Richmond had been complaining about fiscal mismanagement in many counties since 1912.[25] Emerick proposed hiring supervisors to handle administrative functions, noting that the net monthly income of the superintendent was less than any high school principal, yet there were over seventy one- and two-room schools to administer, which represented an unworkable burden for one person.[26] At the time, superintendents were more like clerks than department managers; thus, the principal of Lincoln High School had more day-to-day management responsibility. That would change in the 1920s, when the entire county system was reorganized in a progressive efficiency move, putting hiring and firing of all teachers under the superintendent, who had full administrative control for the entire system.

As in the first era of public schools, salaries in this period continued to give preference for race and gender, although there was also preference when an instructor worked in schoolhouses with three or four rooms versus those who taught in one- or two-room schoolhouses. White male teachers earned more per academic year in Loudoun than Black teachers. In the same period, white female instructors earned more than Black female teachers. Emerick didn't change the salary balance, but he did demand that Blacks, not whites, should supervise Black teachers. They were paid by sharing expenses between the commonwealth, the county, and the Jeanes Fund. Per capita costs in 1937–38 were $31.77 for white schools versus $13.44 for Black schools.[27]

Transportation

At the turn of the century, most students continued to walk, ride horses or mules, and take wagons using roads and cutting through woods and fields to get to their local school. Until 1922, school transportation in a particular district was managed by that district. Poorer districts or municipalities had fewer resources. School consolidation began in Loudoun County in 1910. Led by Superintendent W. G. Edmundson, smaller white schools in remote areas were consolidated into larger ones, and public school transportation of white students began. But Blacks did not benefit from consolidation until the 1940s. "Benefit" is a relative word, of course. Consolidation meant the new schools were more distant, so unless private or public transportation was provided, many students who would have attended now could not.

Public transportation for students started as horse-drawn wagons known as "school hacks," developed in the 1880s. The first recorded appearance in Loudoun was in 1911 in the Jefferson district and was used to transport white students to the Hillsboro school (from the closed Salem and Edge Grove schools). When there was snow, the wagon wheels were replaced with skis.[28] Records indicate that LCPS had a "Transportation of Pupils" expenditure of $1,461 for the 1916–17 school year, likely the cost of new school hacks—by that time, wagons mounted on automobile chassis. There is no evidence that Black students were transported to school using county-provided wagons during this period.

With the advent of the automobile, students in more remote areas could be transported to school by their parents (providing their parents

Horse-drawn school hacks in front of the Hillsboro School (between 1910 and 1917). *Hillsboro School [Photo], 53-0237 Lewis/Edwards Architectural Surveys of Loudoun County 1972–1983 (M 022), Thomas Balch Library, Leesburg, Virginia*

owned an automobile) or by carpooling. Automobile ownership was not a common thing in the Black communities, so their children continued to travel mostly by foot, horse, mule, or private wagon.

Health Inequity

Just as the County School Fair movement was needed to address a potential famine, so too health care policy was a life-and-death matter and an essential factor in attendance and efficiency of schools. Therefore, it is important to read two quotes from the period.

> With the advent of puberty and sexual development there will be an almost total arrest of subsequent mental growth. His people have "gone to seed."
>
> —Paul Brandon Barringer, MD, Chair of Faculty,
> University of Virginia, articulating his theory that
> biology made Black people inferior (1900)

> Without health, and until we reduce the high death rate, it will be impossible for us to have permanent success in business, in property getting, in acquiring education, or to show other evidences of progress.
>
> —Booker T. Washington, the Hampton Institute (1914)

Despite mandatory vaccinations and excluding students with contagious diseases (e.g., smallpox, polio, tuberculosis, and diphtheria), worms, and other diseases, poor sanitation continued to be common in the county and elsewhere in Virginia. This led the state government to create a department of health in 1908. Existing policies were strengthened and new ones were created for student inspections, vaccinations, and other preventive care. The problem of contagion was very real, as seen in 1917 when infantile paralysis (polio), scarlet fever, and so on impacted work at Bluemont, Waterford, and Leesburg. In 1918 the school system was almost completely shut down due to Spanish flu. In 1908 the Department of Health stated, "It is better to exclude one child with a sore throat from class for a few days than to close the school for a week and treat a dozen cases of diphtheria."[29]

To their credit, superintendents and other Loudoun school system leaders made health and sanitation priorities. Each district school board agreed that all schools should have sanitary outhouses versus the old-fashioned kind, which allowed waste to leak into the footpath.[30] They also agreed to require individual water cups instead of common dippers, although interviews lead the team to believe this policy took a long time to be fully accepted. As late as academic year 1946–47, teachers had to be reminded that common cups and dippers were illegal.[31] Common towels were also replaced by paper towels.[32] Sanitary fountains were set up in three schools and a shower bath in one school, but there is no direct evidence that Black schools benefited. However, Black schools did benefit from the county school nurse, who was paid by the civic leagues, not the government.[33]

While health care for poor rural youth of any race was not optimal, there was no equity. For example, although Blacks had access to the segregated wards at Loudoun County Hospital, which opened in Leesburg in 1912, Black nurses and doctors had no access. In addition, the hospital's training school for nurses was for whites only. However, while the health care system was not equitable, it would be unfair to paint everyone as doing nothing. On November 7, 1913, Virginia governor William Hodges Mann personally met with officials of the NOS to build interracial public health cooperation. However, the conversation was also within the context of keeping Blacks on the farm, thus avoiding migration to the labor pools of the great cities of the North where white workers loathed competition.[34]

The records clearly show that inequity existed, but perhaps more important than the details, it is more useful to understand why inequality existed because in the twenty-first century health equity is still only aspirational for many minorities. CIGNA and other health providers and insurance firms have all pointed to the continuation of systemic health inequity, noting in 2016 that "as a group, the African-American or Black population experiences significant disparities with chronic conditions, access to care, preventive screenings, and mental health."[35] In 2017 10.6 percent of Blacks were uninsured compared with 5.9 percent of non-Hispanic whites.[36]

As noted in the introduction, Dr. Barringer's speech of February 20, 1900, was devastating to Black health and education. His use of genetic determinism put an acceptable hard ceiling on the social advancement of Blacks, which were essentially understood by many as biologically frozen, inherently savage, and incapable of survival in a civilized society unless managed by white paternalism. In Barringer's words, "the present school system of the south is but a 'forcing-bed' for racial hatred and antagonism. I do not harbor any antipathy to the negro schoolteacher— I simply deny his capacity for the task at hand."[37]

It is also important to consider a major insurance study out of Chicago that proposed that Blacks were not worth insuring because they were becoming extinct.[38] This derives from an 1896 perversion of Charles Darwin's theory of evolution proposed by Frederick Hoffman, a statistician in the Prudential Insurance Company of America. Extinction, according to Hoffman, would not come from the terrible conditions imposed on Blacks by whites, which were poverty, poor working conditions, and poor access to health professionals. Instead, Hoffman felt racial decline was due to inherited and inferior "race traits." If the race were destined to extinction anyway because of inherited weaknesses, why insure them, why even provide basic medical services?

The impact of the pseudo-science proposed by Barringer and others was of deep concern to Loudoun's Black teachers and parents, as reflected in the agendas of Black teacher institutes and from numerous petitions. Would Blacks obtain medical care equal to whites, especially when it is expensive?[39] In Loudoun, the Willing Workers Club and the Black Odd Fellows were leading proponents of improving health care among Blacks. The Black teacher institutes and, later, Loudoun's County-Wide League also advocated for proper health policies such as placing sanitary toilets in the Training Center in Leesburg, later known as Douglass Elementary School. In a show of determination to accomplish that essential goal, local Blacks even hired a lawyer who threatened a lawsuit.

Unkempt school grounds allowed illness to be spread by contaminated dirt brought in on student's shoes. Tuberculosis was also a serious threat in Loudoun and one of the top three causes of death for urban Blacks. Fighting disease continued throughout segregation. Therefore,

Willing Worker School House in Purcellville (ca. 1940).
Courtesy of EWP Archives

bearing these threats in mind and the need for mitigation, W. E. B. Du Bois stressed the need in 1906 to end the health disparity with whites caused by a maldistribution of resources and poverty, which were symptoms of segregation and prejudice. In 1914 Booker T. Washington, referencing a Tuskegee conference the year before, further appealed for a practical movement that became the National Negro Health Week, which took place for thirty-five years. A simple annual set of easy-to-achieve health goals, Negro Health Week continued to influence Black behavior in Loudoun as late as the 1940s.[40] Promoted by Andrew Carnegie and the Virginia Department of Health, Washington organized the first such week in 1915, which evolved over time into school events, physical examinations, mass meetings, clean-up sessions, and clinics held across the state.[41]

On the matter of not providing proper medical care, apart from racism, there was also a financial philosophy that this was not a taxpayer responsibility; instead, it was the responsibility of parents, regardless of their economic standing, or of churches and philanthropists. This regressive policy inevitably and disproportionality disadvantaged Blacks and poor whites. The problem was that while the policy aimed to save money, it also reduced tax revenue by depressing economic activity—in other words, not investing enough in health caused workers to be out for more sick days, be less productive, and cost the government more in emergency health care. The same should be said about underfunding Black schools. If the schools had been better resourced, Blacks would have obtained better jobs, paid higher taxes, and enhanced local and state revenue.

Although providing actual direct care was not a recognized core government policy for decades and was not affordable, there was a growing consensus about the importance of promoting prevention. In this, both the NOS and the white government had shared goals. Loudoun's Black and white students were required to take vaccinations, undergo physical inspections, and listen to advice on good health practices such as wearing masks during the Spanish flu.[42] Sources of heat and ventilation were also tracked.[43] By 1918 the impact of World War I created a real attitude change in health politics. Virginia's first bill on physical and health education, known as the West Law, did not pass until March 15, 1918, inspired by Sen. Julius West, who realized that 29 percent of draftees were rejected because of health conditions caused by preventable childhood diseases. However, although the law aimed to reduce accidents and disease for all students, in practice the policy of segregation and the growing influence of eugenics continued the disparity. Loudoun County Blacks nevertheless benefited from the influence of the Hampton Institute and the NOS in sanitation, antituberculosis programs, and the like. These positive influences, which were supported by Virginia's Department of Health, underpinned a generation of work on Black health.[44]

Given the impact of the Spanish flu, discussions on good preventive health practices were important to local educators.[45] Our team discovered many references to schools being closed during the pandemic. Tightly packed, poorly ventilated one-room schools prevented social distancing and would have provided an excellent medium for spreading death. Nearly all schools were closed in October 1918, although many white and Black schools reopened in November and December, except for Greggsville Colored, which was closed in December, and Mountain Gap Colored, which was closed in November. Colored schools open in November included Bull Run, Conklin, Hughesville, Little River, Middleburg, Nokes, Round Hill, Saint Louis, Waterford, and Willard.

In the late nineteenth and early twentieth centuries, significant steps were taken by the commonwealth, the NOS, and local Loudoun leaders to improve health. Some steps were aimed at both races. For example, under West Law, all students were to be provided health inspections, health instruction, and physical training. To standardize these activities, the law also mandated that nurses, physicians, and physical directors employed by the schools had to be approved by the health commissioner and the state superintendent of public instruction. County boards of supervisors were also authorized to appropriate funds for these purposes, meaning funds were to be local, not from Richmond. This was essential because Virginia is a Dillon state, meaning counties cannot pass laws or appropriate funds for purposes not authorized by the legislature.[46]

Nutrition is also a health care matter. Students must be well nourished to succeed in school. From interviews of former students at Conklin Colored and discussions with tour docents at Waterford's Second Street School Living History Program, which reenacts a day in the life of the 1880 "Colored School 'A', Jefferson District," it is known that many children brought their own lunches to the one-room schoolhouses, usually in metal pails specially constructed for the purpose or in old molasses tins with handles. At the white teacher institute held October 11–12, 1917, participants discussed food conservation in the home and the provision of hot lunches, although there is no direct evidence that hot lunches were provided to "colored" students until the 1930s. However, in 1914, white schools, and perhaps Black schools, did experiment with augmenting cold lunches. Instead of creating entire hot lunches, which would have been impossible in many one-room schools, the idea was to create a warm dish to supplement the cold lunches brought to school.[47] Records do not show how widely this approach was used.

Sanitation

Instructive are county nurse reports, which compared the sanitary conditions of white versus colored schools, like in Bluemont village in 1919.[48] Bluemont white had a water cooler, whereas Bluemont "colored" only had a common water bucket.

Training center alumnus Jim Roberts showing the location of former sanitary out-houses, July 12, 2020.
Photo by Larry Roeder

In the nineteenth century, some Loudoun schoolhouses had no out-houses, meaning children of either race relieved themselves in the woods. In 1888, for example, there were 86 white schoolhouses and 31 Black, for a total of 117, only 76 of which had outhouses.[49] Similarly, in 1890, twenty years after the start of the public school system, of the 116 buildings in use, only 83 had outhouses.[50] Early outhouses were unsanitary. They were built on level ground and had to be cleaned regularly, sometimes by the older students or teachers. They were swarmed with flies. Students might even have to walk through urine leaking out the structure's side, bringing disease into classrooms and homes. Then a 1913 campaign led by the Loudoun Federated Society for Community Betterment began to provide sanitary toilets to all schools.[51] To minimize flies, these toilets were built over pits, and lime was used to cover the spoor. By 1915 in Loudoun, over forty years after the start of Virginia's public school system, the "School Board agreed to equip every school with two sanitary outhouses," although implementation was not immediate.[52]

Saliva transmits diseases like tuberculosis, hepatitis, viral meningitis, herpes, and other ailments. Therefore, consider the advice provided by Dr. Ennion C. Williams in September 1918.[53] Williams, who was the state health commissioner and a strong proponent of physical inspection, opined as far back as 1910 that "the sanitary arrangements of a majority of country schoolhouses are without doubt deplorable" and "veritable breeding places for contagious disease."[54] However, he felt schools could stay open if students and teachers covered their mouth with a handkerchief, did not spit, avoided placing anything in the mouth that did not belong like a pencil, and avoided the common drinking cup. This sounds not dissimilar to health cautions proposed by health professionals during the COVID-19 crisis. However, Dr. Williams felt preventive medical care was perhaps better than quarantining, and there is no doubt that the advice reduced some disease, much like wearing a mask did during the COVID-19 pandemic. Interestingly, during World War I, wearing a mask was considered patriotic.

The following February 1919 chart on eleven schools, including one Black, is instructive of the thoroughness of the sanitation inspections.

Table 4.1
Sanitary Inspection Chart of Eleven Schools, 1919

Schools	Race	Water	Heat & Lights	Toilets	Floors	Vents	Cups	Towels	Phys[a]
Milltown	W	Cooler	Good & good	untidy	Tidy	fair	✓	No	No
Bluemont	W	Cooler	Good & good	Needs cleaning	Tidy	good	✓	No	Yes
Bluemont (colored)	C	bucket	Good & fair	good	Tidy	good	✓	No	No
Purcellville	W	Not legible	Good & fair	good	Tidy	good	✓	No	No
Clark's Gap	W	Cooler	Good & fair	fair	Tidy	fair	✓	No	No
Waterford	W	Cooler	Good & fair	good	Tidy	good	✓	Yes	No
Oat Lands	W	Cooler	Good & fair	Good, no [illegible]	Tidy	good	✓	No	No
Middleburg	W	Bucket	Good & good	Had repairs	Tidy	fair	✓	No	No
Aldie	W	Fountain	Good & good	Good	Tidy	good	✓	No	No
Hamilton	W	Cooler	Fair & poor	Good	Tidy	fair	✓	No	No
Crossroads	W	Bucket	Good & Good	Good	Tidy	fair	✓	No	No

[a]The term "Phys" could be physical inspection, but this was not explained on forms.

Nurses and Doctors

Blacks across Virginia generally had to rely on white doctors and nurses for care, although the team found no evidence in Loudoun of less-than-professional treatment being provided, often in the form of house visits. As already mentioned, thanks to the Loudoun Federated Society, Loudoun obtained the first rural county nurse in Virginia by the fall of 1914, which was quite an accomplishment, given that the total population was only twenty-one thousand people by 1918.[55] The nurse demonstrated to teachers how to inspect students for hearing, sight, and weight issues as well as dental defects. The nurse also made house calls, offering shots, inoculations, and basic medical care for ear infections and worms, especially hookworm.[56] It is uncertain how much she assisted Black schools directly, but she did make recommendations to parents, teachers, and doctors for future work, and eventually Blacks did significantly benefit, according to interviews the team conducted.[57]

At the time, medical inspections of schools in Loudoun were under the auspices of both the Federated Society for Community Betterment and the State Health Department, which also vaccinated all pupils.[58] The commissioner of health felt that local organizations were needed to respond to local medical problems. The "country [rural] community must find a way to reach the heedless, the ignorant and the poverty-stricken and lift from their offspring the burden of preventable handicap, or the gap between the health of the city child and the country child will never be closed."[59] In 1914 the Federated Society realized that infectious diseases were higher in Loudoun County than elsewhere, such as in the less prosperous Orange County. The federation arranged for the first state director of the hookworm investigations to attend its meetings in Purcellville to establish plans of action "that committees of three influential people, active in good works, be appointed in every school center in the county. These committees [are] to endeavor to interest the various school, social, civic, religious, beneficial and fraternal organizations of their several communities in the health betterment work."[60]

In addition, the county nurse, Mrs. McCulley, a proponent of student inspections, engaged the 1916 white teacher institute in a discussion on how to detect and minimize infectious disease.[61] Her intent was not just to share information. She wanted an action plan, which would have included inspections. This kind of conversation was common by both nurses and doctors. In 1916 the colored teacher institute discussed how to improve outhouses as part of the commonwealth's "War on the Fly."[62]

In January 1914 the Federated Society conducted a comprehensive survey of students, which also covered traveling costs of state inspectors. Loudoun superintendent William Edmondson led overall management. Unfortunately, epidemics elsewhere in the state interrupted work, and the inspectors had to be redeployed the last two weeks of the program. A heavy snowstorm closed many roads, causing more delays. Separate field inspectors under the Rockefeller Sanitary Commission, which was trying to eradicate hookworm, took up the inspection of the remaining schools, and those were completed on schedule. Owing to the presence in Leesburg of exceptional visiting nurse Anne Gulley, the team only had to inspect a few students at Leesburg High School and none at the colored school (meaning the Training Center). The Black students and most of the white students had been previously inspected by Gulley.[63]

The earliest example in Loudoun of a doctor inspecting students was during the academic year 1913–14, when Dr. Roy F. Flannegan, then assistant health commissioner for Virginia, inspected all of Loudoun County's children and did similar inspections of Orange and other counties.[64] In addition to high schools, twenty Black schoolhouses and forty-seven white schoolhouses were inspected, covering around eight hundred white students and four hundred Black students. Children were inspected for defects with eyes, ears, throat, teeth, and glands and for deficiencies in nutrition, which eventually evolved into the Five Point System. Inspections also covered anemia, skin eruptions, vaccinations and prior illnesses, retardation, and organic diseases.

Setting the Stage

This period set the stage for the future battles, arguments for Black subjugation by whites, progressive management of education, and Black resistance to inequity. A basic argument often made by the government was that because Blacks did not pay as much tax as whites, they did not deserve equity. When the county did not provide enough revenue for education, the Black parents or school trustees were forced to open their own wallets to improve education. That might work for some (like Lincoln village or the Quakers), but such a policy is regressive, putting unfair pressure on the poor. From the beginning, Black parents had been doing more than their fair share in supplementing their schools and would continue to do so.

Supplemental funding for public schools was common, including by patrons or parents supporting construction. Volunteers covered salaries or expenses associated with extending the school year, like at Lincoln white or Paeonian Springs white.[65] Interestingly, before the county system was revised in 1922, the superintendent sometimes did not even know the source of funds, only that it was a "large amount of private funds" raised locally.[66] While one cannot fault any parent for doing anything to advance his or her child, the system was inherently regressive because of the disparity of income between the races in rural Virginia. A system that provides an unequal funding of operations also creates an environment whereby poor children of any race are disadvantaged in relation to the middle class or wealthy. The poor are thus unable to catch up with the middle class or the wealthy. In the end, as Ruffner himself posited during his tenure in 1870, that gap in economic production damages the entire society.

Notes

1. EWP: 2.5B Lincoln-Purcellville-Dispute-1926. In the 1950s, this was a serious problem in response to the *Brown* decision, with some southern politicians offering: "If Communists supported racial integration, could there be any clearer sign of its immorality?" Thomas Borstelmann, *The Cold War and the Color Line: American Race Relations in the Global Arena* (Cambridge, MA: Harvard University Press, 2001), 182.

2. "Public Education in Northern Virginia," *Times-Dispatch* (Richmond), November 1, 1908, 12.

3. "United States to Study New School System of Europe," *Miami News*, October 4, 1912, 2.

4. "Will Confer in July," *Richmond Dispatch*, June 27, 1902, 5.

5. EWP: 2.2 Yr. 1919, April 1. Professionalism Recommendations to County School Board by Oscar Emerick.

6. "Virginia Facts Knock Out Coon's Absurd Theories," *The Farmer and Mechanic* (Raleigh, NC), October 12, 1909, 11.

7. Brochure for the 30th Annual Meeting, Negro Organizational Society, State Organization of Community Leagues, November 11–13, 1942, Chatham, Virginia.

8. Biennial Report, State Superintendent of Public Instruction, 1921–22, 1922–23, p. 26. Jackson had been doing the same work prior as supervisor of Rural Elementary Schools.

9. J. L. Blair Buck, *Development of Public Schools in Virginia, 1607–1952* (Richmond: State Board of Education, 1952), 156.

10. John F. Slater Fund for the Education of Freedmen was established in 1882 to create schools for Blacks. It also helped establish the Hampton Institute and Tuskegee Institute and provided salaries in over thirty Black colleges and many secondary schools. It ceased operations in 1937.

11. The training center there was known as the Old Dormitory of the Tangipahoa Parish Training School. It was placed on the National Register of Historic Places in July 1979. See https://npgallery.nps.gov/NRHP/GetAsset/5d5932b5-97e6-4f5c-a03b-91fec018002f?branding=NRHP.

12. Formal name was Peabody Education Fund. See Buck, *Development of Public Schools*, 161.

13. Eugene Scheel, "High Schools Once Flourished Across Area," *Washington Post*, October 21, 2003.

14. Larry Roeder, "The County School Fair Movement," *Bulletin of Loudoun County History* (2019): 76–118.

15. President Taft's letter read at 45th commencement, Fisk University, at Nashville, TN, June 14, 1911.

16. On Virginia Federation of Women's Clubs, see *County School Fairs in Virginia*, issued by Department of Public Instruction in Virginia, J. D. Eggleston, superintendent, December 1912, p. 12. Professor Seaman Knapp of Iowa founded the Farmers' Cooperative Work Division of the Department of Agriculture and originated the concept of having experts demonstrate, farm by farm, new agricultural methods. He was particularly famous for his work in Texas to control the boll weevil.

17. *Quarterly Journal of Economics*, 27 (November 1912–August 1913): 9.

18. *County School Fairs in Virginia*, 1912.

19. Private Contributions and Notable Events in EWP: 3.3 Yr. 1916/17, Superintendent Annual Report.

20. "Harvey W. Wiley Named President," *Staunton Daily Leader*, August 24, 1915, 6.

21. Patrick Arthur Deck and Henry Heaton, *An Economic and Social History of Loudoun County* (Charlottesville: University of Virginia, 1924), 117–18.

22. See bio on Wiley, a national leader: *The Herald* (Jasper, Indiana), February 12, 2011, A14.

23. Grasslands (photo), *Washington Post*, November 16, 1919, 5.

24. EWP: Yr. 1919 Emerick Annual Report, p. 2.

25. "Superintendent J. D. Eggleston Wants System to Straighten Out School Accounts," *Daily Press* (Newport News), January 3, 1912, 8.

26. Notable Events in EWP: 3.3 Yr. 1917/18 Superintendent Annual Report.

27. EWP: 15.17 Special NAACP Papers, Loudoun 2, p. 7.

28. Gene Scheel, Loudoun County-based historian, interview with Nathan Bailey, August 14, 2020.

29. "The Fable of the Country School," *Virginia Health Bulletin* 1–4 (1908/ 1912): 20. See also sec. 1496, *Virginia Code*, in *Virginia Health Bulletin* 1–4 (1908/ 1912): 103.

30. Front section in EWP: 3.3 Superintendent Annual Reports for 1911–12.

31. EWP: 4.1 Yr. 1946–47 Rules and Regulations for Loudoun County Teachers. For a history of the common dipper, see Michael J. McGuire "100 Years of Outlawing the Common Cup," safedrinkingwater.com (blog), October 29, 2012, https://safedrinkingwaterdotcom.wordpress.com/2012/10/29/100-years -of-outlawing-the-common-cup/.

32. Notable Events in EWP: 3.3 Superintendent Annual Reports for 1915–16.

33. Notable Events and Table 6 in EWP: 3.3 Superintendent Annual Reports for 1914–15.

34. Editors, "News of the State Capital," *Loudoun Times-Mirror*, October 24, 1913, 7.

35. "African American/Black Health Disparities," CIGNA, n.d., accessed September 10, 2020, https://www.cigna.com/health-care-providers/resources /african-american-black-health-disparities.

36. Sofia Carratala and Conner Maxwell, "Health Disparities by Race and Ethnicity," Center for American Progress, May 7, 2020, https://www.american progress.org/issues/race/reports/2020/05/07/484742/health-disparities-race -ethnicity/.

37. Paul Brandon Barrington, *The American Negro: His Past and Future* (Raleigh, NC: Edwards and Broughton, 1900), 21.

38. Frederick L. Hoffman, *Race Traits and Tendencies of the American Negro* (New York: American Economic Association and Macmillan, 1896). See also Chicago Commission on Race Relations, *A Study of Race Relations and a Race Riot* (Chicago: University of Chicago Press, 1922), xxiii.

39. Hoffman, *Race Traits and Tendencies of the American Negro*.

40. The US Public Health Service took over the National Negro Health Week in 1932 due to the costs to Tuskegee during the Depression and changed the focus from mainly cleaning and sanitation to medical care.

108CHAPTER 4

41. EWP: 7.4. National Negro Health Week. The program lasted from 1915 to 1951, when it was ended by the Public Health Service in an effort toward integration by closing the Office of Negro Health. Also see Sandra Crouse Quinn and Stephen B. Thomas, "The National Negro Health Week, 1915 to 1951: A Descriptive Account," *Minority Health Today* 2, no. 3 (March–April 2001): 44–49.

42. EWP: 7.1.4 Yr. 1955 Emerick on Vaccinations.

43. EWP: 6.1 Yr. 1886–1892 Register for Clark's Gap and Round Hill Colored in Loudoun.

44. Notes by Barbara Scott and Gertrude Evans to Larry Roeder, July 28, 2020. When Blacks were diagnosed with tuberculosis, they were sent to a sanitorium in Glendale, Maryland, which opened in 1934 and was also used to house victims from Washington, DC. The disease was rampant in the Saint Louis community due to contaminated water.

45. In 1918, of the 354 people who died in Loudoun, 90 perished due to influenza and 18 due to pneumonia. EWP: 3.1 Daybook by Oscar Emerick.

46. William R. Hood, "State Laws Related to Education Enacted in 1918 and 1919," *Bulletin No. 30* (Washington, DC: Department of the Interior, 1920), 324.

47. Emma Conley, "School Lunches," in *Principles of Cooking: A Textbook in Domestic Science* (New York: American Book Company, 1914), 194–200.

48. EWP: 7.8 AY. February 28, 1919. Report on Sanitary Conditions of Schools. Only one colored school (Bluemont) was studied that year.

49. EWP: 3.3 AY. 1888, Superintendent Annual Report, Table 2. The records do not indicate which schools with outhouses were Black and which were white.

50. Reports for AY 1888 and AY 1890 in EWP: 3.3 Superintendent Annual Reports 1887–1918, Table 8. There is no breakdown of white versus Black schools.

51. Notable Events in EWP: 3.3 Yr. 1914, Superintendent Annual School Report.

52. Notable Events and Table 6 "remarks" in EWP: 3.3 Superintendent Annual Report June 30, 1915.

53. Ennion C. Williams was appointed state health commissioner in 1908 and served until his death in 1931. He was previously professor of bacteriology and pathology at the Medical College of Virginia, 1900–1908. He also served as professor of preventive medicine at the Medical College of Virginia, 1916–1924, where he developed the science of the causes and effects of diseases, especially the branch of medicine that deals with the laboratory examination of samples of body tissue for diagnostic or forensic purposes.

54. Ennion Williams, *Annual Report of the Commissioner of Health to the Governor of Virginia ending December 31, 1909* (Richmond: Commisisoner of Health, 1910).

55. EWP: 7.3 Yr. 1913/14, Health Galas and Clinics.

56. Jim Rogers, interview with Larry Roeder, August 6, 2020.

57. Deck and Heaton, *An Economic and Social Survey*, 117–18.

58. See Notable Events in EWP: 3.3 Superintendent Annual Report for June 30, 1914.

59. "Unnecessary Scourges," *Virginia Journal of Education* 8 (September 1914): 187.

60. *Virginia Health, Process and Prospect: Annual Report of Commissioner of Health for Virginia* (1914), 183.

61. EWP: 4.2.A Yr. 1916, October 12–13, White Teacher Institute.

62. EWP: 7.5 Yr. 1916, February, County Nurse Work.

63. *Virginia's Heath, Process and Prospect*, 179.

64. EWP: 7.6.4 Yr. 1921 Physical Exams, Pg. 1.

65. 1905–6 Table 3; 1906–7 Table 3; 1910–11 Table 5 in EWP: 3.3 Superintendent Annual Reports for the appropriate Academic Year.

66. EWP: 3.3 AY 1907–8, Table 10. Superintendent Annual Reports.

5

THE 1920s
Progress through Darkness

We cannot afford to offer our teachers lower salaries, and the 5% increase indicated in the budget is needed to replace our poor teachers with better ones.

> —Annual report from Oscar Emerick to the school
> board, arguing that projected budget shortfalls relative
> to salaries would harm students in the end (1921)

Our present salary is insufficient to meet the high cost of present living conditions.... Therefore we respectfully request that your Board allow us a reasonable increase of pay.

> —Petition by the Black teachers of Loudoun,
> March 6, 1926, to Superintendent Oscar Emerick
> and the school board. The request was denied.

The great mass of Negro children (in Virginia) was almost entirely without standard high school facilities.

> —Observation by Archie G. Richardson, former
> Associate State Supervisor of Negro Education (1926)

It is very much to be regretted the Board gave the impression of antagonism and indifference. We certainly felt that we had been treated like a bunch of suspects—if not criminals—rather than as a group of decent citizens making a courteous petition for the supervisors to do something for a group of people who look to us for help—our little children.

> —Reverend Campbell T. Myers of Middleburg, complaining
> about a decision of the Loudoun County Board of
> Supervisors not to fund a dental clinic requested by 785
> citizens, including Superintendent Oscar Emerick (1926)

111

It is better for all the world, if instead of waiting to execute degenerate offspring for crime or to let them starve for their imbecility, society can prevent those who are manifestly unfit from continuing their kind. The principle that sustains compulsory vaccination is broad enough to cover cutting the fallopian tubes. Three generations of imbeciles are enough.

—Justice Oliver Wendell Holmes, in an infamous opinion
(*Buck v. Bel*, 274 US 200 [1927]) of the US Supreme Court
justifying eugenics and sterilization of the weak

Against a national backdrop of increasing anti-Black violence, white supremacist bodies like the Anglo-Saxon Clubs of America were forming in Virginia in 1922. The 1920s saw significant efforts by Loudoun Blacks to resist white suppression by improving education management and health, which was understood as a foundation of education. As an example, the Loudoun Colored Teachers Association was formed on October 17, 1921, to enhance teacher performance. The first Black supervisor (or industrial supervisor) was also hired in 1920, Mary Peniston.[1]

Whites had held back Black health for generations, so in the 1920s the Negro Organization Society began a campaign to educate both the Black population and white officials about the link between health and education. Health care programs in schools began to improve. Blacks needed fly and mosquito control as well as better access to clinics, hospitals, nurses, physicians, and dentists, both in the school system as well as the general population.[2] The NOS ideas were about self-help—Blacks advancing their own health and education—even without white encouragement. This included petitions and public action. For example, in 1921 Loudon Black educators joined a statewide program called the County School Fair movement, which had been designed to advance agricultural schooling, and staged a peaceful march though Leesburg, the county seat, to celebrate their academic achievements. It was also extraordinarily courageous, with huge physical risks at a time of increased lynching and other violent, racist activities. Although records are incomplete, we believe all of the instructors and most, if not all, of the students participated in the march.

While contemporary white leaders might have been surprised by some of this, none of it was a surprise to the authors because educational

Mary A. E. Peniston (birth and death dates unknown): Mary Peniston was Loudoun's first Jeanes Supervisor for Black teachers. Peniston arrived in Loudoun in 1920 with sixteen years' experience in education. She was likely funded in part by the Jeanes Fund, and this kind of social work in the schools was exactly what Jeanes teachers were most known for. She graduated from Hampton Normal Institute in 1903, then taught in Flatwoods, Alabama, where she wrote a fascinating article on life as a schoolteacher in segregated America.[1] She also served in Snow Hill Normal and Industrial Institute in Alabama. The 1920 *Southern Workman* described her title in Loudoun as "industrial supervisor," which meant she was in charge of all Black teachers. She may also have been a public schoolteacher in Richmond before arriving in Loudoun.

1. Mary A. E. Peniston "Flatwoods, A Back-Belt Study," 43 (1914): 630–35.

determination was already well rooted in the Black experience as early as Reconstruction.

Edwin Washington's story is another example of risk taking to achieve an education. It was bright and brave when race relations were very raw in the town of Leesburg just following the Civil War. Half a century later, in the 1920s, race relations were again raw. The KKK was on the rise across the nation and in 1926 mounted a major march in nearby Washington, DC. In November 1925, a statewide meeting of the KKK was also held in the village of Purcellville. "White-robed and hooded Klansmen marched with torches down the main street of town and back for all to see."[3] Race riots erupted around the nation as well, such as in Chicago in 1919, and some led to outright massacres, such as in Tulsa, Oklahoma, in 1921. Despite those pressures to be compliant, Black parents and teachers exhibited unbowed zeal in their own quest to provide their children quality education.

The 1920s also ushered in major upheavals in how public schools were managed. Originally, superintendents didn't fully manage an entire county system. Instead, the hiring and firing of teachers, the ownership and leasing of school properties, and so on was done at the school district level, which created a major management and administrative burden for the state superintendent for public instruction, Harris Hart, and for county superintendents (formally known as division superintendents). Hart caused the county unit law to take effect in September 1922, which placed full local authority with a unified county school board and superintendent.[4] The new system, which combined multiple districts into one school board, gave real power to the local superintendent and reduced the number of administrative units from about 700 to about 150, thus simplifying communications between counties and Richmond. County superintendents were given full authority over staff, equipment, and resources, only reporting to the county school board and the state. That shift would have significant bearing on Loudoun because it took place during the administration of Oscar Emerick, of which much more will be said. On September 1 Superintendent Emerick held a meeting of the new school board, and they ruled that each school was to have a committee of one man who was to be the "patron," except for the Leesburg white school, which was to be represented by three men or women. Committees of patrons were to be formed no later than October 1 and to then cooperate with the school board.[5] Local leagues of patrons raised private funds for books, encyclopedias, and other supplies. The system worked for white schools, but Black communities were generally poorer, such as those who supported the Training Center in Leesburg. As a result of their relative levels of income, for Blacks to provide financial support for the schools was no small financial feat and must be appreciated as an important, even heroic, component of their larger determination to bolster their children's education. This is perhaps best illustrated through the experience of the Lucien Allen family in the deep southeast corner of Loudoun, now known as Conklin, which borders the community of South Riding.

The Allen Family Story

The Edwin Washington Project team repeatedly saw evidence of Black families demanding better education for their children and, to the extent possible, funding it at great personal sacrifice. While many poor whites had similar issues with poverty, when set against the steep hill of ambition for their children, as seen in this chapter, the educational

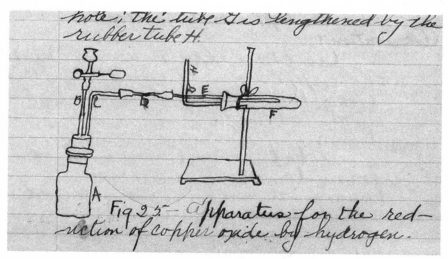

Experiment from Christine Allen's chemistry notebook.
Courtesy of Archives of Prosperity Baptist Church

infrastructure gave most whites a significant advantage. Consider the case of Lucien Allen, a farmer in the 1920s who was scratching out a living in a portion of Loudoun along the Fairfax border with what is generally considered the poorest-quality soil, so he supplemented his income. For example, between May and July of 1926, he engaged in road work for $1.25 a day and did labor for other farmers for 74 cents a day.[6] Allen's income was well below the national income.[7] His family also used its farm to sell or barter in butter, eggs, and chickens. Still, despite his low income and need to support a large family, Allen also managed to send his daughter Christine to Armstrong Technical High School in Washington, DC, where she studied chemistry (see above). After graduation she taught at Greggsville and Conklin colored schools in Loudoun and became an official in the Prosperity Baptist Church.[8]

Struggle for a High School Education

In 1926 Emerick wrote that "education should make it possible for each individual to be an intelligent participant in an everchanging society. Education in the United States should enable . . . every individual to live creatively to the optimism of his capacity in a representative democracy."[9] While Emerick's stated goal was certainly commendable, it is worth repeating that segregation undermined the potential for Black students to succeed because it limited access to higher-branch (high school) courses, which Blacks wanted right after the Civil War. Such courses date back to Reconstruction, like the ones taught by the Quaker teacher Caroline Thomas, who also instructed Edwin Washington.[10] Her teachings and those of other teachers at that time offered the earliest exposure to upper-branch learning for local Blacks. Classes ranged from the basics of writing and arithmetic to physiology, Latin, and algebra; the last three were upper-branch coursework. Latin was never offered to Blacks in the segregated public schools, although algebra would be taught as part of John Walker's program on the second floor of the Training Center in Leesburg beginning in the 1920s.[11]

When constructed in 1882, the Leesburg school for Blacks was simply an elementary school with the humble name of Leesburg Colored School A. A two-story building on Union Street in Leesburg, it was larger than any other Black school in the county and eventually (the exact date is lost) became known as the County Training Center, probably because of James Dillard's negotiations that established training centers as Black alternatives to formal high schools. They were partly supported by the Slater Fund and the General Education Board, stressing industrial and agricultural schools. The initial goals were to teach ethics and farm and home living skills through common elementary schooling as well as a few sessions of secondary education.[12] The training centers were also intended to provide educational leaders in Black schools. Influenced by the Hampton Institute and Tuskegee Institute, they evolved to include language in some cases and offered courses leading to college, but they were also criticized for lacking standard curricula, lacking supervision, possessing uneven teaching loads, and having irregular attendance, among other faults.[13]

By 1924, and perhaps as early as 1920, John C. Walker, an inspiring Black educator who had also been a leader in Black teacher institutes in Loudoun, offered a mix of upper-branch and basic classes on the second floor of the Training Center. It wasn't formally known as a high school, but because of the mix of course levels, many considered it such. The

John C. Walker (1868–1953): John Walker emerged as one of Loudoun's educational giants. His leadership at the Training Center over two decades laid the foundation for the first accredited Black high school in Loudoun. He was born in the county, graduated from what is now Virginia State University in Petersburg, and stood for his exam to be a teacher in Loudoun in 1892, the same year he was an instructor at Waterford—probably with prior experience under his belt. He married Hattie Binns of Loudoun in 1903, and was the leader of a Sunday school at the Mount Zion Methodist Church in Leesburg (the oldest Black church in Loudoun). He appears to have been principal of the Training Center as early as 1903, when he offered eight grades, the only county colored school to do so. By the 1920s he was offering upper-branch courses and the Training Center became known as Leesburg High School. He continued in that role until 1930/31 when Edythe Harris began an official high school program. By 1934 he was no longer principal; he continued teaching at the Training Center until his retirement in academic year 1940–41. In 1916 he was president of a colored teacher institute.[1]

1. One of the problems in this kind of research is that many official records are missing. Loudoun actually has a great wealth of files compared to many other counties, but as in the case of Training Center principals and the teacher institutes, there are gaps that argue for a special project to find them, probably in private holdings.

allegory that often described the work of these "high school" pioneers, given their near universal lack of resources and minimal staffing, was to "make bricks without straw." By 1927 thirty-five training centers emerged in Virginia, and fifty-six by 1932.[14]

Despite the bureaucratic restrictions in the 1920s, while Leesburg was the center for higher-branch offerings for Blacks, other "colored" one-room schools provided some limited offerings. From 1920 to 1923 Edith Blackwell White at Hughesville offered a half hour of daily higher-branch studies.[15] From 1920 to 1926 Alice Scott offered at Purcellville a "small amount of time" for higher-branch vocal music.[16] Saint Louis offered 2.5 hours of higher-branch coursework in academic year 1921–22. Anna Bell Ferrell at Waterford offered a half hour of higher-branch coursework in academic year 1920–21.[17] Beatrice Scipio, one of Loudoun's best-known instructors from the era, offered higher-branch classes at Bluemont in academic year 1923–24 as well as common courses (elementary school).[18]

The existence of inequities is not surprising. Consider that by 1918 there were only three accredited Black high schools across the state. Elsewhere, counties gave only "slight provision for the high school education of Colored children, but in most of them high school education is almost entirely lacking, or negligible," wrote Alexander Inglis of the Virginia Public Schools Commission in 1919.[19] By academic year 1925–26, things were only modestly better, according to the US Department of the Interior. Only eighteen localities in Virginia offered Blacks a public high school.[20] Why? Another study in 1928 "found indifference to Negro education surprisingly characteristic."[21] Emerick reported in September 1929: "[High] Schools have been located at almost every point in the county where the residents asked for one and offered to pay a part of the cost of building."[22] He failed to mention that there was only an unaccredited partial program for Blacks in Leesburg, while there were nine high schools for whites scattered about the county.[23]

John Walker's High School Project

John Walker's program at the Training Center was interesting. According to an August 1929 report by Oscar Emerick, "Leesburg Colored School has three teachers and offers a part of the first-year high school course."[24] Yet the records of a student named Fannie Parkie showed that high school coursework began under Walker as early as 1921, perhaps the 1920–21 academic year. Fannie Parkie (a.k.a. Parkey) of Leesburg also taught at the Sycoline Colored School from 1924 to 1926.[25] In the academic year 1925–26 term report for Sycoline, Parkie was shown as having attended "Leesburg High School," the first instance of records calling the program an actual high school.[26]

The Training Center under Walker offered a divided curriculum. Younger students studied elementary school courses on the first floor. Walker's second-floor program for older students provided two hours of higher-branch lessons per day, which included algebra, general science, and physical geography as well as four hours of primary lessons; in other words, a third of the day went to a form of high school education. In addition, Walker taught math during the summer.[27] High school text-books included Steele's general science book, a popular high school choice for both races.[28] The textbook for physical geography was by Maury, perhaps the one by Matthew Fontaine Maury containing a classic discussion of the ocean.[29] History would have been a special challenge to Walker and other Black teachers. The main history text used during that time, Royall Bascom Smithey's *History of Virginia*, described life under slavery with the following decidedly optimistic interpretation: "As a rule, the negroes were well fed and well clothed; and it cannot be said that they were an unhappy race. Free from all responsibilities of life, they brought up large families and enjoyed to the full extent such blessings as came to them. . . . There is no reason to doubt that the planters were as a body just and humane in their treatment of their slaves."[30] The same book described the 1902 Virginia constitution as "work well done" and as representing the will of the people, and extolled it for restricting suffrage.[31] In truth, voting was restricted to only those who paid the poll tax or passed certain educational qualifications—essentially wealthy whites. This eviscerated the political rights of both Blacks and poor whites.

Like Walker, other training center instructors were determined to improve their school's offerings, but their efforts were made harder because poor funding limited access to the necessary books, laboratory equipment, and other essentials given to white schools.[32] This was the pattern throughout segregation. Walker's salary also had to be supplemented by the local patrons to teach eighth grade subjects before the courses were added to the official curriculum.[33] This would set the stage, described in the next chapter, for the formation of a formal high school program in 1930 by Edythe Harris on the second floor of the Training Center.

All of this is important because of the way Virginia's rural schools were managed. In Loudoun, while school buildings might have been constructed on donated land or built by the community or LCPS, and the salaries of the teachers mostly paid by LCPS, much of the schools' day-to-day expenses had to be supplemented by patrons (parents and interested citizens). The white, largely Quaker community of Lincoln could afford to supplement white teacher salaries, buy the best books and equipment, support the county's best high school, and build a

Lincoln White School, about 1940.
EWP 11 Yr. 1940 Insurance Photos. Also known as Inspection and Survey Report: Property of Loudoun County School Board, Garrett Insurance, Virginia

substantive two-story elementary schoolhouse for Blacks on a side road.[34] However, other Black schools generally could not depend on a similar income base, so the official regressive dependence on patrons for certain activities caused cruel disparities between Blacks and whites because of their relative incomes. A similar inequity continues today in the Parent-Teacher Association (PTA) support of schools in well-off communities as opposed to that provided by PTAs of schools in lower-income areas. Property taxes are the primary source of funds for local schools, so a wealthy county like Loudoun will support more expansive schools than in poorer counties in southern Virginia. In the view of the authors, this system needs improvement so that all citizens have equal access to the best laboratory equipment, properly paid teachers, and other necessities of the twenty-first century. Unfortunately, our research indicates that no state has abandoned this approach, although some supplement with state resources. It should be noted, however, that Loudoun schools also had access to grants and other supplements and, eventually, federal aid.

As for sources of personal income in the 1920s, jobs available to Blacks were not much different from those of previous decades. Many Blacks, like Lucien Allen, were subsistence farmers who raised chickens, turkeys, hogs, and occasionally beef cattle and often sought jobs as day and seasonal laborers for additional income. In the Saint Louis area, further to the west, Blacks frequently worked as servants in white homes. The Quaker community of Waterford, perhaps Loudoun's most famous mixed community, had a high percentage of Black-owned properties in the village. Jobs for Blacks there included being laborers, whitewashers, and washerwomen, all of which appear fairly consistently across the censuses. For Blacks and whites in rural areas and small villages, much of their food was homegrown. Many Waterford Village Black families had their own hogs and participated in multifamily butchering occasions late in the fall behind the old tannery at Bond Street. Many also had gardens supplemented by wild greens in the spring as well as seasonal wild fruit. John Middleton remembered picking wild blackberries as a child with friends on Old Waterford Road for his grandmother to preserve.[35]

Transportation

Until 1922, school transportation was managed by each district. Poorer districts or municipalities had fewer resources. Beginning in 1922, school transportation was managed at the county level in Loudoun to more equitably distribute school funds (including transportation) across the county, so that wealthier districts didn't have all the advantages. But this was equity among whites, not between Blacks and whites.[36] Before the Walker program, Blacks had to go to Manassas Industrial School in Prince William County or one of two Black public high schools in Washington, DC. Walker's program offered a third opportunity, although it was quite limited, especially regarding transportation. No transportation was offered to Blacks by LCPS—students had to make their own way to school. In fact, there would be no transportation for Blacks to any school in Loudoun until 1937.[37] That is important because it meant that many children who were qualified for high school education could not attend. Their parents either could not afford to take them, did not have the physical means, or could not spare time away from their agricultural pursuits to take them. This lack of transportation was a theme throughout segregation of underfunding and underequipping Black schools in general, and it is certain to have exacerbated racial inequality.

In the 1920s the primary modes of school transportation continued to be walking or riding a horse, mule, or wagon, which was unchanged since schools opened in Loudoun County. Students of both races generally attended neighborhood schools no more than a few miles from home; but 1924–25, by way of contrast, was a time of transportation transition for whites as LCPS moved from wagons or school hacks to gas-powered school buses. These buses served only white students at first.[38] The term "wagon" persisted, for at first the new buses were no more than wagons or school hacks mounted on automobile chassis. The terms "bus" and "wagon" were likely used interchangeably for a period.[39] Consider the term "icebox." While it accurately described the method of in-home refrigeration in the late nineteenth and early twentieth centuries, many older Americans continued to use that term well into the twentieth century when speaking of refrigerators. Petitions written after 1925 using the term "wagon" may well have meant motorized school buses.[40]

The following excerpt is from a 1924 petition from the white patrons of Bluemont requesting a school bus for students traveling from Bluemont to Round Hill High School: "In view of the present unsatisfactory means of transportation for pupils from Bluemont to the Round Hill High School, we the undersigned Bluemont patrons of the Round Hill High School petition the school board of Loudoun County to operate a school bus direct from Bluemont to Round Hill."[41]

Research by Loudoun-based historian Eugene M. Scheel has revealed that by 1925, Black parents with the means had formed carpools to transport Black students to the Manassas Industrial School.[42] Some students even used the Washington and Old Dominion (W&OD) railway line.[43] Of course, segregation and Jim Crow continued to be the rule of the land, and the W&OD had required Blacks to sit at the rear of railway cars since 1900.[44] The road conditions were also a problem, regardless of the mode of transportation, a combination of dirt, gravel, and asphalt, with roads in the farther reaches of the county being dirt and gravel. This presented problems in muddy weather for outlying communities. There are accounts of school buses mired so deeply in mud that farm tractors were needed to pull them free.

The Role of Petitions and Teacher Salaries

Encouraged by the NOS, Blacks began to use petitions to lobby for their own rights to open a new school in a community, to keep schools open, to acquire coal for heat, to hire teachers, to improve transportation, or to request increases in salary.[45] Transportation issues accounted for 18 percent of all "colored" petitions that EWP volunteers reviewed, but salary requests became the most political. In some cases Blacks also convinced influential white politicians to support them, such as former speaker of the House of Delegates John Ryan, who argued (unsuccessfully) in favor of keeping the Conklin Colored School open.[46]

The legal basis for the existing system of discrimination was the 1896 US Supreme Court decision *Plessy v. Ferguson*, which is now considered one of the worst decisions in the history of the Court. That decision gave the separation of the races a constitutional backing, essentially creating a legalized form of apartheid in the United States. However, to be consistent with the Fourteenth Amendment, the Court articulated a "separate but equal" doctrine, which allowed for separation based on race as long as there was equality. Because the Fourteenth Amendment to the US Constitution provided for equality under the law for all citizens, the Court had to ensure its ruling did not violate the equal protection clause. Interestingly, as will be seen in future legal actions by Blacks, it was that add-on phrase ("but equal") that ultimately spelled its doom.

The difference in salaries between Black and white teachers was a deliberate form of discrimination. This was not only a violation of the separate but equal doctrine, it was also one of the most clearly documented examples of systemic racism available. In 1926 LCPS Black teachers petitioned for a pay increase—not equal pay—to cover the increasing cost of living. It is important to emphasize that they did not ask to get paid the same as white teachers. Considering the racial violence perpetrated on Black citizens in the late teens and early 1920s (indeed, going all the way back to the end of the Civil War), that decision is understandable; nevertheless, their request was denied. While that initial request for increased salaries was not successful, efforts by the National Association for the Advancement of Colored People (NAACP) outside Loudoun had ripple effects, which are explored in the next chapter.

Although the success rate of the petitions was mixed, the important fact is that Black people stood up and publicly challenged the segregationist government. These actions educated both the government and the white population at large of an important inequity in education and reminded everyone that Blacks cared about their education. Their actions also encouraged fellow local Blacks, regardless of economic background, to publicly advocate for all of their rights. For example, in the 1930s a voter club was formed by Loudoun's County-Wide League of Black PTAs.

Black Schools and the County School Fairs Movement

County school fairs in Loudoun (not to be confused with 4-H and traditional county fairs) were held nearly annually between 1910 and the early 1920s. All were white in Loudoun until 1921, when separate Black and white fairs were offered. The white fairs offered marches and exhibits of skills needed on farms as well as tests of academic achievement, oratorical prowess, carpentry, map making, sports, and drawing, all based on a comprehensive manual of guidelines.[47] Nearly every white school and student in Loudoun was involved, plus faculty and staff. Many records on Loudoun's school fairs have also survived, including official brochures and personal notes of teachers. The intensity of coordinating academic, sports, and agricultural events would eventually overwhelm Loudoun's school system and probably had a similar impact in other counties, which is why they faded out in the 1920s and why, in 1921, they did not include agricultural exhibits.

Interestingly, none of the brochures or planning documents for Loudoun's Black fairs survived. The EWP team became aware of their existence only because faint markings were found on term reports, which led to a closer examination of Black Teacher Institute records and then newspapers. The latter was difficult because the Loudoun County newspapers held at the Balch Library are not fully indexed. What we discovered was that a major Black event took place in 1921, preceded by detailed planning in 1920. Our impression is that every Black school in Loudoun marched through Leesburg. The date is important because of the violence against Blacks then going on, such as the Ocoee massacre in Florida in November 1920 and the 1919 riots in Washington, DC; Norfolk, Virginia; and Chicago, Illinois. Chicago's riot was likely influenced by the significant increase in the Black population from the Great Migration. In May 1921, the year of the Black event in Loudoun, there was also a massacre in Tulsa, Oklahoma, considered the worst anti-Black attack in American history. Although Loudoun was not like Chicago or the Deep South, it is hard to imagine that the risks associated with a march through Leesburg would not have been considered.

Other Virginia counties began their Black county school fairs earlier than Loudoun, like neighboring Fairfax County in 1916.[48] Those continued through 1924 and were different from Loudoun's Black fairs in that they featured both industrial and academic competitions as well as agricultural exhibits of garden vegetables and canned fruits as well as poultry and livestock.[49] These fairs then were merged with the ordinary county fairs. "The object was to encourage education, agriculture and social development of Fairfax and adjacent counties," which included Loudoun, so perhaps Loudoun's students also participated in some way.[50] There was precedent certainly in white fairs to attract students from multiple jurisdictions. Loudoun's Black fair did not focus on agriculture, which surprised the EWP team, given the goals of the state program; but further research indicated that the superintendent had also caused the white fairs to reduce their exhibits due to the burden placed on educators.

John Walker and Mary Peniston, Loudoun's first supervisor for Black teachers, organized the first Black fair in Loudoun. Other leaders in the 1921 fair were teachers with deep experience, the cream of the community. However, despite their enthusiasm, the community faced a similar hurdle to that of the white educators—an excessive workload that detracted from classroom instruction. This is probably why the number of participating Black schools went from nineteen for the October 1921 fair to ten in 1922–23 and only five in 1923–24. Seemingly as an alternative to the school-style fair, the white teachers' institute on September 7, 1922, raised the question of "the schools'" part in the Loudoun County Fair.

Black fairs were less complex than the massive white ones, which required special trains be laid on for guests. The Black fairs also included exhibits of serving, an unfortunate recognition of the prevalent racial

Possible photo of Black school fair, Leesburg.
Courtesy of Archives, Virginia State University

social order. The white fairs were a very labor-demanding element of a system designed by the Virginia State Department for Public Instruction. However, a similar mandate for Black fairs was not so clear, except that they had to have been permitted by the superintendent and towns. That said, the only people directly involved in their management were Black instructors, not even the Negro Extension Service. If the Negro Extension Service had been involved, the exhibits by the Black-oriented fair would have likely included corn and tomato demonstration projects.

Exhibits and other events by the Black fair were displayed at the Training Center; not the Leesburg Opera House, where white exhibits had been shown. Also, unlike the white fairs, there was no evidence in the Black fairs of sports events, debates, or other oratorical competitions. Day-to-day management rested with a committee made up of the following:

- **John C. Walker**, president, then serving as principal and instructor at the Training Center.
- **Bushrod W. Murray**, first vice president, then serving at Mountain Gap Colored School in his thirty-second year as an instructor.

The Scipio cabin, thought to have been used by many Black instructors as a teacherage, still stands on Foggy Bottom Road near Bluemont.
Photo by Larry Roeder

- **Charles. H. Willis,** second vice president, then serving at Bull Run Colored School on New Mountain in Aldie in his second year as an instructor.
- **Annie E. B. Harris,** treasurer, then serving at the Training Center in her twenty-ninth year of education.
- **Beatrice Scipio,** secretary, then serving in the Bluemont Colored School in her eleventh year as an instructor. Scipio, a revered teacher in her own right, was also the aunt of Rosa Carter, another beloved teacher.
- **Mary V. Roberts,** assistant secretary. No records on her have emerged.
- **Mary E. Peniston,** supervisor and executive secretary.

A brass band from the village of Lincoln "furnished excellent music" under the leadership of James E. Bell, probably a Black farm laborer then living on the Lincoln-Purcellville Turnpike.[51] Walter Brown of Hamilton

Table 5.1
Awards Presented for the 1921 Fair

School	Instructor	Prize
Hughesville	Edith V. White	Best collection of embroideries, including a crocheted tie and sleeve holder (shirt garter) for a boy.
Leesburg	John C. Walker, Mary E. Waters, and Annie E. B. Harris	Best collection of ready-to-use articles, including umbrella stands, knife and fork holders, costumes, center table, rabbit gums, a Chinese counting frame of wire and buckeyes to be used in primary grades and bird houses.
Lucketts / Mount Pleasant	Sylvia Wright	Best collection of rafia baskets.
Mountain Gap	Bushrod Murray	Although taught by a man, sent a good display of gingham dresses and hand sewing.
Purcellville	Alice Scott	Displayed a line of sewed-on button and stitched designs.
Sycoline	Mary B. Norris	One of the smallest schools in the county, yet contributed a handsome yoke by an eight-year-old boy.
Willisville	Anna Gaskins	Best collection of schoolwork, including drawings, toy wagons and wheelbarrows, ox yokes, and a large Morris chair.

"presented the Leesburg School with a large United States flag, which is to be displayed from the windows daily."[52] This was probably J. Walter Brown, a Black public school teacher at Brownsville, then living on the Paeonian and Hamilton Turnpike.[53]

Health in the 1920s

The 1920s brought great promise for health care in the public schools of Virginia, particularly regarding the professionalization of the physical inspection of students to detect ailments and then recommend remedies. In addition, students' access to medical professionals generally, such as nurses, improved. However, as in all other aspects of life, race intruded, especially the specter of eugenics. On the practical side were lectures led by Rose Dolan, the county nurse. In addition to keeping the children well, she extolled teachers to stay well, reflecting a reality that school-age students can transmit disease to adults.[54] This was practical, but health officials in Richmond went further. They believed that because of the severity of the Spanish flu virus, segregation of the races was important, so we assume this was the case in Loudoun; but why would segregation even matter? Why would it be a legitimate excuse? This was likely a political statement to support eugenics, then on the rise in Virginia. Consider the infamous Racial Integrity Act, passed by the Virginia General Assembly in 1924 and remaining law until the *Loving v. Virginia* decision in 1967, thirteen years after *Brown v. Board of Education*. Think of the Racial Integrity Act as a pseudo-scientific justification for white supremacy and defining Black people as racially inferior.

Unquestionably as well, the 1895 Prudential study and Brandon Barringer's speech of February 20, 1900, had a continuing negative impact. But there were positive developments in this decade, such as a full-time county health unit, which ran from March 1923 to March 1924 in Loudoun. It included a health officer, nurse, sanitary officer, and nutrition officer. The goal was to make sanitary as many schools as possible and to inoculate children against diphtheria and smallpox. Also included were inspections for dental problems and other ailments.[55] Anne Gulley was the nurse, and Dr. P. M. Chichester was the director. The following year, in 1925, the Loudoun Federated Society for Community Betterment became known as the Public Health Association of Loudoun County.

In 1924 the commonwealth also required certification in medical inspection and physical training for anyone who wanted to be a public school teacher. Based on Dr. Roy F. Flannegan's 1913–14 student health inspection study, discussed in the previous chapter, teachers were taught to inspect for defects with eyes, ears, throat, teeth, glands, and nutrition. The results of the study would eventually evolve into the Five Point System of student inspections. Inspections also covered anemia, skin eruptions, vaccinations and prior illnesses, retardation, and organic diseases.

The Flannegan exercise revealed a lot of exposure to disease and bad dental conditions, all of which inhibited student attendance and performance. Therefore, it became obvious to many that since there were not enough physicians and nurses to do the job, professional inspections by teachers had to be ramped up to provide early warning of problems and early remediation before issues became irreversible. But the concept of teacher inspections was controversial. Some felt it immoral for teachers to strip students, although there is no evidence in the files that students were stripped. But there were practical considerations in favor of teachers doing the inspections. The State Board of Health had estimated that if physicians did the inspections for the four hundred thousand or so public school students in Virginia, it would cost taxpayers at least $200,000, whereas teachers were already salaried, so the cost of them doing the inspections was zero.[56] On September 13, 1921, county nurse Anne Gulley advocated for the continued medical inspection of students by the teachers.[57] The teacher opposition to them doing the actual inspections continued in a debate during the 1923 white teachers institute in Loudoun managed by Mary T. Shoemaker. While engaged in a discussion of a possible health unit, the question was also raised: "Should we recommend repeal of the requirement that teachers make a physical inspection of school children in counties that have a school nurse?"[58]

Initially in Virginia, children were inspected by teachers because of the lack of rural nurses; by the 1920s there were still few rural nurses.[59] In Loudoun in 1920, efforts to follow up such inspections with salaried physicians also faced pushback from Loudoun school officials due to the costs and because by then a county nurse dealing with school health had already been employed by the Loudoun Federated Society for Community Betterment in 1914.[60] Many other counties had no nurse at all. By 1924–25 children were inspected by their teachers under the direction of the county nurse, who prepared a report on white children by October 3 and Black children by October 17. However, to conduct an inspection, the teachers were required to have taken a "physical inspection course" or to find a substitute who had taken such a course. But there was a significant change in the approach to student medical inspections in 1925, when the state boards of education and health officially initiated the Five Point Physical Inspection System, developed by Nancy Vance, the Virginia State School Nurse. Once again, based on the experiences of Flannegan, the Virginia State Department of Public Instruction

1929 May Day Health Wagon.
EWP: 16 Photography Field Health Day, photo #24 in set; photographer unknown

gathered health statistics on both races from the beginning of the new program. The specific five areas or points were: ears, eyes, teeth, throat, and weight. In addition, school term reports submitted to Richmond covered a wide range of diseases and conditions, from rheumatic fever to posture and speech, the latter of which would be used eventually as a rationale for speech clinics.[61] The goal was to use these reports to foster positive change among students and parents through health fairs and events in Loudoun and other counties.

The Five Point Program took advantage of traditional fairs such as May Day. The fairs, at least for white children, hosted health events and special programs to educate youths on the benefits of good health practices. This was both a community and school event for whites, but Black May Days are not thought to have had a health care aspect. Nonetheless, Black people did actively participate in the Five Point Program at the level of inspections. In the case of white fairs, winners wore paper crowns

and were sometimes photographed.[62] There are no surviving photos of
Blacks wearing crowns in Loudoun, and May Day for Blacks was used
for visits to classrooms, games, and dances based on grade level. Food
was a big item as well as baseball games and wrapping the May Pole—
with a king and queen (selected based on funds raised). Prizes were provided for game winners, and the PTA gave out little bags with candies,
and so on. Students were to dress in white.[63]

The EWP team found the actual design for a five-star crown used in
1929, which was the lead discussion item at the county school board,
presented by Harriet Wharton, supervisor for one and two-room
schools.[64] Loudoun's Black teachers took note.[65] On September 23 they
also discussed the program while meeting at the Training Center. In addition, they discussed vaccinations and compulsory attendance. Leading the discussion was William D. Gresham, state superintendent of
Negro schools. What is interesting, especially as this book is being written in the shadow of the COVID-19 pandemic that began in 2020, is
that the teachers were worried that, without the inspections providing
early identification of problems, attendance would decline in "colored"
schools due to an increase of illness.[66] In fact, many believe that this concern and the potential benefits from isolating students with contagions
was an impetus for school nursing in America.

In Loudoun's white health fairs, school health skits highlighted physical education and good health practices. Students who won Five Point
Stars received certificates; winners were photographed in 1928 at the
white health fair on the Mount Hope School grounds. Schools in the
Broad Run School District competed in sports, a parade, and a health
float contest. The floats, called health wagons, were pulled by children
and taught a lesson. Archival photos indicate that Blacks walked among
the crowds, but the team found no evidence of such events at the Black
schools.[67] The only exception might be in March 1954, when Banneker
put on its own health skits, and Black students were recognized for scor-
ing high in the Five Point Program.

Teachers who inspected students had to be appointed by the Virginia health commissioner, who charged the normal schools with pre-
paring teachers for health work.[68] The October 1926 annual report of
the Department of Education included the Five Point Program under

Five-Point Star Certificate Winners, 1929. Notice the barefoot student to the left. Going shoeless was a potential way to contract hookworm.
EWP: 16 Photography Field Health Day, Photo #26 in set; photographer unknown

"Corrections" in the Physical and Health Education section, stating: "The report on correction of physical defects, which is the follow-up work pertaining to the annual physical inspection, shows that a great deal more was accomplished during the past year than during any previous year. A new program known as the 'Five Point Standard'—'Physically Fit School Child' was successfully carried on in one or more schools of fifteen counties."[69]

The program's goal was to achieve a set of minimum standards across the state for the average child. These standards were applied to both Black and white children to determine whether they "had normal or corrected vision, normal or corrected hearing, their teeth were reasonably clean, with no exposed roots or unfilled cavities, normal throats, and are less than ten per cent underweight or not more than twenty per cent overweight."[70] While good health was certainly a result of these activities, memos by Superintendent Emerick also showed that his focus was to reduce absenteeism, which makes sense for a school system manager. For example, in a memo from 1932, Emerick noted various

Five-Point Star Certificate.
EWP: 7.6.3 Five Point Star Standard; photographer unknown

causes of absenteeism since 1919, problems like illness, poverty, weather and "don't care." He also pointed to poor education backgrounds by teachers but noted that requirements by the commonwealth over the past decade had improved things. As of the date of the memo, "all new teachers of elementary grades must complete two years of teachers college work."[71] Indeed, high school principals across the state were extolled to pay attention to the health of those students who participated in sports, but this appears not so much to improve the scoreboard in games but to avoid academic absences.[72]

Data was collected in standard spreadsheets used by both the counties and Richmond. The good news is that statistics in this format were gathered on Black and white students. The data was then converted into Five Point evaluations for each student. The same reports showed whether students were vaccinated or received a diphtheria immunization. Collectively, the data was labeled "Annual Physical Inspection" and studied height, weight and underweight, teeth, vision, hearing (right versus left ear), tonsils, mouth breathing, posture, and other defects. Those reports also looked at vaccinations and whether in the past the pupil experienced measles, malaria, mumps, scarlet fever, typhoid, whooping cough, diphtheria, smallpox, or chicken pox.

Dental Care

According to a 1921 report, preventive dental care for public school students was done through physical exams by teachers in order "to discover cavities and incidentally whether they are clean."[73] The exams were not a substitute for a good dentist or nurse. These inspections were then followed up by the county nurse, the first having arrived in 1914. No records indicate what happened to students before then, probably only a cursory inspection, if any. The nurses' information was then passed on to the parents "to get all teeth that have cavities filled by a dentist" and "to focus attention on the need for clean teeth." Of course, if the parents were indigent or nearly so, carrying out the recommendations might have been impossible. What was good, however, is that the recommendations were made in connection with lectures on proper nutrition, such as reducing sugar intake. The nurses also provided reports to the teachers, thus helping teachers understand other potential reasons why a student might be distracted, such as poor health versus simple inattention.

A dentist appeared on the scene in 1920 available to schools and using the nurse as an advance agent. Records do not indicate under what program this was funded, whether federal, state, county or private funds, or some combination. The nurse's mission was to go to the schools and, having discovered teeth requiring special care, "to get the parents to consent to have the teeth fixed."[74] The name of the dentist is unknown, but there were eight dentists in Loudoun that year, most in Leesburg. All were white except for one Black dentist who operated in Waterford. He was William F. Brounaugh, born 1873 in Lynchburg; he had the title "dental technician." He graduated from Lincoln University in 1893, worked as a dentist in a Manhattan laboratory in 1910, and then moved to Loudoun. By 1930 Brounaugh had left dentistry to work as a butler in Greenwich, Connecticut.[75] There are no school records about Dr. Brounaugh.[76]

As mentioned earlier, in April 1926, 785 petitioners, including Superintendent Oscar Emerick, asked the county board of supervisors to approve a dental clinic for the school system. Even though this clinic would likely have focused mainly on whites, the initiative was defeated by a vote of four to two, based on the stated objection of one supervisor who did not wish to raise a levy of one cent for one hundred dollars of property valuation.

Transitioning to the 1930s

The 1920s was an extraordinarily complex period as education evolved in the state. The state and county administration of schools changed dramatically. Loudoun County saw an upsurge in Black political activity aimed at improving education, for example, the program in the Training Center, the use of petitions, and the march through Leesburg. All of this set the stage for the next decade, when a real high school education appeared in the middle of the Depression. That experience, and the help of the NAACP, would then lead to the construction of a dedicated Black high school building in 1941—what many consider the local Black community's greatest achievement, save for integration.

Notes

1. Hiring supervisors was a controversial move for the school board, which was reluctant to spend the funds. The League of Women Voters supported the idea, which helped tip the vote. Emerick felt compelled again in 1921 to argue to continue to keep Peniston employed. EWP: 2.2 Yr. 1921 Emerick Annual Report. See also "Graduates and Ex-Students," *Southern Workman* 49 (1920): 482. Also see *Southern Workman* 50 (1921): 181; and William D. Gresham, "Supervising Industrial Teachers of Virginia 1921–1922," *Virginia Journal of Education* 15 (1922): 151–56.

2. Frederick Milton Alexander, *Education for the Needs of the Negro In Virginia*, no. 2 (Washington, DC: John F. Slater Fund Studies in Education of Negroes, 1943), 72.

3. Mosby Heritage Area Association (now known as the Virginia Piedmont Heritage Area Association), "Loudoun's Historic Civil Rights Landscape: What Should We Show Our Children?" (2016), retrieved from History of Loudoun County, Virginia, https://www.loudounhistory.org/visit-historical-sites-and-museums/.

4. J. L. Blair Buck, "The End of the District System," in *Development of Public Schools in Virginia, 1607–1952* (Richmond: State Board of Education, 1952), 208–10.

5. *Loudoun Times-Mirror*, September 7, 1922, 2.

6. Private diary records from the Allen family, Archives of the Prosperity Baptist Church, Conklin, Virginia.

7. *Statistics of Income from Returns of Net Income for 1920, Compiled under the Direction of the Commissioner of Internal Revenue* (Washington, DC: Government Printing Office, 1922). The average net income reported for 1920 was $3,269.40.

8. EWP: 4.5 "Christine Allen" in Colored Teacher Cards.

9. EWP: 5.1 Yr. 1926, Oscar Emerick on the Purpose of Education.

10. Caroline Thomas, *Teacher's Monthly School Report for Tate Colored School* (Washington, DC: Bureau of Refugees, Freedmen and Abandoned Lands, April 1870).

11. William. T. Alderson, "The Freedmen's Bureau and Negro Education in Virginia," *North Carolina Historical Review* 29 (1952): 75.

12. Alexander, *Education for the Needs of the Negro in Virginia*, 43, 74, 107, and 190. It is worth noting that Mr. Alexander played a major role in the decision to build Douglass High School in Loudoun County.

13. Leo Mortimer Favrot, *A Study of County Training School for Negroes in the South* (Charlottesville, VA: Trustees of the John H. Slater Fund, 1923).

14. Archie G. Richardson, *The Development of Negro Education in Virginia, 1831–1970* (Richmond: Phi Delta Kappa, 1976), 34 and 38.

15. EWP: 6.3.3 AY 1920/1923, Term reports for Hughesville Colored. Edith Blackwell White was a high school graduate who also went to normal school in Washington, DC, and instructed grades 1–7 at Hughesville from 1914 to 1923. By 1940 she had acquired two years of college. See EWP: 4.5 Colored Teacher Cards.

16. EWP: 6.3.3 AY 1920/1923 and AY 1924/26, Term reports for Purcellville Colored. See also EWP: 4.5 Colored Teacher Cards.

17. EWP: 6.3.3 AY 1920/1921 Term report for Waterford Colored. Anna Bell Ferrell instructed higher-branch coursework for 1.5 hours a day.

18. EWP: 6.3.3 AY 1923/1924, Term report for Bluemont Colored.

19. Alexander J. Inglis, *Virginia Public Schools Education Commission's Report to the Assembly of Virginia* (Richmond, VA: Waddey, 1919), 200.

20. David T. Blose, "Statistics of Education of the Negro Race 1925–1926," *Bulletin* no. 19 (1928): 42.

21. Michael Vincent O'Shea, *Report to the Educational Commission of Virginia of a Survey of the Public Educational System of the State* (Richmond, VA: Superintendent of Publishing, 1928), 290.

22. Oscar Emerick, "Loudoun County Public Schools among Leading Schools of State," *Loudoun County Magazine*, September 5, 1929, p. 1.

23. The high schools were located in Aldie, Ashburn, Leesburg, Lincoln, Lovettsville, Lucketts, Round Hill, Unison-Bloomfield, and Waterford. Hillsboro offered a two-year program and Middleburg a one-year program.

24. Emerick, "Loudoun County Public Schools among Leading Schools of State," 1.

25. EWP: 6.3.3 Term Reports for AY 1924/25 and 1925/26 for Sycoline Colored School.

26. EWP: 6.3.3 Term Reports for AY 1925/26 for Sycoline Colored School.

27. Douglass Alumni Association recollections, 1991.

28. Joel Dorman Steele, *Hygienic Physiology: Fourteen Weeks in Human Physiology* (New York: American Book, 1889).

29. Mathew Fontaine Maury, *The Physical Geography of the Sea* (New York: Harper and Brothers, 1855).

30. Royall Bascom Smithey, *History of Virginia, a Brief Textbook for Schools*, rev. ed. (New York: American Book Company, 1915), 113.

31. Smithey, 258.

32. EWP: 6.3.3 AY 1921/1922 and 1922/1923, Term reports for Leesburg Colored Graded School A.

33. Each schoolhouse had a supportive League of Patrons who provided funds. This is separate from the PTA system adopted in later years. Patrons were parents and others interested in supporting a school.

34. "Loudoun County Leads" in the *Virginia Journal of Education* described Lincoln by saying that "few schools in the State are better fitted by environment and other advantages for good agricultural work as this splendidly equipped school." *Virginia Journal of Education* (1914): 188–89, in EWP 7.6.4 Yr. 1914 Medical Exams.

35. Bronwen Souders, Waterford historian, interview by Larry Roeder, December 16, 2020.

36. Gene Scheel, Waterford historian, interview by Nathan Bailey, August 14, 2020.

37. The first time a school bus was driven by a Black man (Will Brown) was 1937, per Gene Scheel, a well-known Waterford historian. Of note, Brown is also

shown in the fiftieth Douglass High School anniversary book as one of those providing transportation including in a station wagon he had purchased.

38. Gene Scheel, "Timeline of Important Events in African American History in Loudoun County, Virginia," *The History of Loudoun County, Virginia*, accessed September 29, 2020, http://www.loudounhistory.org/history/african -american-chronology.

39. Gene Scheel, interview by Nathan Bailey, August 14, 2020. Scheel, a Loudoun-based historian and mapmaker, with his headquarters in historic Waterford Village, has helped the EWP on many occasions and has been recognized by President Clinton, the government of Loudoun County, and the town of Leesburg for his scholarly work as well as by the Virginia Historical Society, which also operates the Virginia Museum of History and Culture. Scheel is the author of nine books on Virginia history and over fifty historical maps. He also provides Loudoun County school instructors "history in the field courses." Steve Dryden, "Virginia Mapmaker Traces History's Winding Path," *Lawrence Journal World*, June 13, 1999, 37.

40. EWP: 2.5B Yr. 1926, September 6. Request to change direction of Edge Grove School Wagon route from Ebenezer Compher's gate in Hillsboro to Round Hill.

41. EWP: 2.5B Yr. 1924, February 9. Request to transport children from Bluemont to Round Hill High School. Names of children are provided.

42. Scheel, "Timeline of Important Events."

43. EWP: 2.5B Yr. September 9, 1927 . . . permitted to leave school early to catch the 3:18 train going east and the 3:43 going west.

44. Scheel, "Timeline of Important Events."

45. EWP: 2.5.A Yr. 1929, October 4. The Greggsville community requested that a school be opened for their students. In 1927 and 1928, the Black community asked to reopen their school. EWP: 2.5.A Yr. 1928, June 28, and 2.5.A Yr. 1927, October 24, Hughesville; EWP: 2.5.A Yr. 1928, June 28. On hiring teachers, see EWP: 2.5.A Yr. 1924, May 5, Howard Clark of Hamilton PTA asked for a Female Teacher and New School.

46. EWP: 2.5.A Yr. 1924, June 13, Conklin John Ryan supports keeping Conklin Colored School Open.

47. EWP: 2.5.A Yr. 1924, June 13.

48. Phyllis Walker Ford of the Laurel Grove School, interview by Larry Roeder, March 2019. Ford discovered a set of annual fair programs for the Fairfax County Colored School Fair Association in a trunk. See http://www.laurel groveschool.org/.

49. All documents on the participation of Loudoun in these special school fairs are in the Edwin Washington Archives, section EWP: 15.21.

50. Bylaws of the Colored Fair Association of Fairfax County, 1922, courtesy of Laurel Grove School Museum, Alexandria.

51. US Census for 1920, Loudoun County, Lincoln Village.

52. According to the term report for 1920–21, that year only a small flag hung from the front window. See question 27 in EWP: 6.3.3 AY 1920/21. Term Report for Leesburg, AY 1920/21, note by John C. Walker, May 5, 1921. Mention was confirmed by report by Annie E. B. Harris.

53. US Census for 1920, Loudoun, Jefferson District.

54. EWP: 4.2A Yr. September 11, 1928, White Teacher Institute, Leesburg High School.

55. Patrick Arthur Deck and Henry Heaton, *Economic and Social History of Loudoun County* (Charlottesville: University of Virginia, 1924), 118–19. See also "Loudoun Organizes County Health Unit," *Times Dispatch* (Richmond), March 12, 1923, 7.

56. "Inspections by Teachers," in *Report of the State Health Commissioner for the Biennium Ending Sept 30, 1923* (Richmond: Superintendent of Public Printing, 1924), 13. See also EWP: 7.2 Yr Abt 1921, Rationale for Physical Examinations, an informal memo by the school nurse in Loudoun.

57. EWP: 4.2A White Teacher Institute, September 12–13, 1921, Leesburg School House.

58. EWP: 4.2A White Teacher Institute, September 6–7, 1923, Leesburg High School, Superintendent O. L. Emerick, Presiding.

59. EWP: 4.1 Rules and Regulations for Loudoun County Teachers, 1924–25.

60. EWP: 7.6.4. Yr. 1921 Physical Exams, 1.

61. Guidance and Testing Service, Division of Special Services, in *Guidance Handbook for Virginia Schools* (Richmond, VA: State Department of Education, June 1965). See also B. S. Andrews, "Report on Speech Defects in Loudoun," May 1952, Medical College, Richmond, VA, which dealt with treatment of white and Black students. EWP: 4.11 Visiting Teacher Files, Yr. 1944–1954.

62. EWP: 7.6.4 Inspections and the Five Point Standard Health Program.

63. Barbara Scott, interview by Larry Roeder, May 3, 2017. See also Bridget Houlahan and Lilianna Deveneau, "The Promotion of Early School Nurses in Virginia . . . ," *Journal of School Nursing* (2019): 7.

64. EWP: 4.5 White Teacher Cards.

65. EWP: 4.4 Superintendent of Schools, 1946; Superintendent's Record of Teacher's Certificates, 1915–1946. See also EWP: 5.1 Curriculum: 1929, Five Point Star.

66. EWP: 4.2b Colored Teachers Institute, September 23, 1929.

67. EWP: 7.3.1 Letter from Fred Drummond, Principal of Banneker Colored School to Oscar Emerick, Principal.

68. William R. Hood, *State Laws Related to Education Enacted in 1918 and 1919*, Bulletin no. 30 (Washington, DC: Department of the Interior, 1920), 324.

69. Harris Hart, *Annual Report of the Superintendent of Public Instruction* (Richmond, VA: Superintendent of Public Printing, 1926), 36.

70. *The 1927 Annual Report of the Superintendent of Public Instruction*, the text of which was provided by Zachary Vickery, senior reference librarian, Library of Virginia, Richmond.

71. EWP: 3.1 Yr. 1932 Some Random Facts about Our Schools. See also "Normal Professional," in *Regulations Governing Certification of Teachers in Virginia*, Bulletin of the State Board of Education (Richmond: Division of Purchase and Printing, January 1931), 7.

72. References to the need to enhance attendance are throughout the annual reports of state superintendents of public instruction, such as a state-sponsored study in Montgomery County, Virginia, in 1931. See *Annual Report of the Superintendent of Public Instruction of the Commonwealth of Virginia, 1930–41* (Richmond: Division of Purchase and Printing, 1932), 95.

73. EWP: 7.6 Physical Exams about 1921, Report by Oscar Emerick.

74. EWP: 7.6 Physical Exams about 1921, Report by Oscar Emerick.

75. "Death Notice for William Brounaugh," *News Journal* (Wilmington, DE), August 21, 1961, p. 30.

76. Brounaugh (niece Sarah Rucker Gordon spelled it "Bronough") married Caroline (Carrie) Minor ca. 1890, daughter of Daniel Webster Minor, one of Waterford's five trustees in 1866. They moved to New Jersey sometime after 1890. Research by Bronwen Souders.

6

1930–50

A Twenty-Year Sprint

Before the segregated public schools began in 1870, individuals like Edwin Washington had to stand up for their rights in the absence of institutional support—except, of course, for the aid of the Quakers, who were very important in Loudoun, and the Freedmen's Bureau. Then, in the early years of the twentieth century white philanthropies like the Slater Fund, and Black institutions like the NOS as well as the official Black teacher institutes brought collective Black intellectual power and influence to bear on educational excellence in Loudoun and elsewhere in Virginia, despite the rise of Jim Crow and racial violence. We must also not forget the Virginia Teachers Association, which began in 1887 to organize Black educators in the commonwealth.[1] The 1930s and 1940s marked some important transitions. Black leadership continued to make measurable advances, especially toiling for secondary school learning. Toward the end of the period, as the NOS declined in influence, the National Association for the Advancement of Colored People (NAACP), the County-Wide League of Black PTAs, the Loudoun County Teachers Association, and lawyers would increase their own mark, using arguments based on the Fourteenth Amendment to improve sanitation, health, transportation, teachers' salaries, and general education.[2] However, the constant barriers of white supremacy remained.[3]

What Drove Emerick?

Advances by Blacks in education required agreement from the division superintendent, the local school board, and Virginia's government—all segregationist by law and temperament. So was Oscar Emerick at least fair? Did he listen and make accommodations? Since taking the helm of Loudoun's schools in 1917, Emerick had proven to be a skilled, often progressive administrator, capable of juggling the political and financial headwinds that inhibited critical investments or the latest administrative techniques.[4] However, considering the real contemporary systemic inequality as well as the gentleman's upbringing, answering the question of his fairness is complicated.

Emerick permitted significant advances in Black education in the prior decade such as John Walker's limited upper-branch (high school) classes on the second floor of the Training Center, as well as the march through Leesburg at a time of national racial strife. He also found funding partnerships to supplement official financial support and hired a Jeanes Supervisor in 1920, which was controversial to a parsimonious board of supervisors. In 1930, a decade before Douglass High School was built, he encouraged a true high school program in the Training Center. However, the floor on which the program was run could not have objectively been considered sufficient for the growing Black high school–qualified student population, nor were the programs being offered sufficient for college entry. In the 1940s, decades after whites had them, Emerick finally permitted modern consolidated Black elementary schools. The permission was based on a plan developed by the County-Wide League of Black PTAs. However, related transportation needs were not handled well. This seriously stifled the ability of Blacks to attend their high school program, thus forcing them to turn to outside assistance to make their cases, such as to Charles Hamilton Houston, the dean of Howard University's law school. Importantly, however, Emerick's official writings did recognize that the system was unfair and, if not put into balance (as he narrowly understood the concept), he feared the schools would be taken over by the courts.[5] Walter White of the NAACP wrote about some of this unfairness in a letter of March 20, 1940, saying that the school system spent "three and half times as much for the salary of white janitors (there is no janitor service in Negro schools) as it spends on the total bus transportation for Negro schools. Though taxed at the same rate as anyone else, Negro parents had to pay for wiring school buildings and have to pay the electric bills."[6]

Stark contradictions abounded. In 1933 Emerick said, "Throughout our entire education experiences, the resistance of the aristocrats of Virginia has been a powerful factor in retarding the progress of our schools."[7] While true, Emerick issued public statements supporting the separation of the races. For example, in 1941 Emerick said, "We do not haul white and colored children in the same bus, and we haven't thought of allowing both races to attend the same school."[8] After the 1954 *Brown v. Board of Education* Supreme Court decision, he was a vocal supporter of Virginia's massive resistance campaign against integration.

Emerick said in 1949 that the "real deterrent to education progress in the county" hinged on the number of white high schools and the funds to improve conditions and then blamed the commonwealth for inadequately supporting the State Literary Fund, "another block to orderly educational development in the county."[9] While the second observation might have been true, what is also true is there was systemic underfunding of Black education. That was both a county and commonwealth decision.

Emerick's intellectual blinders were symptomatic of the white-dominated culture, as seen in a memo shortly after World War II in which he wrote, "Not all of the colored children are black. It is really a surprising and shocking condition to observe how many of the 'colored' children in several of our schools are 'white.'"[10] The real shock might have been that he was surprised. Emerick was born in Loudoun, and interracial unions and their offspring had existed since the horrid days of enslavement. However, this was a perennial issue, even with Walter White, head of the NAACP from 1929 until his death in 1955. White, with his blond hair and blue eyes, was often mistaken for being white.

To be fair to Emerick, limited budgets were not just about prejudice. There was also a national context. The 1929 stock market crash led to economic despair in America, especially for Blacks, although Virginia was not as hard hit as other states. Reductions in teaching staff and budgets took place across the state, including in Loudoun. Black and white instructors in Loudoun saw salaries cut in academic year 1929–30.[11] Whites and Emerick did fight for increases, but while the 1936 call to arms on salaries was good philosophy, it ran up against the reality of reduced tax revenue. The state and the county had to tighten belts. Charities were also in trouble. Across the South, Blacks had a hard time finding or keeping jobs, and there are many reports that employers were asked to hire whites, not Blacks, although the team did not find evidence of that phenomenon in Loudoun.[12] However, Black workers were at the bottom of the wage scale, resulting in poverty that impacted future generations.

For Loudoun Blacks to emerge out of this cycle required extra determination and creativity, especially as schooling for Blacks was oriented around industrial education rather than being a steppingstone to non-agricultural professions like the law, medicine, or managing a factory. In fact, pressure to learn farming was part of the larger economic and political context of Loudoun with which Blacks of the 1930s and 1940s had to contend, such as during the heavy push to return to farming in the 1930s. Farming as a profession in Loudoun rose to 16.3 percent for whites and 23 percent for Blacks in 1930. The size of farms diminished between 1930 and 1935, but the number of farms increased.[13] Ethel Smith, a long-time Loudoun teacher, recalled that while farming could cause students to be delayed arriving at the Willisville school, none dropped out.[14]

Health, Sanitation, and Heat

During the Depression food security and health care for both the Black and white communities suffered from the lack of government funds. In addition to the decline in tax revenue and increase in unemployment, Virginians faced a philosophical view by many conservative political leaders that it wasn't a core job of government to subsidize either food or health care. Regardless of ability, all parents, white or Black, were expected to pay for their family's basic medical care, surgeries, or dentistry. However, as described elsewhere in the book, the Franklin Roosevelt (FDR) administration quickly assessed that the traditional approach to relief by President Herbert Hoover, with its heavy reliance on charities, was not sufficient to properly deal with the national crisis and established programs to address food and health issues.[15] However, Black people still faced the inequity of the system. It does need to be said that while denying funding for a school dental clinic or a dentist might not always have been overtly directed against the Black community, the primary harbor for funds, when they were made available, was for whites.

Quite apart from the systemic inequity of Black access to health, transportation, and high school education, the actual physical environment critical to health (especially deteriorating buildings) was also challenging. Based on the government's own estimate in 1940 that frame buildings only had a useful life of twenty-five years, versus forty years for brick or masonry, many Black schoolhouses were in trouble.[16] In 1940 Loudoun's Blacks had access to nineteen schoolhouses—all frame except a few, like Lincoln, that sat on bricks or stone—the average age of which was sixty-one years.[17] The 1883-constructed Training Center benefited from an additional room in 1935, but it was constructed from a nineteenth-century frame Black schoolhouse. During the same period, whites used forty-two schoolhouses, eight of which were brick, thirty-one frame, and three stone, plus some teacherages and buildings dedicated to shop classes.[18] Blacks had no teacherages, unless Beatrice Scipio's cabin in Bluemont counted, or shops. The average age of the white school buildings was just thirty-three years.[19]

Poor sanitation and improper heat also beset Black schools. In the winter of 1941, the Ashburn Colored School's only heat came from an ineffective wood stove, forcing students to huddle close to the teacher. "The cold was brutal, with kids having to dress very warmly, shivering for one or two hours before the room heated enough."[20] According to one alum a decade later, a man was supposed to manage the stove, but if he didn't arrive, the students sat in the cold, sometimes for months if the heater broke.[21] At the consolidated Black school of Banneker built in 1948 in Saint Louis, the school only had a drain field and, according to one student, no septic tank, or at least not a working one, which meant the raw sewage leaked into the field behind the school. "The smell was horrible in the warm weather, and when we played ball, quite often, the ball went into the field, and we ducked and dodged the sewage. Between the horse and cow manure, and the raw human sewage, the water supply in Saint Louis was horrible."[22]

Some health threats were exposed in a 1930 report by an inspector hired by Virginia's Department of Health, the Loudoun County Board of Supervisors, and Oscar Emerick. Of the forty-nine schools inspected, thirty-nine had antiquated systems, with the water supply in danger of contamination.[23] The school list was not released, but some surely must have been Black. This surmise comes from examining systemic resource inequities identified by a 1927 study that reported that no "colored" school was equipped with modern heating, the very problem Ashburn faced. As Emerick put it, "by modern is meant either a furnace or jacketed stove. A plain stove heating by direct radiation is not a proper system for heating a school room because it does not give off uniform heat, one side of child is often cold while another is hot."[24] In some schools, the stove also used soft coal, which generated abundant dirt and obnoxious gases. Some white schools were as bad, but the important observation is that not a single Black school had a modern system. Inequality of resources went on throughout the period, even with the advent of consolidated schools in the 1940s and the construction of Douglass High School in 1941.

There were some bright spots in health support; for example, immunizations covered both Black and white pupils.[25] The 1937 federal government appropriations also helped so-called crippled and subnormal children and adults to correct defects or to be trained to be self-supporting. Emerick immediately surveyed all the schools to identify the names and conditions of anyone with defects, "e.g., crippled, defective vision, hearing, speech, organically defective (e.g., bad hearts), mentally incompetent, mentally abnormal and epileptic."[26] This was followed by dental inspections of all students in 1938 and 1939, when county funds for Black health care were also expended for the first time, including $100 for a "dental clinic for colored children."[27] An examination of the files indicates that once again the relative positive impact on Blacks was less than for whites.

Across the races, students in overcrowded conditions were always threatened by viruses. Therefore, during a 1935 polio outbreak, the Loudoun County Health Board ordered that no child under sixteen be admitted to movie houses, dance halls, swimming pools, ball parks, school or church, anywhere people congregated, including circuses and medicine shows.[28] To bolster the weak health budget, Emerick found partnerships with the 4-H Club, the Lion's Club of Leesburg, and the Junior Board of Trade, the latter of which helped fund an X-ray clinic in 1939 and 1943.[29] To develop a strategy for fighting tuberculosis, the Northern Virginia Tuberculosis Association also met in Leesburg in October that year; the association directly engaged Black educators at Douglass High School in 1943 with three cash prizes for the best essays on the topic, which was important since the death rate from tuberculosis for Blacks was three times that of whites.[30]

Some health threats were specific to Blacks, such as the 1932 Tuskegee Study of Untreated Syphilis in the Negro Male, which extended into the Saint Louis hamlet. Researchers searched for young Black males with "bad blood," meaning syphilis, anemia, and fatigue.[31] The study would continue for forty years and never offer treatments, the very definition of a crime against humanity. Even after penicillin was determined in 1947 to be the drug of choice for syphilis, it was never offered to the men in this study, causing untold suffering and a legacy of mistrust in medicine by Blacks that exists into the COVID-19 pandemic era.

A reluctance to raise taxes complicated implementation of effective broad-based health policies in rural counties. Where would the money come from for dentists, doctors, and other medical expenses when insurance did not exist, and social security did not emerge until 1935?[32] If from taxes, that meant asking the County Board of Supervisors, not something they were inclined to support. In 1935 a dental clinic, which the EWP team understands to mean use of a dentist's office or travel by a dentist to a school, was denied by the supervisors for lack of funds. For many decades, the board did not allocate funds for the one-room schools to store even simple medical supplies, so any material useful for cuts, scrapes, and minor illnesses was maintained in "loan closets," from which supplies were lent to a home or to students when needed and then resupplied by the school patrons.

Some citizens were so upset about the government's lackluster response to the need for basic health care, what some might call a crisis, that they became philanthropists. A great example that supported both poor whites and Blacks was the free health service operated by the Foxcroft School for girls in the Mercer School District, between the town of Purcellville to the north and the Black hamlet of Saint Louis to the south.[33] Services were managed by registered nurse Helen Pittman MacDonald. Care was not just for minor medical issues like supplying a toothbrush, although that was an essential gift. Care included tooth extraction and dental surgery. Foxcroft also financed medical care for two Black children needing brain tumor operations.[34] Once a school dental clinic was established, Foxcroft promised five dollars to any school that completed 100 percent corrections of defects identified in their student inspections.

Operations of the long-awaited dental clinic began on January 29, 1938, providing examinations to 1,505 children in fifteen schools.[35] There were at the time twenty-nine white and twenty Black schools.[36] A white dentist, probably Dr. Charles Brown or Dr. Bernard Brann, inspected Black students from November 26, 1938, to March 26, 1939. In that period, he examined 710 pupils and treated 453 from Ashburn, Bull Run, Conklin, Hillsboro, Hughesville, Leesburg, Lincoln, Lovettsville, Marble Quarry, Middleburg, Mountain Gap, Powell's Grove, Rock Hill, Round Hill, Saint Louis, Waterford, and Willisville.[37] Middleburg, Willisville, Waterford, and Lincoln had no work done.

Inspection records for nineteen Black schools show that of the total population of 862 students, 42 percent had dental defects and 47 percent had corrections.[38] There are also records for twenty-three white schools.[39] They show that in a population of 3,441 students, 57 percent had dental defects and 21 percent had corrections made, which indicates that Black teeth were in better shape. One possible reason is that, because of their relative poverty, Blacks had a leaner diet as well as less access to sugar. Records also show that the clinic inspections yielded results, with 489 children being treated in schools and 350 others in dental offices. No racial breakdown is given, although the board of supervisors did agree to appropriate dental funds for both white and Black schools in academic year 1938–39.

In 1943 the school dentist examined 706 pupils in seven schools (hardly comprehensive), and the records do not indicate if Blacks were treated or only examined.[40] A decade later, in 1952, preschool dental clinics were not funded and parents were advised to take children to their own doctors for examination. "The most important time for teeth examination is in the first three years of life. Care and treatment then prevent malformations and shows if the teeth are growing and being formed properly."[41] Once again the question is, what if the parents were poor? Could they afford to use a private dentist? If not, would the government help?

Why wasn't the government doing more? While underfunding Black health was a symptom of overt prejudice and pseudo-science, this does not explain the lack of support for health care for white schools, workers, and the poor. The philosophy that funding health services was not a core government function was deeply rooted both in Virginia and at the national level. Even today, some political conservatives feel that way.

The United States lagged well behind Europe in providing medical insurance and health care for the poor or the working classes. Germany in 1845 provided compulsory smallpox vaccinations for all its citizens, and by the early twentieth century mutual benefit societies and government health services existed throughout Europe. But America was different, leaving health care in the hands of the states, local governments, churches, and charities until World War II, when companies began offering health insurance.

The lack of health care for Loudoun Blacks was not an arcane historical point. Lack of private or government insurance had a disproportionally negative impact on Black health since in a segregated, stratified society, benefits first adhered to whites. There were government efforts to improve preventive health care such as the establishment in June 1944 of the white-only Manassas Vocational School, which included an urgently needed thirteen-week practical nursing program.[42] However, the school was of no direct help to Blacks.

The Five Point Standard Health Program was an integral part of the school health program during the 1930s and 1940s and continued to at least 1951.[43] It began with physical inspections. The team gathered statistical evidence of inspection of students' eyes, ears, throat, teeth, and weight. For example, the inspection of fifteen boys and ten girls at the Marble Quarry Colored School in academic year 1938–39 revealed:[44]

- Eyes: One girl had an eye defect, which was corrected.
- Ears: There were no ear defects.
- Throat: Two boys had throat defects, which were corrected.
- Teeth: Seven boys and four girls had teeth defects, which were corrected.
- Weight: Three boys had weight defects, which were not corrected.

The data was then converted by the school system into Five Point evaluations and certificates for each student. Of the same twenty-five pupils, twenty-one were given high marks for the Five Point Program and one girl was gauged as good. An interesting story on the Five Point Program in Hanover County appeared in the *Richmond Times-Dispatch* on November 20, 1932. "Close competition marked the award of the

Federation prizes for the schools, white and Negro, for the school having the highest percentage of pupils who qualified under the State Board of Health standard for a "five-point" child in health covering physical perfection."[45]

Nutrition

HOT LUNCHES[46]

Hot dinner lunches are just the thing,
To make the children laugh and sing,
They twist and turn, and fro
In the house and the door.
Some bring potatoes, some bring hash,
A few have bread and succotash.
Now and then a bone is seen
A little fat with a little lean.
Of times on a gloomy day
The children romp and then they play
With a spoon, not a scoop
They stir and stir their dainty soup.

Banneker, which was built in 1948, offered sandwiches and four lunch periods.[47] The students at Willisville also purchased canned lunches at Schenck's store.[48] According to the EWP chief docent, Gert Evans, "one of the teachers, Isaac Daniels, sold snacks to students that were probably delivered by this company."[49] A victory garden in the 1940s was also a source of vegetables.[50] However, interviews of former Black and white students from this period reveal that children were mostly expected to bring their lunch, often sandwiches in paper bags or soup. Students often used red King Molasses tins to carry their lunch because the brand had metal handles. In 1941 at the Ashburn Colored School, there was a small table with a common water bucket and sandwiches that the teacher, Lola Jackson, had made with peanut butter supplied by the county. She paid for the bread herself as well as for hot chocolate on cold days. Her efforts were primarily aimed at the indigent.[51] The diet for some children was also supplemented by rabbit, squirrel, pork, and chicken.[52] In the winter at the Saint Louis School, before Banneker was built, "parents volunteer at least once a week to provide a nice hot lunch, bean soup, vegetable soup, chicken and dumplings, and dessert, e.g., bread pudding, pound cake, or Jell-O with fruit cocktail. They also prepared special holiday meals."[53] Sometimes teachers, even into the 1950s, would heat up food on the wood stoves, such as at Bull Run Colored on New Mountain Road, although the students also brought their lunches in paper bags.[54]

A former white student told the team, "My dad carried two biscuits with homemade jelly when available every day for lunch. That was 1934 forward. He would often have fried fatback on the biscuits."[55] Another said, "My mom said she had saltine crackers crushed in milk in the morning for breakfast." Her father had died in combat in World War I, leaving their family destitute during the Depression, so her mother had to dig up vegetable roots for food.[56] A more fortunate student's father, on return from World War I, cured hams and shared the meat with students, but one day dogs got into the school and ate all the lunches, so the kids could not eat anything until supper. A Black former student also said that in "1945 when I started, until 1957 when I graduated, the only food we got was some apples when I was in seventh grade. Mrs. Craven [Ruth Craven, a teacher] sold hot dogs and chocolate milk. It was brown bag for twelve years."[57] In the 1930s, according to teacher Mildred Gray (née Boyd) of Waterford, her landlady made a bucket of hot chocolate on very cold days to warm the children after their walk to school. The one-room schoolhouse had a coal stove for heat, but Gray also had a hotplate. The 1930–40s students remembered US surplus beans and cheese being used in Waterford.

Fortunately, federal programs such as a home economics effort that provided inexpensive meals and hot lunches in the harsh winter of 1934, helped both Blacks and whites, although unequally. Aid was given to twelve white and three Black Loudoun schools, paid for by the Civil Works Administration (CWA), the first public employment program under FDR.[58] The short-term goal was to feed children, and the long-term goal was to train adults in food preparation. Loudoun County social caseworkers Blanche Melvin and Matilda Garner assisted with the program: "It is hoped lunches can be arranged for all white one-room schools and a few negro schools," opined the *Loudoun Times-Mirror* in 1934.[59]

However, CWA funds were only to pay for CWA contractors like Mildred Weadon, a CWA home demonstration agent, not for supplies. Therefore, an appeal went out for donations of "canned tomatoes, corn, soup mixtures, beans, salmon, carrots, peas, tomato juice, peanut butter, rice, macaroni, oatmeal, raisins, prunes, sugar, dried peas, dried beans, cocoa, Irish and sweet potatoes, turnips, cabbage, apples, onions, dried chip beef, salt pork, milk, canned, dried or fresh."[60] Weadon traveled the county every day in her Model T Ford, averaging 222 miles a week between January 1 and April 13, 1934.[61]

Food was provided to white schools: Arlington, Brooklyn, Carter, Coleman, Emerick, Little River, McGraw Ridge, Mountville, Neersville, Philomont, Sunny River, and Woodland.[62] The Black schools that received food were Marble Quarry, Mountain Gap, and Watson.[63] Supplies and labor were provided by the Loudoun Tuberculosis Association and the Leesburg Rotary Club as well as two Black teachers, Gertrude Stewart (of Middleburg) and Mattie Berryman (of Marble Quarry), who helped with summer community canning. As a result, one hot meal was prepared and served to 193 children every day by women in need of work, paid by Blanch Melvin, the director of relief.[64] In addition, 172 children brought food in jars. The program had positive results; children began to gain weight. A ceremony was then held at each school at the end of the lunch project on March 30, 1934, which was then replaced by the Works Progress Administration (WPA; renamed in 1939 as the Work Projects Administration).

In August 1935 the county provided milk, hot lunches, and cod liver oil to underweight children.[65] Lincoln High School also developed a home economics program in academic year 1938–39 "serving hot food to underweight children . . . during winter months," funded by the Lincoln PTA for one meal a day for about twenty-nine children, likely all white.[66] The home economics classes were a high school function, so Blacks did not benefit until under Edythe Harris. In 1939 Edith Eustis of Oatlands Plantation, a close friend of FDR and his wife, provided lunches to nine white and fourteen Black schools.[67] The previous year she had done the same thing for thirteen white and fourteen Black schools.

The issue of proper nutrition had been around a long time, even discussed at the white teacher institute in October 1917. Despite the awareness of need, official hot lunches were likely not provided to Blacks until the 1930s. In January 1943 five schools were served hot lunch daily. Food served was whole milk, cocoa, soup, vegetables, fruits, and whole grain cereals from surplus commodities and foods canned by parents during the summer of 1942 and from individual donations. Again, there are no references to Blacks receiving this support.[68]

Although a home economics program appears to have existed at the Training Center under Edythe Harris, the details are missing; however, at Douglass in 1942, after it was discovered that Blacks could not pass their armed forces entry physicals, the new high school's home economics classes were used to bolster the physical condition of the prospective servicemen. "Our pupils became more conscious of the importance of nutrition. Each took a great personal interest because relatives were subject to be called for service at most any date."[69] Food was purchased from a nearby grocer and then prepared by the girls.[70]

Edythe Harris's High School Program

Thanks to John C. Walker, Black students during the 1920s were exposed to many high school–level lectures and even demonstrated Black pride by marching through the county seat of Leesburg as part of the state-sponsored County School Fair movement. However, more was needed; therefore, thirty-three Black citizens sent a petition to Emerick in May 1930, asking to upgrade the Training Center staff.[71] The petitioners weren't lawyers or major businessmen, although some, like Wilson Townsend and his wife, Mozelle, did have a business. One petitioner owned the famous Robinson Barbershop, still a Leesburg fixture. Robert R. Coe of Leesburg, who led the group, and others were lime kiln laborers, in an important and dangerous industry that provided material to keep agricultural production high and outhouses sanitary.[72] Other staff had occupations as cobblers, servants, cooks, carpenters, a laundress, a truck driver, and houseworkers, the foundation of the economy. One had three years of high school; another rose to the eighth grade, but the rest had completed less schooling. One had only reached the second grade, while another was functionally illiterate, only leaving a mark on the petition. The important thing is that all shared a keen understanding of citizenship rights and did not let their humble status prevent them demanding better education for the next generation.

Also interesting was the carpenter George H. Russ. Russ had been enslaved on the Oatlands Plantation in 1859 but by 1889 was one of three members of the "Colored Republicans" of the 8th Congressional District who joined a meeting to "redress the wrongs perpetrated upon the colored people of the South in their rights to suffrage and the frauds committed upon them at the ballot box."[73]

Emerick did not like petitions and said in 1931 they "will not be considered in relation to the appointment of any teacher."[74] Still, the 1930 petition convinced him to hire a university graduate from Pennsylvania named Edythe Harris (also known as Edyth) (see photo at right). Harris and other educators in the 1930s and 1940s brought educational magic to the Black students of Loudoun by combining social leadership and professionalism. Building upon the legacy of Walker and Jeanes Supervisor Mary Peniston, these people steadily beat with oral and written hammers at the hard metal of prejudice. They also constructed a steel stage upon which an educational rights movement stood, capable by 1941 of creating the important Douglass High School building, which continues to inspire people of all races in Loudoun as a living civil rights monument. However, as Emerick's study from 1927 showed, Blacks had difficult conditions to overcome. Racial prejudice was still the rule, but that reality just made their accomplishments more remarkable.

Many African Americans stood out as determined to argue for excellence in education, but those with biggest impact in this era were Edythe Harris, John Wanzer, Charles Hamilton Houston, Gertrude Alexander, Janie Redwood, and Archie Richardson. The story begins with Pittsburgh-born Harris, who exemplified what Rep. John Lewis of Georgia spoke about in 2020 when he advocated "good trouble." Protests can be loud and boisterous, but they can also be subtle, as initiated in Leesburg by Harris when she began the reorganization of the high school program at the Training Center. Thirty-nine students were in the opening class in 1930 and enjoyed a sophisticated agenda reflecting Harris's zeal and university education. Offerings included chemistry,

Edythe Harris in front of her
log cabin.
EWP: 4.5 Colored Teacher Cards;
photographer unknown

human and plant biology, algebra, spelling, and English, including study-
ing *Hamlet*. That this play was chosen is particularly fascinating from a
political perspective if the plot's interpretation (there are many) is not
simply about "to be or not to be." In Harris's classroom the play could
have been interpreted as an examination of the social cost of seeking
nearly impossible justice, a phenomenon anyone in the Black community of that generation understood. Indeed, the message resonates today.

Harris's history lessons included the Mexican War and Civil War as
well as decisions by individual states on enslavement and squatter sovereignty. The latter topic would have been interesting to Harris's students
because it was the doctrine that gave federal territories the right to enter the Union as free or slave states. Why would one territory choose to
enslave and another oppose, students may have wondered. Sectionalism

was also raised, the philosophy, in one perspective, that some citizens were more concerned over local interests than the good of the whole nation. Although interviews indicated that segregation was not directly discussed very widely, Harris's pupils did examine the Emancipation Proclamation and abolition movements. The Civil War and segregation were rejections of political change being urged on the South, so if the mission of the founders of the American experiment was to constantly evolve a more perfect union, a discussion of sectionalism could have been interpreted as a direct repudiation of the South's rationale for war or justification of segregation.

This narrative about Harris's teaching program says a lot about the instructor, of course; but it is more important as a discussion about the use of the curriculum, which was evolving. Instead of memorizing minutiae, facts were placed into context. In the beginning of this book, we introduced the reader to an 1883 book used by Loudoun's Black students which portrayed adult Blacks as indigent, dirty, and lazy in the protection of children.[75] The story only told one interpretation of a drawing of a tired family leaning against a wall. However, what if the family were escaping some physical threat? What if the parents were on a long journey to a better job and life? Context is important.

Typical for many public schools at the time, individual military battles came up in Harris's courses, but political context was also provided by focusing on the attitudes of France and England. For example, the class studied British prime minister William Ewart Gladstone's speech on the CSS *Alabama*, a great adventure story that was always appealing to youths but was also a narrative with elements of international intrigue, maritime law, and a weak nation's search for justice from a global power. The story then could take on new meaning, especially to a disadvantaged people wanting to take on an unfair system. In the case of the *Alabama*, it was a Confederate commerce raider sunk off France by a United States warship in 1864, one of several raiders constructed by the United Kingdom for the rebel navy. The *Alabama*'s mode was to fly under a false flag to overtake United States merchants through deception. In the 1860s this was considered a violation of the contemporary rules of neutrality, and the matter eventually went to international arbitration, leading to a legal and financial victory for the United States and eventually a fresh treaty between the United States and the United Kingdom.[76] The implication of this and other lessons is that Harris was managing a covert curriculum using standard materials to highlight the struggle of American Blacks. Letters are missing that would document this intent, but such a transparent assault on the social order, were that to be made public, would have been dangerous. Still, her intent does seem obvious with the passage of time. She clearly was a determined lady.

Harris initially faced a daunting workload and equipment challenges and in 1931 said to the school board and Emerick that she was using all her energy to develop a permanent high school program. It began with the first and second years and would expand to a third year, but without additional resources, accommodating students from across the county was impossible. She wanted an additional room, an assistant, and an increase of fifteen dollars a month in salary.[77] Keep in mind. these requests were made at the start of the Great Depression. Determination worked, however, and the program was expanded—although more slowly than she wanted—and included the addition in 1935 of a room on the first floor built with the lumber from the discontinued Sycoline Colored School.[78] Because the county did not provide much money to heat the Training Center, supplementary funds from parents and concerned citizens were always needed.[79] Proper equipment was also not provided for biology or chemistry, so parents had to provide it from their kitchens.

Students of civil rights often focus on famous names like Thurgood Marshall, but in the EWP team's opinion, lesser-known people like Edythe Harris deserve equal recognition for advancing her people up the rickety ladder to equality through the simple act of offering relevant lessons and helping students think and understand, not just recite. Black teachers had been calling for this kind of education in Loudoun since at least 1916.[80] Harris would eventually expand the program to four years, according to Emerick in February 1938: "The Leesburg Colored school has recently started a four-year high school course. More space, more land, and increased teaching staff were needed to provide suitable high school courses."[81] The curriculum Emerick referred to in 1938 seems to have also been offered in 1935 by covering grades 8–11.[82] This was further evidence of a highly active Harris, who also formed a choir, organized plays, and raised funds to provide textbooks to the indigent. The later would traditionally have been done by the government. She also covered "high school grades from AY 1930/1931 to AY 1939/1940, and even taught French, which was a novelty in Black schools, though whites had been learning French and Latin for years."[83] Her determination also led to accreditation the year before Douglass High School was formed.[84]

Harris was probably paid by the Slater Fund (called the Jeanes/Slater Fund in some quarters[85]) in cooperation with the Commonwealth of Virginia and the county. Later, Jeanes supervisor Gertrude Alexander, hired in 1938, would be supported by the same sources. What is clear is that some support was given in 1932, perhaps in response to another petition by eighty Black and six white citizens supporting the continuation of teachers Annie E. Harris and Mary E. Waters in the elementary department of the same school.[86] Among the white signers who supported the school was Charles Harrison, mayor of Leesburg (1913–17 and 1923–34).[87]

The budget for the 1932 venture covered one high school teacher (Edythe Harris) and three elementary teachers. Total monthly salary for eight months was proposed to be $243 split between the Commonwealth of Virginia, Loudoun County, the Black community, and the Slater Fund.[88] The monies were entirely used to instruct students in the high school and lower grades. Surviving records are imperfect, but this kind of financial support continued for the 1933–34 academic year.[89] Emerick's application also indicated that vocational training included home economics and manual training.[90] Edythe Harris also requested a second high school teacher to effectively teach what she saw would be ever-growing classes. That occurred in the 1934–35 academic year, when grants of $1,000 from the state, $1,100 from Loudoun County, and $100 from the Slater Fund were approved. At the time the Training Center included two high school teachers and three elementary school teachers. The high school program also increased to three years of instruction.

Petitions as Political Tools

Political action was needed to keep schools open and to protest the lack of adequate space, transportation, and critical repairs. The archives

Table 6.1
Breakdown of Petition Topics

Subject	Black Petitions (*n*)	Black Petitions (%)	White Petitions (*n*)	White Petitions (%)
Conditions of schools	10	14	0	0
Miscellaneous	19	26	24	15
Opening/reopening or expanding a schoolhouse	16	22	42	25
Teachers	15	20	77	47
Transportation and safety	13	18	22	13
Total	73	100	165	100

contain copies of 73 petitions by Blacks and 165 by whites, all during the administration of Oscar Emerick. The EWP team also believes that some petitions were developed in prior administrations but have been lost. There is no formal indication that petitions were used after Emerick retired in 1957, but it is entirely possible. A table listing all the petitions is published in the 2021–22 edition of the *Bulletin of Loudoun County History*.

A complete set of the text of each petition is also available on the project's website along with photographs of the original documents. The site also contains a video about the petitions.

As in prior decades, Blacks resorted to formal petitions, as did whites, especially concerning school closures, often caused by low attendance. Attendance for boys was always problematic in a farming county because they were inexpensive labor, and during the Depression parents could not afford to hire laborers. There also was no county-supported transportation for Black students until 1937, and then only for twenty-five elementary and fifteen high school students attending the Training Center.[91] Unless parents could provide transportation, which was difficult for farm laborers, or could pool their resources, children had to walk. Distances were often great and sometimes in unsafe conditions. Inevitably, some students just missed school completely.

Harris was right that many wanted to go to the Training Center. In the 1930s nearly one hundred parents and teachers petitioned the school board to provide bus transportation for Black students from

Willisville, Saint Louis, Middleburg, Bull Run, and Gleedsville to the Loudoun County Training School in Leesburg.[92] In 1937, twelve years after school buses were introduced in Loudoun County, the first school bus serving Black students was placed into service. Driven by Will Brown, it ran from Purcellville through Hamilton and Waterford to the Training Center.[93]

An example of a typical transportation petition is shown in a letter from patrons and parents of Black students attending the Saint Louis School before Banneker was built. It is notable that not only was the road to the school in terrible shape, the patrons did not think the school system would consider a remedy unless the parents and patrons contributed the labor.

Middleburg, Virginia
January 21, 1932
Mr. O. L. Emerick
Purcellville, Virginia

Dear Sir:
We, the patrons of St. Louis School, are very anxious to have the roads entering the school grounds improved. It is in a terrible condition, making travel upon it almost impossible. If possible, we should like very much to get help from the School Board. We are willing to contribute labor towards the work.

Sincerely yours,
James S. Grant, Robert T. McQuay, Dudley Gaskins, Sam Hamblin, Myrtle McQuay, Clarence Howard, Mollie Evans, Laura Cook, Teacher.[94]

Imagine living in an agricultural county with dirt or gravel roads, then learning that the one-room schoolhouse serving your community is about to close in the next school term. Since the approach of winter comes with the threat of impassable roads for days or weeks at a time, concern about safe travel to a new school location is an understandable one. In October of 1934 patrons of the Bluemont Colored School addressed the condition of school closings with the following petition:

On account of the enrollment of the Colored School at Bluemont being too small for a legal school, our school has been closed.

In view of this condition, we the patrons of the Bluemont Colored School are asking the Loudoun County Board of Education to give us transportation for seven pupils, to Rock Hill School with the teacher; as she passes through Bluemont going from Purcellville to Rock Hill School.

We the undersigned persons believe that this request is reasonable.[95]

The Bluemont Colored School closed in 1932–33, and yet by 1934 LCPS still had not provided transportation for their students.

Conklin Colored, where the EWP project began, was under constant threat of closure, due to reduced attendance in the 1920s, 1930s, and 1940s and sometimes their students walked quite a distance to another school. In similar fashion, in 1934, the Black citizens of Paeonian Springs complained that a lack of transportation made it impossible for children to reach the nearest village of Waterford.[96] This also happened at Mount Pleasant Colored, which serviced Lucketts and Mt. Pleasant. In June 1938 those families feared their children would not acquire any public school education without transportation.[97] Saint Louis was also the focal point in the 1930s for several petitions to expand an overcrowded schoolhouse, make repairs to the road, or improve the staff. In fact, before Banneker was built, children in the Saint Louis area attended classes in shifts and used a nearby church or café.

Middleburg's Black community offered a good example of a petition using science. It involved Dr. Maurice Britton King Edmead, who practiced in the village from about 1933 until 1952 and was Loudoun's second Black physician.[98] A Howard University Medical School graduate, Edmead was not allowed to practice at Loudoun Hospital in Leesburg, although the facility treated Blacks and had a dedicated wing, largely paid from the estate of a local Black man. However, by the 1940s Edmead was chair of the Building Site Committee of the Middleburg PTA and Community League. He would use the science of medicine in petitions to address the appalling conditions in the schools. Local Blacks were worried that if Grant Colored School was not expanded, respiratory disease might spread from overcrowding. Indeed, overcrowding in

Grant Colored School, about 1940.
Courtesy of EWP Archives

Black schools had been a problem for at least thirty years, with Black one-room schools in 1914 averaging thirty-four students as opposed to twenty-eight students in white schools.[99] The school had no plumbing, a potbelly stove heated with wood supplied by families, and a common ceramic cooler for water.[100] The multiroom structure still exists today, although as a small office building; old pictures and records on class sizes show that Edmead had a point. When the school closed in 1947, it hosted 3 teachers and 110 students.[101] The local Baptist Church had to be used as a supplementary school room. Further, to have something to sit on, children used homemade orange crates created by their teacher Rosa Lee Carter. The same thing also happened at Bull Run where, according to Ethel Smith, the teacher's desk and student chairs and benches had to be homemade.[102]

On November 16, 1944, Edmead employed the support of famed attorney James. H. Raby, who petitioned Emerick directly.

You have received a letter from a number of the parents in Middleburg complaining of the crowded condition at Grant School. As they stated to you, there were two rooms of which ninety-six children had to be cared for by two teachers. Under these conditions, there is no way that these children can get adequate training. This condition should not exist and there is not any reason for such condition because there is ample space to enlarge the school building.[103]

The real problem was politics. Blacks had proposed a location for a new school on a lot in the hamlet of Maxville to the east, potentially placing a large new Black school in plain view of Route 50, the main east–west highway.[104] Instead, Emerick chose Saint Louis, which was out of sight of the highway, for the consolidated school of Banneker.[105] Edmead and Raby had lost that battle because, as Black supervisor Gertrude Alexander put it, the government wanted Black schools placed on out-of-the-way routes. That described Saint Louis; however, it is also true that Banneker was well constructed and still stands today as a fully functional school building with a vibrant alumni association.

Consolidation of small elementary schools into larger graded schools was considered an important evolution in education because it permitted teachers to focus their lectures. In a one-room building, students from every grade and age had to listen to the same thing, causing problems of concentration and comprehension. The first white consolidated schools appeared in 1910 and increased with better road construction and bus transportation. Yet despite the deteriorating age and condition of Black schools, Emerick did not provide Black students the same benefit. In other words, Black children who should have been in consolidated schools could not attend them because the government refused to provide transportation or adequate facilities. As a direct result, an official LCPS report from October 2, 1939, noted that for academic year 1938–39, only 60 Black children were in high school (the Training Center), yet 329 were eligible![106]

In the 1940s, with increased Black community pressure, court cases, and the work of Charles Houston and Gertrude Alexander, Emerick changed his approach, leading to the approval of Banneker in 1945 as a modern consolidated school. To accomplish this, Black leaders lobbied the scattered Black communities because many children would have to travel farther and because, just as in white villages, the loss of a one-room school was often considered an assault on local pride. The EWP team heard the same pride described by former students and their descendants during a field trip to one-room schools in Fredericksburg, Texas, in 2016 under the auspices of the Country School Association of America as well as to Black and white one-room schools in Frederick, Maryland. The County-Wide League of Black PTAs designated an instructor named Janie Redwood as its ambassador to both lobby the white government to permit consolidation and to build Black support around an operational plan. After an exhaustive effort, her recommendations on locations, staffing and equipment were then forwarded to Emerick on March 20, 1945. The result was not only Banneker, but also Carver, both modern schoolhouses with up-to-date heating and toilets—clearly an example of organizational skill and diplomacy, as Redwood had to negotiate not only with the government but also the many Black communities.

In some cases, the petitions were requests to retain great teachers like Esther Randolph in 1937 at the Hughesville Colored School.[107] In similar fashion, in 1930 and 1935 Purcellville Colored (the Willing Workers School) parents asked to retain Elizabeth M. Norton as principal. In Waterford in 1932 the parents and patrons used petitions to protest performance of a teacher, felt to be so strict as to be ineffective.[108] Yet harsh discipline was not uncommon. One teacher used a paddle called Dr. Pepper. Another used group punishment, including with a strap called Susie. Another had students cut branches from a tree for switches.[109]

While the records show a clear path from offering limited access to higher-branch courses to a full high school curriculum at the Training Center, the Black community also understood the need to do a more effective job petitioning for a dedicated facility. This is seen in the efforts of the County-Wide League and individual pleadings of ordinary citizens. A good example is William McKinley Jackson of Middleburg, a stone mason with a fourth-grade education. Jackson wanted more for his daughter, Eva. He complained that the absence of an accredited high school in Loudoun prevented his daughter from gaining entrance to college, forcing him in 1939 to send her to the more expensive Manassas Industrial School in the next county.[110] His letter is also referenced in a complaint to Emerick by the NAACP and the County-Wide League and included his expenses to demonstrate his financial hardship.

Teachers' Salaries: A Step Toward Dismantling Segregation

In 1936, when the Depression was driving down county budgets across the commonwealth, Emerick asked to increase white teacher salaries, saying, "The public school presents the county's best opportunity to improve the human race. As an agency of society for improving our civilization it has the great possibilities, greater than the church because it can reach all people, greater than the home because it can exercise more discretion in selecting those who will guide and influence the destines of our youth."[111] However, he wasn't asking for Black salary increases. When looking over the whole of Emerick's career, it is clear he believed the philosophy he articulated in 1936; salaries for whites were greater than for Blacks with the same qualifications, so his observations were ironic when laid next to the inequality. In academic year 1938–39 salaries of Black teachers with a normal professional certificate and experience of three or more years were frozen at $65 a month. With experience of only two years, the starting salary for whites of $66 could rise to $78. There were exceptions for senior Black instructors such as Edythe Harris, who was paid $70 a month, outpacing John C. Walker, who was paid $60.[112] Walker had over fifty years teaching experience and served as Training Center principal but lacked Harris's professional credentials. Then in January 1938 Black teachers petitioned for an increase and the right to provide a nine-month academic year. If the extension of time was impossible, they wanted at least to return to pre-Depression salaries. The petition was denied.[113]

In the late 1930s and early 1940s, through a combination of legal cases, grassroots campaigns, and discussions with local school board officials, Black teachers were eventually able to move Loudoun toward a single salary schedule for both Black and white teachers. The main influences on this civil rights development were the organization of teachers and parents along with support from the NAACP.

In December 1940 the Loudoun County Teachers Association officially appealed to the school board for salary equity between the races. According to Emerick, the board accepted this principle but indicated it was impossible without reducing white salaries because they didn't have the authority without an appropriation, which meant the board of supervisors.[114] There was a series of court cases in which Black teachers, principals, and supervisors challenged the local school board on race-based inequality in pay when qualifications and tasks were similar. The two most notable cases with national implications that took place in 1939 and 1940, respectively, were *Mills v. Board of Education of Anne Arundel County*, in Maryland, and *Alston v. School Board of the City of Norfolk*, in Virginia. They argued that race-based salary differences violated the 1896 *Plessy v. Ferguson* decision. By violating that "equal doctrine," the school system was also violating the Equal Protection Clause of the Fourteenth Amendment. However, the clearest threat to segregation and Jim Crow was *Alston v. School Board of the City of Norfolk*.[115] The plaintiff, a schoolteacher named Melvin Alston, argued that Black teachers were being paid on a lower salary scale for no other reason than their race. The court ruled that the salary scale violated the Fourteenth Amendment, thus fundamentally weakening the hold of *Plessy*.

Following these cases, several groups of Loudoun County Black teachers and other school employees joined together in opposition to the unjust salary system. They proposed the implementation of a single salary schedule on the grounds that a race-based salary scale was unconstitutional. Specifically, they cited the ruling in *Alston*, pointing out that the board would not want to "maintain a practice which is not only in contravention of [the petitioners'] democratic ideals, but which is also unconstitutional." Identical copies of this petition were sent to the school board by the Leesburg PTA, the Loudoun County-Wide League of Black PTAs, the Loudoun County Teachers Association, and the Loudoun branch of the NAACP.

The teachers noted that local superintendents and school boards were designed to prescribe and regulate salaries based upon the "laws and regulations of the State of Virginia and of the United States." Amid this debate, the public school system leadership searched for ways to keep the salary system segregated in favor of white teachers. Emerick and the school board suggested that the reason for the salary differential was that white teachers were better credentialed, had higher test scores, or had more experience in the classroom. Their excuses were clearly attempts to maintain the status quo.

The teachers and the County-Wide League of Black PTAs compared specific salaries for teachers of equal qualifications and experience, noting that the uniform bias toward white teachers could not reasonably be based on anything besides race. In addition, they mentioned that teachers of all races were required to take the same test and earn the same certificate, so the claim that Black teachers were somehow less capable than white teachers did not withstand scrutiny. Finally, they argued that the perceived difference in pay "is even greater than is indicated on the face of the schedule because [white teachers] are paid for 12 months of the year, while the Negro teachers are paid for 10 months."[116] The teachers concluded by stating that the intention behind their proposal for the equalization of salaries was not to reduce the salaries of the white teachers but instead to use the same pay scale for all groups of teachers.

In case after case, the NAACP presented clear evidence from the government's own documents that the school system was separate and unequal. With Thurgood Marshall as the lead attorney, they built a record that proved an undeniable fact—"separate" was never meant to be equal. It was meant to institutionalize white supremacy. Finally, a plan to equalize salaries was approved by the school board. It was a small victory in a long fight, yet within that victory there were continuing inequities. It would take three years to implement the new salary schedule.

Gertrude Alexander Takes the Stage

In 1937 Edythe Harris and many other Black teachers petitioned the county to use "Jeanes/Slater Funds" to hire a supervisor for Black teachers. This led to Gertrude Alexander, the third Jeanes Supervisor hired by Emerick. The first was Mary Peniston in 1920, who played an important role in the Black version of the County School Fair and the march through Leesburg.[117] Emerick made the request for Gertrude A. Alexander official on July 9, 1938, and it was approved the following month, with service to begin on September 1. She came with both bachelor's and master's

The county hired several "colored" supervisors (supported by the Jeanes Fund), although not every year. There were gaps in hiring, and in one instance, a white teacher had to be hired to fill the slot because no Black teacher was available. The reasons for no Black teacher applying are not known.

- 1921–22 Mary A. E. Peniston
- 1930–32 Mary E. Tyler McCoy
- 1938–41 Gertrude Alexander
- 1941–49 Ruby Gilford Vaughan
- 1945–46 Cora P. Campbell, listed as elementary supervisor.
- 1949–51 Marian J. Sands
- 1952–55 Helen M. N. Cauthorne
- 1955. No Black teacher could be found for this position, so the unprecedented step was made to use Ruth Schulke in that slot.

Gaps were frequent, and in the other instances the specific slot was not filled. Instead, all teachers fell under management of one white teacher.

degrees, having been educated at Atlanta University, and she had a Collegiate Professional teacher's certificate issued by the State of Virginia. At the time, she also had three years of teaching experience but none as a Jeanes Supervisor. Alexander was paid $900 for nine months' work, with $150 provided by the Southern Education Foundation, $450 by the commonwealth, and $300 by Loudoun County. She supervised twenty-eight Black teachers.

Alexander is one of the most remembered historical figures in Loudoun's Black educational movement, partly because she caused the creation in 1938 of the County-Wide League of Black PTAs and because of her work to convince Emerick to allow the erection of the Douglass High School. In addition, she worked with NAACP legend Charles Hamilton Houston on surveys of citizens to document how much they were handicapped by the lack of public transportation. Houston was known for defeating Jim Crow on transportation and high school matters and for laying the groundwork for many of the battles and lawsuits against segregation in the 1940s and 1950s. As a Jeanes Supervisor, Alexander was a true force for social change, which is seen in her personal reports to donors in the archives of the Atlanta University.

The Jeanes Supervisor model was to survey the schools in their district, report back to the Slater Fund, and make suggestions for improvement. While some schools were well constructed, Alexander said of the Black schools standing in 1939–40 that maintenance had been poor and construction not on par with that of white buildings; furthermore, the education conditions for Blacks was extremely limited. Emerick agreed on the quality of construction, across the board, noting in 1938 that despite Loudoun being among the wealthiest counties in Virginia per capita, "our buildings have been cheaply constructed and have a low value compared to Virginia as a whole."[118] Alexander also pointed out that most of the buildings for Blacks were in "small communities away from main highways, which makes transportation in winter months quite difficult."[119] Two schools were in churches and one in a lodge hall. The buildings were all old, and many were dilapidated, with improper lighting and ventilation. All toilets were outhouses. Five had electricity, but this was only thanks to the intervention of patrons, not the county; none had janitors. In fact, interviews by the EWP team indicated that in Willisville there was no money for linseed oil to treat the wood floors, so students had to rub the planks with old motor oil—an interesting choice, given poor ventilation and the presence of an open stove fire. While motor oil is not classified as flammable, it is toxic to breathe and is combustible.

Alexander also noted that each teacher was responsible for obtaining his or her own wood or coal and "building her own fire." At the Bull Run school, boys hauled water from a nearby well in the mornings, and each child had to bring a lump of coal to heat the room before the teacher arrived. While the county did provide coal to the Training Center by truck, students were required to haul it from the street into the coal bin and the rooms' stoves. The study also pointed out the lack of transportation for Black students. There was only one bus available, which was privately owned and rented by the county. It made two trips a day to connect children with the Training Center, twenty-nine students for nine miles and eighteen more for five miles. Alexander's damning assessment of conditions extended as well to attendance: 725 children of school age were not enrolled, including 173 of elementary school age, and 329 eligible for high school but not enrolled. To remedy some of this, Alexander visited the parents of unenrolled children.

Alexander's achievements went well beyond her report, including sponsoring beautification and cleanup programs, an NOS priority. She worked with the county health unit to sponsor dental, diphtheria, and tuberculosis clinics, and she secured donations of food as well as money for cod liver oil and hot lunches for at least five months. Alexander also formed a voter's club to increase the number of Black registered voters.[120] She brought into the county lay workers and specialists to hold teacher forums as well as supervisors and teachers from adjoining counties to observe classrooms and make recommendations. In addition, she developed the first detailed breakdown of industries and property ownership/rental by Black males and females, covering 1,307 males and 545 females. It was the most detailed economic breakdown of the Black community up to that point. In effect, Alexander was a sort of "mayor."

Grassroots Tools: The NOS and County-Wide League of Black PTAs

Despite economic hardships, significant progress was made in challenging the limitations of school segregation, thanks in part to how lobbying by Virginia Blacks changed in the mid-1930s. Counties formed County-Wide Leagues of Black PTAs. Established in 1938, Loudoun's league became a unified voice for nearly all Blacks and remained active at least until 1958. There is little published literature on this important political tool, and minutes of meetings have not survived, but some material exists at the Library of Virginia, Virginia State University, Hampton University, and in contemporary media reports. The EWP team also drew on conversations with descendants of former league officials from Botetourt, Henrico, Loudoun, Prince William, Sussex, and Warrick Counties as well as Norfolk to understand how their leagues operated. Archie Richardson wrote about them briefly in his study. Loudouners remembered their league as unique, but research indicates that Alexander likely organized it in cooperation with the NOS, a grass-roots advocacy body. The concept also had the support of the NAACP.[121] The ties to the NOS continued with Marian J. Sands, Loudoun's Jeanes Supervisor from 1949 to 1951. Sands had been a field agent for the NOS. At that time, she organized the first state-wide survey of county objectives and progress reports, which would have prepared her very well for her tour of duty in Loudoun.[122]

Alexander's own role cannot be overstressed, nor that of Edythe Harris, who served as publicity head. Until then, PTAs focused on their specific schools and their parochial interests, which were important, but the league leveraged the power of many at the all-white government's negotiating table.[123] Harris was also critical because she had to speak directly to every PTA about the links between their own interests and league policies. Unifying all interests into one strong fabric could not have been easy, especially regarding consolidation, and the league did not always get its way. Middleburg disagreed with the league on how to expand its school. Purcellville Blacks wanted the new Black high school to be in their village, not Leesburg, as the league proposed, but that was simply democracy at work.

To understand the league's origins and its relationship with the NOS, the authors also studied Loudoun records in the archives of Atlanta University, where Alexander graduated in 1938 with a master's degree, and in the NOS files at Hampton University. Initially, the organization was about "the social, civic, intellectual, industrial and moral betterment of the black man" but, by the 1930s, fostered local networks such as the County-Wide Leagues. Both organizations and citizens could join the NOS; Hampton University files showed that Loudoun members in 1941 included Elizabeth C. Jones of the Leesburg PTA and Phyllis Smith of the Purcellville's Happy Pals Junior School League. The later probably refers to a Junior League of the NOS. From its inception in 1912, adults attended annual conferences along with children, but the youths had nothing to do. By November 1935 the NOS formed junior leagues to prepare "youth for intelligent participation in affairs of the community and state."[124] Evidently one formed in Loudoun but went inactive; then the Loudoun County Teachers Association reorganized the Junior County-Wide league in 1943, which is perhaps the same body.[125]

The counties that the EWP team contacted felt their leagues were unique. This is probably because their operations were based on local synergy, not solely from state-level NOS organizers based at the Hampton Institute. Thus, success was really about the labor of local volunteers, parents, teachers, and other interested citizens, like Charlotte Noland, an aristocratic white educator and owner of Foxcroft School for girls, just north of the traditionally Black village of Saint Louis. To this day, some local Blacks remember her efforts to support Black one-room schools as well as victory gardens during World War II, which involved both white and Black students.

At the recommendation of Dr. Margaret T. Haley, an educator advocate in neighboring Manassas, Prince William County formed its own league in 1935 with the help of the NOS. She continued with it until 1945, when she joined the Virginia State Department of Education.[126] Haley found NOS leadership to be essential, and during her ten-year tenure they often visited to advance access to dental care, preschool, tuberculous clinics, diphtheria immunizations, and hot lunches. Members included both parents and adults without children, as in Loudoun.

Loudoun's County-Wide League was managed under the iron will of Middleburg blacksmith John Wanzer.[127] In fact, one of the most impressive photos of the period is of Wanzer banging metal into form, symbolic of efforts to bend the will of the white government. Wanzer served as league president until his death in 1957, earning respect from both whites and Blacks. The records are not clear when the league folded, but it was still in operation in 1958, according to Peggy Drummond, wife of the principal of Douglass Elementary that year.[128]

Loudoun's County-Wide League of Black PTAs Officers (1938):

John Wanzer, president (Middleburg)
Elizabeth Quisenberry, vice president (Leesburg); Annie Ferrell, second vice president (Waterford); Charles H. Willis, secretary (Aldie); E. Sanford, assistant secretary (Hamilton); Irene Roberts, treasurer (Leesburg); Reverend Williams, chaplain (Leesburg); Edythe O. Harris, publicity (Leesburg)

John Wanzer, head of the County-Wide League, in his Middleburg shop.
EWP Archives, loose file; photographer unknown

Loudoun's league focused on (a) moving students out of the Loudoun County Training Center, considered a death trap by many; (b) gaining an accredited high school building for Blacks, eventually Douglass High School; and (c) moving children out of the dilapidated Grant School in Middleburg, also considered a death trap. For the league's efforts, the NOS presented Loudoun's league a prize at its annual meeting in Warrenton, November 6–8, 1946. Wanzer and the County-Wide League were also strong partners with Charles Houston prior to the NAACP formally being brought in.

Black Cavalcade

An important event in Black pride took place in the form of a two-act play at the Ashburn Colored School in 1941.[129] Called the *Cavalcade of*

```
                                      B ox 302
                                      Leesburg, Virginia.
                                      November 12, 1938.


     Dear Parents and Teachers:

          Please accept my deep appreciation for the way you
     cooperated in making our first County-Wide meeting a
     success.

          This first gesture is only a beginning of the many
     worthwhile things we hope to do this year to make our
     community a better place in which to live.  As Mr. Hender-
     son told us - "our duty as citizens is to provide the
     best educational facilities possible for our children".
     This, as you know, makes for better community living.

          We know that by working together toward this end our
     rewards will be measured not by the outside manifestations
     but by the attitudes and ideals.

          We need to get closer together now more so than ever
     before to provide the right kind of education for our child-
     ren.  Parents cannot work successfully without the aid of
     the teachers, and teachers need your assistance, parents,
     in order to best care for the physical and mental needs of
     your child.

          Again let me thank you for your presence and may we
     meet again soon with as much enthusiasm and interest.

                         Very truly yours,

                         G. A. Alexander,

                         Jeanes Supervisor.


     s/c

                    OFFICERS OF COMMUNITY LEAGUE

     President             Mr. John Wanzer              Middleburg, Va.
     Vice-president        Mrs. Elizabeth Quizenberry   Leesburg, Va.
     2nd vice-president    Mrs. Annie Ferrell           Waterford, Va.
     Secretary             Mr. C. H. Willis             Aldie, Va.
     Assistant Secretary   Mrs. E. Sanford              Hamilton, Va.
     Treasurer             Mrs. Irene Roberts           Leesburg, Va.
     Chaplin               Rev. Williams               Leesburg, Va.
     Publicity             Miss E. O. Harris            Leesburg, Va.
```

1938 Opening meeting of the County-Wide League.
EWP: 15.5 Yr. 1938 Nov 12 County Wide League.pdf

Negroana, the event was based on a 1940 event by the Illinois Writer's Project at the Diamond Jubilee Exposition in Chicago.[130] Also known as the American Negro Exposition and the Black World's Fair, the Chicago event was held from July to September 1940 and celebrated the seventy-fifth anniversary of Emancipation and the 1865 conclusion of the Civil

War. Black achievement was honored using twenty dioramas. Health was also a feature, mainly regarding the fight against tuberculosis as well as exhibits by the Public Health Service.[131] The Ashburn event honored with statues many of the same historical figures as in Chicago, but the main activity appears to have been the play, which involved all the Black schools in the county.

Perhaps written by an attendee at the 1940 exposition, the setting for the Ashburn event was the office of Uncle Sam, and the characters were Frederick Douglass, Uncle Sam, Secretary, Guide, a chorus, rhythm band, and a dance group. Like the exposition, the goal was to speak about Black accomplishments to, in this case, a resurrected Douglass. The Ashburn play must have taken a great deal of time to prepare and memorize the dialogue. In addition, statues were erected in honor of Booker T. Washington (leader and educator), Phillis Wheatley (poet), Paul Lawrence Dunbar (poet), James Weldon Johnson (poet and reformer), George Washington Carver (scientist), Marian Anderson (artist), Dorothy Maynor (artist), Mary McLeod Bethune (college president), Arthur Mitchell (member of Congress), Maggie L. Walker (bank president), Joe Louis (prizefighter), Jessie Owens (athlete), Benjamin Banneker (inventor), C. C. Spaulding (businessman), Richard B. Harrison (actor), Col. Charles S. Young (soldier), Henry O. Tanner (painter), Robert S. Abbott (painter), and Madam C. J. Walker (beauty products manufacturer).

As a follow-up, the Edwin Washington Project is planning to sponsor a reprise, considering Black accomplishments since 1940. More about this can be found on the project website.

A Dedicated High School and Transportation

As seen already, by the 1930s, whites had far more exposure than Blacks to higher-branch coursework and high schools. Blacks were provided, as far back as Reconstruction, only a limited number of higher-branch lectures that evolved to more formal schooling at the Training Center in the early 1920s. The 1920s experience was then upgraded in 1930 to a one-year high school program by Edythe Harris and further evolved into a four-year accredited high school by 1940–41, the year before Douglass was created as the first dedicated Black high school building (1941).[132] This could only have happened as a result of heroic efforts by underpaid staff who worked in a significantly underequipped building.

Emerick permitted the projects, but the evolutionary change was slow. In a memo of April 13, 1936, on construction needs, Emerick wrote that "the colored high school at Leesburg [the Training Center] is in its beginnings. It will undoubtedly grow considerably in the next few years."[133] Despite that, Emerick also said that the school board did not intend to have multiple Black high schools, unlike what was offered whites. "We can expect to find a rather pressing need for future building enlargement," Emerick predicted, "as it is the present idea that all high school facilities for colored children will be entered there." Emerick was suggesting keeping Blacks in the rapidly declining nineteenth-century structure, but perhaps reflecting the increased pressure on him by parents, the County-Wide League, and the NAACP, he struck a different tone after Douglass was constructed, saying to the school board in 1944 that if they did not deal with the maldistribution of resources between white and Black students, the courts would force action within four years.[134]

Educators were concerned about the number of Black students who did not continue their education beyond elementary school. While interviews archived at the Founders Library at Howard University reveal a zeal by many parents to send their children to high school, some were satisfied with farming or the service industry as a future for their children, probably due to the realities of the Depression.[135] To understand the scope of the problem between 1906 and 1945, it is useful to examine a study by Archie Richardson on the sharp disparity between white and Black high school enrollment populations across the state.[136]

Although 329 Blacks in Loudoun were eligible in 1938 for high school, only 60 continued their studies. In other words, 269 eligible students did not go further. Richardson theorizes that the average one-room school student had parents who held less than a sixth-grade education. Loudoun was heavily agricultural, so many students also likely felt a seventh-grade education provided enough opportunity for farming. Also, most Black children lived in a home bereft of literature, did not usually have experiences that fostered careers beyond a rural environment, and thus found

Table 6.2
Black Versus White Pupil Secondary School Enrollment in Virginia

	Session 1906–7		Session 1926–27		Session 1944–45	
	Blacks	Whites	Blacks	Whites	Blacks	Whites
Census of secondary school-age children	85,661	146,585	86,721	193,892	70,940	194,153
Actual enrollment	910	12,974	6,189	59,258	24,140	99,941
Percentage	1.0	8.8	7.1	30.6	34.0	51.5

employment chiefly as domestic servants and laborers. They were made to believe that they would have "few chances in life."[137]

Transportation was also a significant hurdle, so even if they wanted to attend high school, some parents felt they lived too far away. Since the school system did not provide transport, alternatives such as a private bus or station wagon were required but unaffordable to many. Other Black students relied on friends with private vehicles, often using donated gasoline. Black parents drove their children to the Saint Louis School until it closed in the late 1940s. As recounted by Barbara Scott (née Evans) who attended the school from 1944 to 1947: "When we lived near Middleburg on Benton Farms, my father and Mr. Anderson had a carpool arranged. We were driven to school every morning, first to a two-room schoolhouse in Saint Louis for three years and then to Banneker Elementary in Saint Louis. We'd walk the 1.5 miles home in the early fall and spring unless there was inclement weather. In late fall and through the winter we were driven both ways."[138]

The confluence of poverty and a lack of public transportation was the theme of a letter in 1940 to Charles Hamilton Houston. Henry Young, representing the Willisville parents, wrote, "We certainly need a bus for our children and above all a High School, for we have too many boys and girls ready for High School to be turned out in the world to go to destruction when they can be in school."[139]

Similarly, Elizabeth Warner of Bluemont wrote in March 1940, "I am poor and have no way of getting [my children] to Leesburg."[140] According to M. K. Jennings, who lived in Hughesville, a feeder village to Willisville, "There are children who have finished from the Willisville School

Table 6.3
Study of Student Transportation, Loudoun County, 1935–39

| | Black Student Transport, 1935–39[a] | | | | | | | |
| | 1935–36 | | 1936–37 | | 1937–38 | | 1938–39 | |
Category	Transport	Walk	Transport	Walk	Transport	Walk	Transport	Walk
High School								
(Leesburg)	0	40	15	45	15	51	22	35
Grade Schools[b]								
Leesburg	0	100	0	92	10	92	10	109
Rock Hill	0	33	0	40	15	24	15	30
All Others	0	675	0	722	0	700	0	586
Total Grade	0	808	0	854	25	816	25	725

| | White Student Transport, 1935–39 | | | | | | | |
| | 1935–36 | | 1935–37 | | 1937–38 | | 1938–39 | |
Category	Transport	Walk	Transport	Walk	Transport	Walk	Transport	Walk
High Schools								
(9 schools; 7								
in 1938–39)	266	390	340	368	350	265	465	232
Grade Schools	160	243	165	240	170	209	180	187

Sources: For Black student transport, EWP: 9.3 Yr. 1940 Report of Survey Committee on Long-Range Planning, p. 23; and for white student transport, EWP: 9.3 Yr. 1940 Report of Survey Committee on Long-Range Planning, p. 20–22.

[a]Notice the disparities in each year. In 1935–36 no Black children were transported versus 266 white high school students and 160 white grade school children who were transported. In the same period, 40 Black high school students had to walk to school, and 808 Black grade school students had to walk, versus 390 white high school students and 243 white grade school students.

[b]We don't know why LCPS singled out Leesburg and Rock Hill, but we kept them itemized in the interest of historical accuracy.

for three years or more and no provision has been made for them to get to high school."[141]

To put pressure on the government, beginning in 1940 the County-Wide League began asking its members to send the school board bills for reimbursement for the expenses Blacks incurred because they were not provided buses. As an example, Annie Wyatt of Sterling, Virginia, sent a letter in 1940 with her itemized bill for the transportation. It read in part: "I am sending in my bill for the transportation of my daughter Ruth Elizabeth Williams to the Loudoun High school, for the year 38–39 and the year 39–40. She is transported by the Washington and Old

Dominion railway. The fare per month is $6.70."[142] Such complaints placed political pressure on the school system to resolve these inequities and are another vivid example of Black determination.[143]

Table 6.4 is an excerpt from NAACP papers for Loudoun County revealing the disparities in transportation costs for Blacks and whites in 1938–39. Note the reference to "Brown" next to Leesburg. This is likely the same Will Brown who began transporting Black students for LCPS in 1937. The county spent $1,260 for Black transportation and $22,472 for white transportation, putting Black transportation costs at 6 percent of white transportation costs. This percentage cannot be explained away with statements such as "the Black student population was 6 percent of the white student population in the 1938–1939 school year."[144] In reality, this is misleading because a lack of transportation prevented many Black school-age children from attending school. What could have become of those transportation-deprived Blacks had they been able to attend high school? In this, the first in-depth study of the impact of segregated education on Blacks in Loudoun County, our conclusion is that the system inhibited the contemporary population and, thus, future generations from finding economic opportunities equal to whites.

In 1938 the county operated twenty school buses for whites. The county proposed to add three buses for whites the following academic year (1939–40) and one for Blacks. The records don't show if the purchases were actually made.[145]

It was a vivid reminder of inequity to read a 1939 article by Lloyd Womeldorph, principal of Lovettsville High School, who complained—

Table 6.4

Excerpt showing Transportation Costs for Black and White Students in 1938–39

Leesburg (Col) Brown	900.00
Special contracts at $2.00 per pupil	
15 Sycoline (Col)	270.00
10 Bluemont	90.00
[Total costs for Black student transportation]	1,260.00
White	22,472.00
Total 1938–39	23,732.00

Source: EWP: 15.18 Charles Houston Papers.

speaking of whites—that too many pupils were not completing sec-ondary schooling.[146] "Due to the easy accessibility of high schools to all sections, no child in Loudoun should be denied the privilege and opportunity of securing a high school education." He reiterated, "This is [the child's] birthright and a great injustice is being done when he is deprived of that right." However, Blacks only had the Training Center then, and as Emerick said in 1936, there were no plans for a second or third high school for Blacks. Bushrod Murray at the Mountain Gap one-room school reported that of the twenty pupils who had graduated from the seventh grade since 1930, only six went on to high school, due to poverty and lack of transportation.[147] The broad access for Black students did not occur until integration in 1968. What could have become of those transportation-deprived Blacks had they been able to attend high school?

The Training Center to Douglass High School

The Training Center was the largest building for Blacks until the 1940s. The land had been purchased for $400 in 1883 by the Leesburg school district from John R. and Mary V. Beuchler.[148] Mr. Beuchler was a white baker who had served as a private in Company D, 2nd Regiment, Virginia Cavalry. When he died in 1931, Beuchler was buried in Union Cemetery, right next to the school. This historical structure played a key role in Black education beginning with the pioneering work of John C. Walker in the 1920s and Edythe Harris in the 1930s. After the high school program was moved to the new Douglass High School in 1941, the building became Douglass Elementary until that program was moved to a second Douglass Elementary School in Leesburg. As with many other Black schools the EWP team visited throughout Virginia and in Fredericksburg, Texas, for comparison, the team feels the original Loudoun Training Center building should be preserved as county school museum property for the use of the public, even though this will be expensive. It is structurally weak and prone to animal infestation but would be a significant physical monument to Black achievement and a natural location for a cultural center.

The Training Center about 1940. The attachment on the left was from the lumber of the old Sycoline school.
EWP: 11 Yr. 1940 Insurance Photos; also known as Inspection and Survey Report: Loudoun County School Board; photographer unknown

One of the most famous issues for Loudoun's County-Wide League evolved out of a realization that the old Training Center potentially threatened the lives of both students and teachers. The league and the NAACP noted on March 16, 1940, an oil drum under the main set of stairs. This particular issue of student safety even came to the attention of Walter White, head of the national NAACP.[149] Interestingly, when the team first visited the Training Center with some LCPS staff in 2018, they found an empty fifty-gallon drum under the stairs. To move the children to a safer environment, one undated petition by the league called for a new high school building to be erected on the Gibbons lot in Leesburg, which the Black community ended up purchasing for $4,000 because the white government refused to buy the land. Unfortunately, the white government would then only agree to take the land if they could purchase it for $1.[150] Still, the effort by the Black community worked. To kick the government into action so the children could be quickly moved from the Training Center to the new property, the league and Charles Houston used the fire trap argument when writing to Superintendent Emerick and to the Fire Chief of Loudoun.[151] The fire escape on the second floor was considered inaccessible and missing a sash cord to hold the window up in an emergency. In other words, if a child tried to evacuate, someone would need to hold up the window to prevent the heavy frame from falling, perhaps impossible during a rush.

There was also the matter of the oil-saturated floor. If, as the league insisted, an electrical short circuit caused a spark or if a careless match were tossed, scores of children might have been killed. Archie Richardson considered the situation so dire that he recommended moving both the elementary and high school children to the new structure.[152] However, only high school students were transferred, probably due to the limited space. Elementary students would be not transferred until 1958. The question remains, why the delay? After all, the elementary school children left behind were surely as much at risk of being burned alive as the former high school pupils. Surviving records do not reveal an answer, but the EWP team is of the opinion that the white government was adamant about not spending the money and could not be budged. This is especially interesting since at least from 1931, the State Department of Public Instruction had been concerned about the loss of schools to fire, noting that year "the heavy losses to the State by school buildings burning, fully justify the construction of only the more fire resistive types of buildings."[153]

Some Blacks disagreed with the County-Wide League's choice for the replacement for the Training Center. Instead, they preferred Purcellville. This was according to an undated document from sixty-two citizens asking for a suitable high school building at a site to be determined by the school board.[154] A letter of April 8, 1940, to the Mt. Gilead District School Board by Blacks from Purcellville made the same point. This group felt the County-Wide League's assertiveness might prove embarrassing and offered to engage in their own set of negotiations.[155] However, a separate petition generated by the league and signed by more than 160 citizens from across the county specifically asked for an accredited high school to be constructed on the William S. Gibbons pasture, the current site of Douglass. We suspect all petitions were done the same year, 1940.[156] To be fair, Purcellville was a reasonable choice. It was once the cultural center of Loudoun and had access to highways and a railroad, which was excellent for school transport, and it had been the location of the annual Emancipation Day celebrations since 1910. However, most Black residents in the county preferred Leesburg.[157]

Because the government was reluctant to provide sufficient funding to purchase land, in a show of political will by Blacks, financing was done through bake sales and other efforts led by Wanzer, Alexander, and the one-room schoolteachers. The league took ownership of the Gibbons lot and ended up essentially donating the land, but only because it had to.[158] The land should have been purchased for market value by the school board, as was the case for white high schools. Still, demonstrating its power to inspire political action, teachers, parents, and other private citizens from the communities of Bull Run, Hamilton, Hillsboro, Leesburg, Middleburg, Purcellville, Rock Hill, Saint Louis, Waterford, and Willisville signed the petition for a new high school building. They also raised funds for equipment, including the curtains for the stage.

One thing is certain. Walking down the hallways of Douglass is a visit with civil rights history. However, while creating Douglass was a monumental civil rights achievement, it was from the beginning too small to adequately accommodate the high school students, having been designed with only an auditorium and four rooms.[159] Issues of size kept coming up, leading to complaints in 1945, 1948, 1950, and 1951 about overcrowding and other inadequacies. For example, the auditorium had to be used for classes, putting children within earshot of the shop, with its loud saws, hammers, and machinery. People had to eat in shifts because the cafeteria was too small to accommodate everyone. As a remedy, the league asked for six additional rooms, a hot water system for showers, and a gas line for the laboratory.[160] Plans for expansion were eventually approved in 1953. Additional furniture and science equipment purchases were also approved in 1954.[161]

Douglass found itself with a role during World War II. Jim Roberts remembered the dearth of male students in classes following the attack

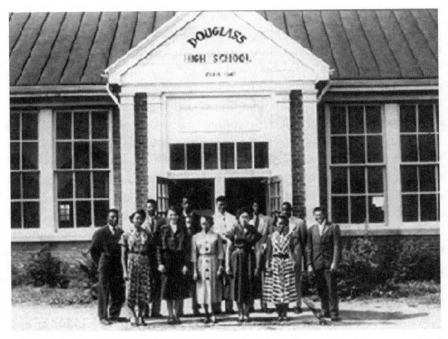

Early faculty photo from Douglass High School.
Courtesy of EWP Archives

on Pearl Harbor; many students enlisted right away.[162] Douglass students also developed aircraft models for the military so that our ships and land based anti-air guns would shoot enemy planes, not our own, an early issue for our naval vessels.[163]

The Edwin Washington Society reached an agreement in 2022 with Loudoun County Public Schools to turn a portion of the venerable structure into a living museum and research center. The goal is to add a library full of documents from the segregation era as well as interactive maps and databases to study that era and be the foundation for similar research across the region. The team wants to invite scholars to compare notes and teach people from across the commonwealth and the nation how to study their past and learn together how segregation was fought so that those lessons can be used in the future around the world, where any people are suppressed.

Janie Redwood
Courtesy of EWP Archives

The Pace for Change Increases

The use of formal written petitions and the work of Alexander, Harris, the County-Wide League, and local activists and teachers caused specific changes, especially after Janie Redwood negotiated a deal on practical consolidation. There was also Harris's important work improving the curriculum at the Training Center and her ability to convert the partial high school program on the second floor of the building into an accredited high school. Those were monumental achievements in the middle of segregation. But the community also recognized the need for legal action as well as new Black leadership in the State Department of Education. The new leadership in Richmond was able to marshal state-level resources in support of local causes. Attorneys like James H. Raby and Edwin Cicero Brown Sr. had also proven the utility of taking Emerick, the school board, and the board of supervisors to court. What was needed now was national legal support, federal lawsuits, and the support of the NAACP.

At the state level was Archie G. Richardson, PhD, the senior Black official in state government and the first appointed Black in the Virginia Department of Education. Using his network of government officials and his ties to philanthropies that supported Black education, Richardson regularly consulted with Oscar Emerick on how to improve school equality and quality in the county. Richardson also strongly supported Gertrude Alexander and the County-Wide League on the need for a dedicated high school building and signaled to Emerick that the school system needed to listen to them. This direct approach required diplomacy navigating the white governments in Richmond and Loudoun, whose leaders had other priorities. Still, Richardson pushed progressive change, as in November 1939 at the "Colored High School" on the Training Center's second floor. He sought facts for practical recommendations and provided guidance; and his diplomatic skills were evident when he informed Emerick in December of the results of his latest visit. Richardson said, "My greatest impression was the complete confidence of the Negro people in you and the school board, and their willingness to cooperate fully."[164] It is doubtful this was true about the local community, but Richardson was trying to avoid confrontation while he pushed ahead to advance the construction of a new school building. He also made specific recommendations on placement of the structure relative to the highway and pointed to the services of the Department of School Buildings in Richmond for assistance.

On the legal front, Charles Hamilton Houston deserves a lot of attention. To make their legal case, the County-Wide League and various school patrons employed Houston, then the dean of Howard University's law school, a national legal scholar, and the NAACP's first litigation director.[165] However, the NAACP wasn't yet prepared to handle many cases on facility inequality for either elementary or high school students, so Houston in 1940 worked as a private lawyer in this matter, essentially donating his time to investigate issues of concern to Loudoun's Black community, such as transportation.[166] Many say that Houston was "the man who killed Jim Crow." Thurgood Marshall was also trying numerous civil rights cases on behalf of the NAACP, with Houston's guidance and support. All those cases were about inequality in some form.

When Houston became involved in Loudoun's educational struggle, there was no local NAACP chapter. He didn't want the NAACP to be formally involved until a local chapter had been established, so he recommended that one be created.[167] He also agreed to represent the Black community through the County-Wide League for one dollar. Like Alexander, with whom he had a strong relationship, he began his work by assessing the situation on the ground. The two conducted surveys of Loudoun parents to understand their transportation needs and how the unaddressed need inhibited access to high school and lucrative careers. This work further stimulated parents to petition Emerick for redress of grievances.

A good example is a simple petition sent to Houston on March 8, 1940, from Mary Page of Upperville: "I have a girl who is ready for high school this fall and there is no means of transportation made yet. I do hope that you will work in our behalf in helping to provide ways for them to get in high school."[168] These various efforts had an impact on Emerick. Although he was a segregationist and would make speeches in favor of that system, he said he opposed inequality—at least his version. His personal files show he followed the news on lawsuits around the commonwealth and understood that the future was grim for proponents of inequality. Relatives who knew him said that, and there is evidence in his 1944 memo to the school board:

> We have housed most of our white school children in reasonably comfortable buildings with central heating plants, drinking fountains, indoor toilets, etc. Nearly all colored elementary school children are housed in comparatively poor buildings. During the next four years the school board will either make plans for improvements in the housing of colored children voluntarily or can expect to be required to do so by court action. Very clearly there has been discrimination here.[169]

The point Emerick made was not casual. While *Plessy v. Ferguson* is now abhorred because it made separate but equal the law of the land, the superintendent interpreted the decision literally to mean specific inequality violated the Supreme Court's decision. Were it to be proven unequal, a school system could be forced to integrate. The NAACP's first staff attorney, Nathan Margold, and Houston decided to use this argument to integrate the University of Maryland school of law in 1936. In tandem, they also used the Equal Protection Clause of the Fourteenth Amendment, which eventually became their most powerful weapon. In

Loudoun, four years before Emerick's memo, Houston was very direct in this regard on March 20, 1940, hitting all the points on equality—buildings, transportation, teacher salaries, and access to high school, which he opined could support 612 students, not the 60 or so in the Training Center. He also said this was a constitutional right. Houston was unbending as to Emerick's responsibility and that of the school system. "I can't say how improvements can be made; only I say they must be made. There must be only one system in Loudoun County public schools, with two branches, colored and white."[170] It is important to also note that Houston did not only deal with Emerick by memo. He also effectively used the media as a tool, letting them know when he would visit Emerick and what the result was, thereby putting public—even national—pressure on the superintendent. A good example of this is a 1940 letter from Houston to Virginius Dabney, a journalist for the *Richmond Times-Dispatch*, obviously not only to gain the attention of local citizens in Loudoun but also the state government in Richmond. Houston made several key points:

- Despairing of convincing the district superintendent or the County Board of Education to make needed improvements to "Negro education," Houston was engaged to represent the County-Wide League and many patrons and parents in Loudoun.
- Houston requested a reporter to cover his upcoming conference with the superintendent and the board of education on March 12.
- Although opposed to the dual school system, the purpose of the fight was not to attack the system itself but its inequities, and thus to equalize the two branches, perhaps knowing that the two separate systems could never be made equal, thereby setting the foundation for the argument that segregation must be dismantled.
- The plan of attack was to sue the superintendent and the board, plus any other responsible county officials for damages in federal court because the discrimination against Blacks "denies them the equal protections of the law."[171]

Emerick grasped the economic and legal challenges before him of Blacks demanding equality, and he spoke about it in 1941 to F. F. Jenkins, director of administration and finance at the State Board of Education in Richmond. In this instance he was less sensitive. The context was a request by Charles Dean to keep the Conklin Colored School open. Dean was in the family of Jennie Dean, a famous regional evangelist and a founder of the Prosperity Baptist Church. Emerick realized the complaint had strategic implications. He said to Jenkins, "We do not haul white and colored children in the same bus, and we haven't thought of allowing both races to attend the same school. These two things are what are really in the minds of the colored people and their white friends who are agitating this question the most."[172] In reality, all Emerick had to do to understand inequality was to look around and compare conditions based on rules set by his own school board or the board of supervisors. At the same time, he was keenly aware Blacks were willing to assert real legal pressure.

Interviews conducted by Houston and Alexander with ordinary Loudoun citizens to support the legal case are often poignant stories that reveal deeply committed parents who could not afford to send their children to Leesburg for a high school education while also lamenting that segregation would damage the economic futures of their children. Alexander and Houston were thus able to form a strong partnership with the citizens to push for everything from proper toilets and equipment to transportation.[173] Sometimes the citizens would argue over tactics, but the partnership was strong and the strategic goals the same, as was the determination, as noted in Houston's threat in his March 16, 1940, letter to Emerick when speaking of the dangers lurking in the Training Center.[174] "I have advised my clients that in my judgment you and the Board of Education can be enjoined from continuing to hold school in a building dangerous to life and limb, and that . . . you and the Board of Education are personally liable for any harm which may befall the children from continuing to force them to go to school in a death trap."[175]

Houston continued the pressure in May 1940. In a letter to Emerick he mentioned attending a meeting of the school board on April 9 and being impressed that "the Board and Superintendent recognized the necessity of a progressive program for ultimate equalization of Negro education, with immediate beginning." He also felt that Emerick's approach was in the right direction, if not as progressive as needed. But he was appalled to discover that on April 22 the Loudoun Board of Supervisors "eliminated entirely the proposed supplementary appropriation for the improvement of Negro education for 1940–41 recommended by the School Board." This, Houston felt, put things back to square one, so his position was to threaten litigation, if required.[176] It was a legal and political struggle that would not end until 1968, when Loudoun finally fully integrated.

It is useful to point out that by 1948 the Loudoun County government was in serious financial trouble due to low taxes, particularly on merchants, which made capital investments of any kind a challenge. The budget had to support the educational needs of four thousand students, of which nine hundred were Black. Except for a single one-room school, all white facilities had central heat and indoor toilets. Blacks, nearly 25 percent of the student body, used twelve schools, including one high school, seven one-room schools, one two-room school, and three five-to eight-room elementary schools: Banneker, Carver, and the Training Center. Only Douglass and two elementary schools had central heat and indoor toilets. Across the board, in Emerick's estimate, the schools lacked adequate space, equipment, and instructional material.[177]

Therefore, Loudoun's Black leaders in this period faced severe challenges, but their community was also courageous and mature and strove to augment their efforts with great academic and legal scholars. The next period would prove to be as challenging, especially in the face of the government's massive resistance strategy, requiring the skills of the best lawyers and supportive politicians. It also required the resolve of citizens not to bend in 1956 when faced with a choice between better schools and making a deal with the devil by agreeing to segregation. The Blacks would choose resolve. Improvements were real. Banneker and Carver were better schools. Douglass was also a great achievement. But none of these achievements changed one major hurdle to progress. Racism and prejudice still were cultural norms that caused economic and social disparities, ones that continue to this day. Just as wars do not eradicate the philosophy that underpins terrorism, neither do laws on equality or well-constructed buildings eliminate classism or racism.

Notes

1. J. Rupert Picott, *History of the Virginia Teachers Association* (Washington, DC: National Education Association, 1975).

2. See EWP: 1.1.2A Yr. 1940 Various Petitions for Equal Salaries. The Loudoun County Teachers Association was an unincorporated association of Black school teachers.

3. An example of exposing prejudice that was dangerous comes in an undated letter to Mr. Houston from Mrs. M. K. Jennings of Howardsville, who complained that a lack of transportation meant that children were missing school for two to three months. Further, "There is a bus provided for the white children coming from the same sections. The driver goes so far as to run our children off the road and to throw stones out of the windows of the bus at our children." EWP 15.17 Special NAACP Papers Loudoun 2, p. 12.

4. EWP: 4.5 White Teacher Cards.

5. EWP: 1.1.1 Yr. 1944 Emerick on Resource Equality.

6. Letter from Walter White, Secretary of the NAACP, to Mr. and Mrs. James Van Alen, Middleburg, March 20, 1940, in EWP: 15.17 Special NAACP papers Loudoun 1, p. 42. See also EWP: 15.17 Special NAACP Papers Loudoun 2, p. 5.

7. EWP: 3.1.1 Yr. 1933, June 23, Emerick on Funding School and Tension with Road Construction.

8. EWP: 2.5A Yr. 1941 Mr. Dean of Conklin Wants School to stay open.

9. EWP: 3.1 Yr. 1949 Status of Loudoun County Schools, p. 2.

10. EWP: 3.1 Yr. Post WWII, Memo by Oscar Emerick.

11. "Supervisors Turn Thumbs Down on School Plea," *Loudoun Times-Mirror*, April 30, 1931, 1.

12. Shirley Robinson Lee, "Schools and the Great Depression," in *Trails and Trailblazers: Public Education and School Desegregation in Lunenburg County, Virginia, 1870–1970* (Pittsburgh: Dorrance, 2017).

13. EWP: 9.3 Yr. 1940 Report of Survey Committee on Long-Range Planning, p. 10.

14. Ethel Smith, interview by Larry Roeder and Maddy Gold, August 5, 2017.

15. US Federal Works Agency, *Final Report on the WPA Program, 1935–1943*, 1935–1943 (Washington, DC: US Government Printing Office, 1947).

16. EWP: 9.3 Yr. 1940 Report of Survey Committee on Long-Range Planning, p. 25.

17. EWP: 9.3 Yr. 1940 Report of Survey Committee on Long-Range Planning, p. 28.

18. Teacherages were accommodations for teachers.

19. EWP: 9.3 Yr. 1940 Report of Survey Committee on Long-Range Planning, p. 26–27.

20. Former Ashburn Colored School students, interview by Larry Roeder, October 23, 2017.

21. Luvinia Bowles Taylor, interview by Larry Roeder, October 18, 2017.

22. Written undated recollections of Barbara Evans Scott, received 2017, EWP Archives; confirmed by interview by Larry Roeder, March 4, 2021.

23. EWP: 2.2 Yr. 1930 "Sanitary Systems in Schools Here Are Found Faulty," *Loudoun Times-Mirror*, October 14, 1930, p. 1.

24. EWP: 3.1 Yr. 1927 Emerick Study on school conditions.

25. EWP: 7.1 Yr. 1936 to 1937 Public Health Nurse Reports.

26. EWP: 3.1 Yr. 1937, March 16, Oscar Emerick "News Item," informal mimeograph note to staff.

27. EWP: 7.1 Yr. 1938 to 1939 Annual Health Report.

28. "Loudoun Prohibits Assembly of Youths," *Washington Post*, July 30, 1935, p. 15.

29. EWP: 4.8C Yr. 1943 Memos to Teachers by Ruby Vaughn Kelly.

30. EWP: 7.1.1 Yr. 1945 Tuberculosis Control in Virginia.

31. Barbara Evans Scott, interview by Larry Roeder, August 15, 2020.

32. Medicaid emerged in 1965.

33. Saint Louis is now an eastern suburb of Middleburg, although the villages have little in common.

34. EWP: 7.5 Yr. 1938–39 Nurse Reports.

35. Reports for July 1937–June 30, 1938, in EWP: 7.5 Yr. 1935/37, Nurse Reports.

36. EWP: 7.3 Yr. 1935–41 Nurse Reports.

37. EWP: 7.5 Yr. 1938–39 Nurse Reports.

38. Data derived from inspecting Term Reports for AY 1938. EWP 6.3.3 Studies of Teacher Term Reports.

39. Some probably combined high school and elementary schools, such as Middleburg and Leesburg. The records the team examined covered Aldie, Arcola, Ashburn, Bluemont, Carters, Emerick, Hamilton, Hillsboro, Leesburg, Lincoln Lovettsville, Lucketts, Mt. Gap, Middleburg, Mountville, Philomont, Pleasant Valley, Purcellville, Round Hill, Sterling, Sunny Ridge, Taylorstown, Unison Bloomfield, and Waterford.

40. EWP: 7.5 Yr. 1943 Helen Einstein Report.

41. EWP: 7.2 Yr. 1952 Alice Cady Visiting Teacher memo to Principals.

42. State Board of Education, "The Manassas State Vocational School," *Bulletin of Information* 1, no. 1 (Alexandria, VA: George Washington High School, October 1945), 13–14. See also EWP: 4.11 Visiting Teacher Folder; and EWP: 9.9 Manassas State Industrial School. (Not Jennie Dean's Manassas Industrial School for Blacks.)

43. Zachary Vickery, senior reference librarian, Library of Virginia, interview by Larry Roeder, November 2, 2017.

44. Statistics on the program are reported in the annual Virginia Teachers Term Reports in EWP: 6.3.2. In addition, personal evaluations of students appear in the annual Term Reports in EWP: 6.3.1. EWP: 6.2.3 Yr. 1938/39 Marble Quarry, p. 3.

45. "Hanover Negro School Makes Great Record," *Richmond Times-Dispatch*, November 20, 1932, p. 34. The term "Federation" referred to a Federation of Community Leagues in Hanover County, likely very similar to that formed in Loudoun.

46. Poem crafted by an anonymous Black citizen in Loudoun in 1934; and EWP: 5.2 Yr. 1934 April, Mildred Weadon Report on Hot Lunches.

47. Ethel Smith, interview by Larry Roeder and Maddy Gold, August 5, 2017.

48. Schenck Foods began in nearby Winchester in 1928 as the Valley Food Company, manufacturing potato chips. It then became a distributor for Kraft Foods, becoming Schenck Cheese Company and distributing food within a thirty-mile radius through the 1940s. It then became Schenck Foods in 1952.

49. Reminiscences of Gert Evans to Larry Roeder, May 15, 2022.

50. Ethel Smith, interview by Larry Roeder and Maddy Gold, August 5, 2017.

51. Former students of Lola Jackson, interviews by Larry Roeder, October 23, 2017.

52. Nellie Dean of Conklin, interview by Larry Roeder, August 28, 2016.

53. Written undated recollections of Barbara Evans Scott, received April 16, 2017, EWP Archives." BarbaraEvansScottMemories.docx, provided by Gertrude Evans to Larry Roeder.

54. Ethel Smith, interview by Larry Roeder and Maddy Gold, August 5, 2017.

55. Dana Keating, interview by Larry Roeder, February 20, 2020.

56. Lisa Prosser Aktug, interview by Larry Roeder, February 20, 2020.

57. Guthrie Ashton, interview by Larry Roeder, February 20, 2020.

58. EWP: 9.4.1 Yr. Civil Works Administration Folder, created November 9, 1933, by Executive Order No. 6420B.

59. "C.W.A. Approves Hot School Lunches at Project in County," *Loudoun Times-Mirror*, January 4, 1934, p. 1.

60. "C.W.A. Approves Hot School Lunches."

61. Mildred Weadon of Waterford, later Purcellville, was a 1932 graduate of the State Teachers College of Harrisonburg, Virginia, and a member of 4-H. She would later become a dietician. See also "Seniors As We See Em," *Breeze*, 11, no. 8 (Senior Issue, November 16, 1932): 3.

62. Memo by Mildred Weadon, April 13, 1934, "Report of Mildred Weadon, Special Loudoun County Home Economic Teacher." EWP 5.4.2 Yr 1934 April, Mildred Weadon Report Home Econ and Hot Lunches.

63. EWP: 5.2 Yr. 1934, April, Mildred Weadon Report Home Econ and Hot Lunches.

64. The records do not say if Melvin was a county, state, or federal employee. She was likely a county employee but paid through a variety of funds run by the Federal Emergency Relief Administration, which employed over forty thousand Virginians.

65. EWP: 7.3 Yr. 1935/41 Nurse and Dental Reports.

66. EWP: 5.4 Yr. 1937–39 Home Economics.

67. EWP: 7 Yr. 1937 to 1939 Public Health Nurse Reports. The home is now known as Oatlands House and Gardens.

68. EWP: 2.1 Memo 3431 Dealt with the School Lunch Program.

69. EWP: 5.2 Yr. 1942–43 Report for Douglass (part II narrative, p. 1, item 2).

70. EWP: 5.2 Yr. 1943–44 Report for Douglass (part II narrative, p. 2, item 6).

71. EWP: 2.5A Yr. 1930, May, Leesburg wants HS and Normal School Graduate.

72. The working conditions of these workers was dangerous and exhausting. Despite that, they took the time to lobby for their children.

73. *The Leader*, February 9, 1889. (*The Leader* was an important Black newspaper.) They were also elected delegates to represent the 8th in the National Colored Convention that was to meet March 6.

74. EWP: 4.3 Yr. 1931 Role of Petitions in Hiring.

75. Emma Elizabeth Brown, *Jack, Jill and Tot* (Boston: D. Lothrop, 1883).

76. Richard Guilliatt and Peter Hohnen, *The Wolf: How One German Raider Terrorized the Allies in the Most Epic Voyage of WWI* (New York: Free Press, 2010), 24–25.

77. EWP: 2.5A Yr. 1931 Edythe Harris Requests more resources.

78. EWP: 9.4.1 Yr. 1935 Addition to Leesburg Colored.

79. In 1938–39, John Walker complained that he did not have access to a large dictionary or encyclopedia, and although he had a case of maps, they were outdated. See EWP: 6.3.2 Virginia Teacher's Term Report for 1938/39 for "Leesburg Negro."

80. EWP: 4.2 Yr. 1916, "Colored Teacher's Institute," *Loudoun Mirror*, March 10, 1916, p. 8. A paper was presented by Erline Fox, "How Can We Help the Child to Think," then discussed by C. L. Murray. John C. Walker presented "Relationship between Teachers and Patrons." The closing address was "War on the Fly" by John C. Walker, president. The war was the Health Department's effort to build sanitary outhouses.

81. EWP: 9.2.3 1938, February, Draft article by Oscar Emerick, "Additional Physical Needs of Our Schools."

82. EWP: 6.3.3 Loudoun County Training Center, Preliminary Annual High School Report for September 23, 1936.

83. EWP: 1.1.1 Yr. 1944 Emerick on Resource Equality.

84. EWP: 6.3.3 Yr. 1940 Report of Progress for Virginia Accredited High Schools, notes by G. William Liverpool, Principal of Loudoun County Training

Center. Note was also made in the same report of the effort to purchase a large plat of ground (for Douglass) described as "a new and adequate school plant."

85. Also known as the Rosenwald Foundation, the Julius Rosenwald Fund, and the Julius Rosenwald Foundation. See also Aisha M. Johnson-Jones, *The African American Struggle for Library Equality: The Untold Story of the Julius Rosenwald Fund Library Program* (Lanham, MD: Rowman and Littlefield, 2019).

86. EWP: 2.5.A Yr. 1932, May 18, Leesburg Supports Annie Harris and Waters.

87. EWP: 2.5.A Yr. 1935, June 9, Leesburg supports Mamie R. Waters.

88. Application for Slater Fund Aid for County Training School made July 20, 1932, Jeanes-Slater Funds, Box 17, Southern Education Foundation Archives, Robert W. Woodruff Library, Atlanta University. The application was approved in August 1932 by Dr. William D. Gresham, state agent in Virginia for Negro Schools, and on October 29, 1932, by Arthur Davis Wright, president of the Slater Fund.

89. Application for Slater Fund Aid for County Training School made July 26, 1933, Jeanes-Slater Funds, Box 17, Southern Education Foundation Archives, Robert W. Woodruff Library, Atlanta.

90. Home economics was a high school phenomenon. Exactly what Harris taught in this class is unknown.

91. EWP: 9.3 Yr. 1940 Construction and Pop Study, p. 21.

92. EWP: 2.5.A Yr. 1930s Petition No. 28 Req for Buses to Transport Pupils to Training Center.

93. Eugene Scheel, *The History of Loudon County, Virginia*, accessed September 29, 2020, http://www.loudounhistory.org/history/african-american-chronology.

94. EWP: 2.5A Yr. 1932 St. Louis Road Needs Improvement. Inscriptions of names are sometimes hard to transcribe exactly.

95. EWP: 2.5A Yr. 1934 Bluemont Needs Transport to Rock Hill.

96. EWP: 2.5A Yr. 1934 Paeonian Springs wants a school.

97. EWP: 2.5A Yr. 1938 Lucketts and Mt. Pleasant.

98. Medical Register for Maurice Britton King Edmead, Archives of the Balch Library. Dr. Edmead received his license June 16, 1934. Loudoun's first Black physician was Benjamin Franklin Young, who apprenticed with white physician George Plaster just after the Civil War.

99. "Colored Schools Crowded," *Virginia Journal of Education* 8 (September 1914): 189.

100. Undated recollections of Barbara Evans Scott, received 2017, EWP Archives.

101. EWP: 6.6 Yr. 1917 to 1947 Middleburg Colored, Grades 1–7.

102. Ethel Smith, interview by Larry Roeder and Maddy Gold, August 5, 2017.

103. EWP: 2.5.A Yr. 1944, November 16, Raby Complains about Transportation and Overcrowding at Grant. See also EWP: 2.5.A Yr. 1945 Grant Expansion Petitions. The Blacks in Middleburg considered Emerick condescending and said that the County-Wide League did not speak for them.

104. EWP: 2.5.A Yr. 1946, February 6, Middleburg Propose Maxville for new school.

105. EWP: 2.5.A Yr. 1945, February 12, Grant Site Proposal. See also EWP: 2.5A Yr. 1946, February 6, Middleburg PTA notifies Emerick that Edmead is Chair of site Committee.

106. EWP: 1.7 October 2, 1939 Distribution of Negro Children of School Age.

107. EWP: 2.5.A Yr. 1937 Hughesville Requests Miss Esther V. Randolph.

108. EWP: 2.5.A Yr. 1932, July 6, Waterford wants removal of instructor.

109. Former segregation-era students, interviews by Larry Roeder and Maddy Gold, August 12, 2017.

110. EWP: 1.1.1 Yr. 1940, March 18, McK Jackson to Emerick.

111. EWP: 3.1 Yr. 1936, March 2, Cost of Personal Services, p. 2. This source is about white teachers but is informative. See also EWP: 3.1 Yr. 1936 The Problem with Reducing Teacher Salaries.

112. EWP: 8.1 Yr. 1941–42.

113. EWP: 2.5.A Yr. 1938, January, LPTA wants salary increase.

114. EWP: 1.1.2A Yr. 1940, December 11, Problem Funding Equal Salaries.

115. EWP: 1.1.2D Norfolk Case June 18, 1940, US Circuit Court of Appeals, Fourth Circuit. No. 4623.

116. EWP: 1.1.2a Yr. 1940 Various Institutional Petitions for Equal Salaries.

117. EWP: 2.5.A Yr. 1937, January 9, Loudoun PTA wants a Jeanes Slater Fund Supervisor.

118. EWP: 3.1 Yr. 1938, February, School Need More Resources.

119. Special Report of Jeanes Teacher for School Year 1939–1940 for Loudoun County, Robert W. Woodruff Library, Atlanta University, James-Slater Funds, Box 17 of the collection known as Southern Education Foundation Archives.

120. Voting club records have been lost, but the Circuit Court of Loudoun does have voting rolls organized by year and district. Minutes of County-Wide League meetings have also been lost.

121. Archie G. Richardson, *The Development of Negro Education in Virginia, 1831–1970* (Richmond, VA: Phi Delta Kappa, 1976), 71–74.

122. Letter from Marian J. Sands, Field Secretary, the NOS, to Dr. Luther P. Jackson, Virginia State College, in Elizabeth Cobb Jordan, "The Impact of the Negro Organization Society in Public Support for Education in Virginia 1912–1950" (PhD dissertation, University of Virginia, Charlottesville, 1978), 198.

123. School leagues were eventually called PTAs. See EWP: 15.26 1978 NOS Interview No 1, Lorenzo White.

124. Jordan, "The Impact of the Negro Organization Society," 102–3.

125. EWP: 1.5 Yr.1943, May 26, Memo to coworkers from Ruby Vaughan, Supervisor of Colored Teachers.

126. Frederick Milton Alexander and Southern Education Foundation, *Education for the Needs of the Negro in Virginia* (Washington, DC: Southern Education Foundation, 1943), 167–73; and Interview of Dr. Margaret T. Haley, March 3, 1977, in Jordan, *The Impact of the Negro Organization Society*.

127. EWP: 1.5 Yr. 1938, November 2, First Meeting of County-Wide League of Loudoun.

128. Peggy Drummond, "Lines from Loudoun," *Loudoun Times-Mirror*, November 13, 1958, reporting on a party celebrating the twenty-fifth anniversary of the League at Douglass and honoring the founding members.

129. The exact date is unknown. See EWP: 5.2 Yr. 1941 Cavalcade of Negroana.

130. Workers of the Writers' Program of the Work Projects Administration in the State of Illinois, sponsored by the Diamond Jubilee Exposition, Chicago. EWP: 5.2 Drama Cavalcade of 1941.

131. The 1940 fair developed as counterpoint to the stereotypical depictions of Blacks at the 1933 World's Fair as indolent and uncivilized. The 1933 fair had other problems, including the presentation of a story about the value of accommodation. It also was a showcase for FDR's programs, set up in a predominantly white area of Chicago, and used as a tool for FDR's reelection.

132. EWP: 6.3.3 Yr. 1940 G. William Liverpool, Report of Progress for Virginia Accredited High Schools, Principal of Loudoun County Training Center.

133. EWP: 9.2.3 Yr. 1919–1952.

134. EWP: 1.1.1 Yr. 1944 Emerick on Resource Equality.

135. Personal papers of Charles Houston, Founder's Library, Howard University, Washington, DC.

136. Richardson, *Negro Education in Virginia*, 23.

137. Richardson, *Negro Education in Virginia*, 37.

138. Barbara Scott (née Evans), interview by Nathan Bailey, July 29, 2020.

139. Henry Young, March 12, 1940, letter to Charles H. Houston, retrieved from personal papers of Charles Houston, Founders Library, Howard University.

140. Elizabeth Warner, March 1940, letter to Charles H. Houston, retrieved from personal papers of Charles Houston, Founders Library, Howard University.

141. Mrs. M. K. Jennings, 1940, letter to Charles H. Houston on behalf of Howardsville and Bluemont parents, retrieved from personal papers of Charles Houston, Founders Library, Howard University.

142. EWP 1.1.1 Equal Education re Transportation: March 31, 1940, letter to Emerick from parent Annie Wyatt requesting reimbursement for Transportation costs. Ruth Elizabeth Williams would have been required to sit in the rear of the railway car.

143. EWP: 1.1.1 Yr. 1940, March 12, Complaint by County-Wide League. See also EWP: 1.1.1 Yr. 1940, March 27, Daisy Allen to Emerick on Transportation Reimbursement.

144. In the 1938–39 academic year, there were 60 Black students in high school and 838 in elementary schools. There were also 725 school-age children out of school. EWP: 1.7 Yr 1939 Distribution of School Age Negro Children. The average attendance of white students in elementary school in 1939–40 was 3,628, whereas the high school enrollment was 891. EWP: 6.15 Enrollment Yr 1889 to 1940.

145. EWP 15.17 Special NAACP Papers Loudoun 2, p. 8.

146. Lloyd Asbey Womeldorph, "Encourage Pupils To Complete Work Is Parents' Duty," *Loudoun Times-Mirror*, September 1, 1939, 2:1.

147. The six students went to Hampton, presumably to become teachers. For details, see Gertrude Alexander, Survey, Washington, DC: Law Offices of Charles Houston, 1939, in personal papers of Charles Houston, Founders Library, Howard University.

148. EWP: 9.1 Yr. 1883, June, Copy of deed for Leesburg Colored.

149. EWP: 2.5A Yr 1940 County-Wide League on Fire Trap.

150. This issue of unfairness was explored in a study commissioned by the Board of Supervisors in 2022, an initiative led by Supervisor Juli Briskman of the Algonkian District and Chairwoman Phyllis Randall, the first African American to lead a county board in Virginia. Nathaniel Cline, "Committee to Study 1940 Douglass High School Sale; Supervisors Look to Hire Expert to Study Desegregation's Impact in Loudoun," *Loudoun Times-Mirror*, March 17, 2022.

151. EWP: 2.5.A Yr. 1940 Training Center Called Fire Trap, Letter from Charles Houston to the Fire Chief of the Fire Department, Loudoun County, March 12, 1940; and EWP: 15.17 Special NAACP papers Loudoun 1, p. 42, Letter from Walter White, Secretary of the NAACP, to Mr. and Mrs. James Van Alen, Middleburg, March 20, 1940.

152. EWP: 1.1.3 Yr. 1939, December, Richardson Recommendations on Douglass.

153. *Annual Report of the Superintendent of Public Instruction of the Commonwealth of Virginia . . . School Year 1930–31* (Richmond, VA: Division of Purchase and Printing, 1932), 95.

154. EWP: 2.5.A Undated Petition Asking for an Accredited High School.

155. EWP: 1.1.3 Yr. 1940, April 8, Letter from Lewis Rector and George A. Brown to William T. Smith.

156. Eugene Scheel, "From the Outspoken to Soft-Spoken, Remembering Black Communities Heroes," *Washington Post*, February 6, 2000; and Eugene Scheel, "For Blacks, a Thriving League of Their Own," *Washington Post*, July 24, 2003.

157. EWP: 1.1.3 Yr. 1940, April 8, Purcellville Option.

158. EWP: 1.1.3 Yr. 1940, December 4, Meeting of County-Wide League to Transfer Title; EWP: 1.1.3 Yr. 1940, December 11, School Board Appoints Harrison to handle Gibbons Lot Transfer; EWP: 1.1.3 Yr. 1940, December 17, Emerick Acknowledges Donation of Gibbons Lot; EWP: 1.1.3 Yr. 1940, December 19, Action in Circuit Court on Gibbons Donation; and EWP: 1.1.3 Yr. 1940, December 22, County Wide League Opinions of Transfer of Gibbons Lot. See also EWP 15.17 Special NAACP papers Loudoun 1, Letter from K. Monroe Allen and Daisy L. Allen to Charles H. Houston, March 7, 1940, p. 9.

159. EWP: 9.2.3 Yr. 1941–42 Douglass HS.

160. EWP: 2.5.A Yr. 1951 Douglass and County-Wide League Say Repairs Needed.

161. EWP: 2.2 Yr. 1953, August 25, Construction Decisions on Douglass and Leesburg HS; EWP: 2.2 Yr 1954, April 12, School Board Agenda; and EWP: 4.2 Yr. 1958, March 6, Negro Consolidation Plan program.

162. Jim Roberts, interview by Larry Roeder, July 12, 2020.

163. EWP: 5.2 Yr. 1943 Douglass HS War Effort Model Planes.

164. EWP: 1.1.3 Yr. 1939, December 15, Archie G. Richardson Recommendations to Emerick.

165. EWP: 1.1.1 March 8, 1940, Houston to Emerick on Equalization. Announces appointment by the County-Wide League.

166. Mark V. Tushnet, "The Strategy of Delay and the Direct Attack on Segregation," chapter 7 in *The NAACP's Legal Strategy Against Segregated Education, 1925–1950* (Chapel Hill: University of North Carolina Press, 1987), 105. See also EWP: 1.1.1. March 8, 1940, Houston to Emerick on Equalization. Houston made the same point in a letter of March 10, 1940, to Thurgood Marshall, Walter White, and Roy Wilkins of the NAACP. "I have not said anything about the NAACP at the present time. However, in my power of attorney from each person I represent I have authorization to call in the NAACP, and of course will promptly do so, as soon as the refusal is made and the fight is on." EWP: 15.17 Special NAACP papers Loudoun 1, p. 13.

167. Memo from Walter White to Thurgood Marshall of March 18, 1940, noting Houston's opinion that NAACP should not join the case until a branch was formed "and then he will call us in." EWP: 15.17 Special NAACP papers Loudoun 1, p. 36.

168. Letter from Mary Page to Charles Houston, March 8, 1940. EWP 15.17 Special NAACP papers Loudoun 1, p. 11.

169. EWP 1.1.1 Yr 29 November 1944, Emerick on Resource Inequality.

170. "In Loudoun," *Richmond Times-Dispatch*, March 13, 1940, p. 5.

171. Letters from Charles Houston of March 10, 1940, to Virginius Dabney, the *Richmond Times-Dispatch*, to Carl Murphy, Editor, the *Afro-American*, Baltimore, Maryland, P. B. Young, Editor, the *Journal and Guide*, Norfolk, Virginia. EWP 15.17 Special NAACP papers Loudoun 1, p. 13.

172. EWP: 2.5.A Yr. 1941, January 18, Conklin Wants to Stay Open.

173. EWP: 15.18 NAACP Charles Houston Papers.

174. On arguing over tactics, see EWP: 15.18 Yr. 1940, March 21, Houston to Emerick on local dissent.

175. EWP: 1.1.3 Yr. 1940, March 16, Houston to Emerick.

176. EWP: 1.1.1 Yr. 1940, May 5, Houston to Emerick, Expressing Dismay at BOS Decision.

177. EWP: 3.1 Yr. 1949 Oscar Emerick, Status of Loudoun County Schools.

7

1950–68

Change and Fear

Whatever integration may come to mean, it will mean a great change; and change, however deeply willed, is always shocking; old stances and accommodation, like the twinge of an old wound, are part of the self, and even as we desire new life and more life, we must realize that a part of us— of each individual person, black or white—has to die into that new life. And there is, of course, the unappeasable resentment that many Negroes must carry, and the suspicion of anything white. . . .

The doctrine of states' rights has frequently been used, and is being used, as an alibi and a screen for some very unworthy proceedings—often quite cynically used and only for some special ad hoc advantage, with total contempt for the principle as principle.

—Robert Penn Warren, 1965

No person in the United States shall, on the ground of race, color, or national origin, be excluded from participation in, be denied the benefits of, or be subjected to discrimination under any program or activity receiving Federal financial assistance.

—Title VI of the 1964 Civil Rights Act

The infant Negro plaintiffs, through their parents and for themselves and others similarly situated, bring this suit against the County School Board of Loudoun County, Virginia, C. M. Bussinger, its Division Superintendent, and E. J. Oglesby, Alfred L. Wingo and E. T. Justis, individually and constituting the Pupil Placement Board of the Commonwealth of Virginia, seeking admission to Loudoun County High School and a temporary and permanent injunction restraining and enjoining the defendants from any and all action that regulates or affects, on the basis of race or color, the initial assignment, the placement, the transfer, the admission, the enrollment or the education of any children to or in any public school.

— *Samuel Eugene Corbin v. County School Board*
of Loudoun County, 1963 (the result was full
integration by the 1968–69 school year)

It appears to the outsider that federalism stands in the way of nothing that the national government actually wants to do; but it is always used as an excuse for the national government's not protecting the rights of Negroes.

—French participant at an international
seminar in Salzburg, Austria, 1958

The work of the American propagandist is not at present a happy one. [Segregation] mocks us and haunts us whenever we become eloquent and indignant in the United Nations. . . . The caste system in this country, particularly when as in Little Rock it is maintained by troops, is an enormous, indeed an almost insuperable, obstacle to our leadership in the cause of freedom and human equality.

—Walter Lippmann, 1957

Blacks had "a sense of kinship with other colored—and also oppressed— peoples of the world," a belief "that the struggle of the Negro in the United States is part and parcel of the struggle against imperialism and exploitation in India, China, Burma, Africa, the Philippines, Malaya, the West Indies, and South America."

—NAACP Secretary Walter Francis White, 1945

By the mid-1950s southern politicians unified an overtly racist strategy known as the Southern Manifesto—massive resistance that rejected integration as a concept and used a theory called interposition, which rejected the historical primacy of the federal judiciary to decide constitutional matters.[1] But segregation was also gaining new foes. The Cold War was becoming a growing, long-term global struggle, and by 1954, when the Korean War ended, the communists were using race relations in the United States as a propaganda tool in Africa, Asia, and Latin America. Allies were also critical.

For entirely practical reasons, to advance national security concerns, the federal government needed to bleach the national character of segregation's stain. Enter the odd mix of President Dwight Eisenhower, civil right lawyer Thurgood Marshall, Chief Justice Earl Warren, and the Supreme Court's *Brown v. Board of Education* decision. The president's campaign had focused on fairness, and after his election Eisenhower ordered the desegregation of military schools, hospitals, and bases and eventually ended segregated units; but those were federal matters. He didn't want to interfere in local affairs. As attorney general of California, Warren had supported the forced internment of Japanese immigrants and citizens during World War II and was not considered a great believer in civil rights. But there was also Thurgood Marshall, NAACP chief counsel, who made the compelling argument that Jim Crow laws were unconstitutional. Although Eisenhower was not an ardent supporter of civil rights and had concerns over the accuracy of *Brown*, he felt a duty to support the courts and would order troops to enforce integration at Little Rock High School after the governor of Arkansas rejected the courts; but research indicates his focus had more to do with rejecting anarchy than advocating desegregation.

> Our personal opinion as to the accuracy of the decision has no bearing on the matter; the responsibility of the Supreme Court to interpret the Constitution is unquestioned.
>
> —President Eisenhower, Address to the nation explaining
> his decision to send federal troops from the 101st Airborne
> Division to Little Rock to allow integration, September 24, 1957

Segregation was still strong in Loudoun. An early typical example occurred twenty years before in September 1931 in the village of Airmont. A little white schoolhouse was closed that year due to poor attendance; the prior academic year had only attracted five students and attendance had been on a steady decline since 1925.[2] With the closure, the building could have been available to Blacks, but that did not happen due at least in part to a letter from a farmer who wrote to the school board, saying "I am very much opposed for the colored to use our school room at Airmont."[3] Along the same lines about thirty years later, the modern

Carver Colored School could have been immediately available for everyone following integration in 1968. Yet according to interviews with former Purcellville residents, this did not occur because whites refused to use a "colored school." Instead, the building was relegated to storage and is now a senior center, although it is much revered in local circles as a focal point for sharing stories about Black history, civil rights, and the exploits of past generations.

The point of the Airmont (1931) and Carver (1968) stories is that despite the changing political climate in Washington and around the globe, segregation was deeply ingrained in Loudoun's educational fabric. Therefore, as Robert Penn Warren alluded to in his article from 1965 in *LOOK* magazine, despite the monumental *Brown* decision, segregationists were not going to give up quietly. Still, what the EWP team calls "blackboard bravery" worked because of the Black community's vibrant and unstinting determination to articulate and effectively advocate for the written vision of the nation's flawed forefathers. Alexis de Tocqueville and US Rep. John Lewis were right. Democracy is hard work and must be defended every day.

The events of this period are also a reminder of the many heroes who were the cast in the desegregation drama, such as Ethel Rae Stewart Smith of the Willisville Colored School who refused to let the social status of being Black prevent her from demanding coal to warm her students during two bitter winters. Pleading for wood and coal in 1955 and 1956, she explained the obvious to Emerick, "that [dirt] doesn't quite burn."[4] There was also Janie Redwood, a charismatic Black teacher who played a key role in developing plans for consolidation in the mid-1940s. Rosa Lee Carter of Bluemont famously worked at Middleburg's Grant School in the 1930s under a leaky roof, without water, and with little heat. To rectify things, she worked with parents to raise money for books and furniture, including a bookcase and chairs made from orange crates, which were painted by the students. The Edwin Washington Society recommended in 2022 to the school system that a monument of two Black students from segregation be erected in front of the Douglass High School atop a base showing the categories of groups of people who supported education through history—parents, teachers, janitors, bus drivers, and organizations like the County-Wide League and the NAACP.

1951: The Battle for Toilets

Segregation ended because of the confluence of external national forces and myriad local pressures, a good example being the 1951 struggle to install toilets at the Training Center, then known as Douglass Elementary (one of three structures to hold that name). The 1882 two-story wooden structure still used outhouses. Sanitation had plagued both white and Black schools since 1870, which is why it was a huge issue for the Negro Organization Society (NOS).[5] Today one can walk along the back of the school property, which is the edge of the Union Cemetery, and track the progression of outhouses for boys and girls, each a mild depression not dissimilar to the graves on the other side of the fence. The community wanted sanitary toilets. Keep in mind that all schools in Loudoun should have had at least sanitary outhouses by 1915, and by the 1950s many of the white schools already had indoor toilets.

Leesburg's Black community saw Charles Hamilton Houston and the NAACP dismantling Jim Crow and decided they were done "asking" for proper toilet facilities. Lawyers were needed, and so Edwin Cicero Brown Sr. courageously stepped in. A lawyer with a past worthy of Jack London, Brown partnered with local leaders and used a federal lawsuit to effect change. The Loudoun branch of the NAACP and the PTA of Douglass Elementary School hired Brown, who threatened a federal lawsuit in 1951 if their demands for proper sanitation facilities were not met. The school system tried to hold off court action, indicating that costs of litigation would require deferral of expenditures for construction and repairs of Waterford, Ashburn, and Mountain Gap schools.[6] Leaders called the government's bluff, stayed firm, and the suit worked. The toilets were constructed in the fall of 1952.[7]

Brown **Is a Judicial Earthquake**

Across the state and the nation, ordinary citizens and civil rights organizations like the NAACP were hard at work, seeking court action to remedy all forms of segregation. The arguments, as articulated by Blacks, had been evolving since the 1930s—Thurgood Marshall and Charles Houston were making the case that separate was unlawful because it

Edwin Cicero Brown Sr.
Courtesy of Christopher Brown,
his grandson

was not equal. This was different from the prior theory supported by Emerick that aspects of inequality could be rectified when addressed narrowly simply through providing better building stock and salaries, busing, and so on. The fresh argument was that segregation itself was inherently unequal and therefore should be swept into history's wastebasket.[8] This new thinking, developed by Charles Hamilton Houston, culminated in the US Supreme Court's *Brown v. Board of Education of Topeka*, Kansas, May 17, 1954. School segregation was banned because it violated the equal protection clause of the Fourteenth Amendment to the US Constitution. *Plessy v. Ferguson* (1896) was overturned. This was a judicial earthquake.

Brown, due to its strong language, should have killed the notion that Blacks and whites should learn separately. Not unexpectedly, however, it sparked resistance among white supremacists across the South and in

Edwin Cicero Brown Sr. was born July 1, 1908, on an Indian Reservation in Guthrie, Logan County, Oklahoma. Later he crossed the Cimarron River in a covered wagon as his parents migrated to Wichita, Kansas, where he attended an integrated school. Brown picked cotton and shined shoes, which were the only jobs available to him, but he also learned the saxophone and clarinet. After earning enough to buy a used Model T Ford and eight spare tires, he drove with other musicians to Washington, DC, and entered Howard University. He paid his tuition by scrubbing floors at the YMCA. After graduating he entered Howard's School of Law and began a legal dynasty of Brown family lawyers, which to this day advises the Edwin Washington Project. Ed Brown remains an unheralded civil rights hero.

Most noteworthy was his role in the lawsuit he filed on behalf of the NAACP in the Eastern District of Virginia, Alexandria Federal Court, successfully seeking—and being successful on several appeals—an order requiring Arlington County Public Schools to comply with the US Supreme Court decision in *Brown v. Board of Education.* See *Thompson v. County School Board of Arlington County,* 144 F. Supp. 239 (D.V.I. 1956); *School Board of City of Charlottesville, Va. v. Allen,* 240 F2d 59 (4th Cir., 1956); *Thompson v. County School Board of Arlington County,* 159 F Supp. 567 (D.V.I., 1957); and *County School Board of Arlington Co., Va. v. Thompson,* 252 F.2d 929 (4th Cit., 1958).

Virginia, like the politically militant Defenders of State Sovereignty and Individual Liberties; but the biggest resistance leader may have been Senator Harry F. Byrd Sr. The Byrd machine controlled Virginia politics; few could hope to be elected or even appointed to high office without Byrd's okay. He promoted the Southern Manifesto, a document attacking integration, which was signed in 1956 by over one hundred southern members of Congress and led to specific segregationist measures to block integration under Gov. Thomas Stanley of Virginia (1954–58). In response, the NAACP, local Black and other civil rights organizations, and their attorneys took on a heavy lift.

Massive Resistance and Interposition

Responding to *Brown,* and with the encouragement of Byrd, Governor Stanley appointed a commission to examine its impact on Virginia and make recommendations. The goal was to prevent or at least delay integration, relying on the concept that states' rights superseded those of the federal government—a theory not too dissimilar to those used by the Confederacy a century earlier. In other words, since the US Constitution gave the states and people all rights not reserved to the federal government, such as the right to public education, the segregationists argued that Virginia was authorized to "interpose" its sovereignty between its citizens and the federal government. Sometimes called nullification, the theory suggested that if a state felt a federal law violated its own constitution, it had the right to ignore the law or actions by federal courts, even the Supreme Court. The approach was strongly supported by prominent Virginians like conservative columnist James J. Kilpatrick, then editor of the *Richmond News Leader*, and other prominent Virginians and organizations. In the view of the Defenders of State Sovereignty and Individual Liberties, the state legislature should "restore the States to their rightful place in our Federal system by interposing the sovereignty of Virginia to check the Supreme Court of the United States in its unconstitutional assumption of power."[9]

The Defenders of State Sovereignty and Individual Liberties was a Virginia grassroots organization founded in October 1954 in Petersburg. Stirling Murray Harrison, the commonwealth's attorney in Loudoun, led the local chapter. John Janney of Loudoun (then living in Nevada), said at a January 1960 meeting of the Defenders that "since the federal government was created by a contractual agreement among the states, federal agencies are in effect employees of the states. When those agencies overstep the authority given it by the Constitution, the states as employers should call it down." He then urged passage of a state law stating that US Supreme Court decisions Virginia felt "to be unconstitutional or illegal would be void in the state."[10] Janney felt this was justified because the courts (in his opinion) were operating outside their authority. The Janney connection is important because his family's heritage went back to the formation of the Republic and because the Janney family in particular, and Loudoun Quakers in general, had been immensely helpful to Blacks, especially in education. For example, Cornelia Janney set up a fund in the 1930s that supported the Lincoln Colored School.[11]

The Janney family is usually spoken of in terms of its support for Black rights. The family certainly had impressive roots. John Janney's great-grandfather was attorney general under George Washington and John Adams. The exception was John Janney. He was born in Leesburg in 1877, graduated from Virginia Military Institute, and over his life proved to be a highly controversial member of his clan. He was frequently involved in litigation related to his many commercial enterprises. He was also outspoken in right-wing politics, anticommunist activities, and—like other conservatives then and today—sought constitutional limits to government.

The Supreme Court rejected the power of states to declare federal laws unconstitutional, reserving that function to the judicial branch of the federal government—the Supreme Court and its various district and appellate courts, all of which played important roles in enforcing integration. *Cooper v. Aaron* (1958) put the nail in the concept's coffin by specifically stating that the states are duty bound to enforce the actions of federal courts:

> The constitutional rights of children not to be discriminated against in school admission on grounds of race or color declared by this Court in the Brown Case can neither be nullified openly and directly by state legislators or state judicial officers, nor nullified indirectly by them through evasive schemes for segregation whether attempted "ingeniously or ingenuously." ...
>
> The interpretation of the Fourteenth Amendment enunciated by this Court in the Brown case is the supreme law of the land, and Art. VI of the Constitution makes it of binding effect on the State "any Thing in the Constitution of Law of any State to the contrary notwithstanding."[12]

In the interests of the rule of law, states are not allowed to postpone implementation of federal laws, even if a governor or legislature is defiant. In other words, while it is true that education is the concern of states, it is also true that all state activities must conform to federal constitutional requirements such as equal protection under the Fourteenth Amendment. President Eisenhower also supported this.[13]

Governor Stanley's commission was never meant to be balanced, leaving out pro-integration supporters, and did not care about the opinions of the Supreme Court. It was led by Garland Gray, a lumber and banking executive and head of the Democratic Caucus in the Virginia Senate who was vehemently opposed to school desegregation. Gray had also been part of a state commission that adopted textbooks that presented the Civil War conflict through the lens of the Lost Cause.[14] Two interim reports were made, the first on January 19, 1955, and the second on June 10, 1955, followed by a final report on November 11, 1955.[15] They ultimately recommended tactics declared in 1958 in *Cooper v. Aaron* as "evasive schemes for segregation."

Probably recognizing that the fight over restricting public education for Blacks was a losing proposition, the commission wanted workarounds to the Supreme Court. The idea was to use a constitutional convention of elected delegates to change section 141 of the Virginia Constitution, which stated that "State appropriations are prohibited to schools or institutions of learning not owned or exclusively controlled by the State or some subdivision thereof . . . with specified exceptions."[16] In other words, Gray supported private academies as an escape pod, with taxpayer funds, that could not be done under section 141, until amended.

Supporting the 1956 convention referendum was the Leesburg-based *Loudoun Times-Mirror*, which said in an editorial: "The people of Virginia will vote on a proposition that none of us can escape. It is not a political vote, nor is it a vote for or against candidates, rather the people of Virginia are asked to give power to their elected representatives that the great Virginia tradition, public schools and the right of individual, is to choose for themselves how their children will be educated, will be preserved."[17] This so-called rival to public schools was also supported by the Loudoun chapter of the Defenders of State Sovereignty and Individual Liberty.[18]

The vote by Loudoun's citizens for the convention was 2,012 in favor and 859 opposed.[19] Leesburg's delegate, Lucas D. Phillips, also registered his support for the Gray Commission.[20] Following the referendum, delegates to the constitutional convention "limited to the question of Section 141" assembled in the Virginia House of Delegates on March 5, 1956. William Harris Gaines represented the 27th District, which included Loudoun County, as well as Culpepper and Fauquier Counties. Across the state, the approval by voters was 2 to 1, exceeding votes cast in the 1952 presidential election.[21]

Despite the widespread support for massive resistance, the attitude of religious leaders was mixed. On December 29, 1955, several Virginia

Baptist pastors and religious figures announced their opposition to the amendment to the Constitution.[22] Loudoun members of the Potomac Baptist Association were James Cates (Hamilton), William Calhoun (Ashburn), Ed Clark Jr. (Purcellville), Lorenzo Clemens (Sterling), Charles Dick (Manassas), John Edens (Manassas), William Engels (Garrisonville), Joseph Grover (Elkwood), Guy C. Heyl (Warrenton), and James Weaver (Triangle). About the same time, twenty-six Episcopal clergymen also opposed the Gray Commission, but there were others who spoke in favor.

The entire set of commission recommendations had the strategic aim of preventing compulsory integration. The Pupil Placement Act of 1956, which remained in existence for a decade, was one of several bits of legislation to emerge from the legislature because of the convention, creating Pupil Placement Boards in each county, with the power to assign specific students to schools—or to refuse entry by Blacks.[23] Such power, ordinarily held by superintendents like Emerick or local school boards, was divested. Tuition grants were also to be provided to students who opposed integrated schools. In addition, state funds were denied to any integrated public school, which were then to be closed. There were opponents who worried that tuition grants "would weaken or destroy the public school system, bring about higher state taxes, and other otherwise jeopardize the educational future."[24] But their voices were drowned out.

The federal government continued attacking segregation and other inequalities by passing the Civil Rights Act of 1957, which created a civil rights section in the US Department of Justice. Federal prosecutors were also empowered to obtain court injunctions against interference with the right to vote, later amended in 1960 to include penalties for anyone who obstructed another person's attempt to register to vote. While those were not educational bills per se, by strengthening the ability of Blacks to vote, the bills meant more Blacks and more officials sympathetic to integration would be elected. Then came the Civil Rights Act of 1964, which created a national clearinghouse for denials of equal protection. It outlawed discrimination based on race, color, religion, sex, and national origin in public accommodations and in private institutions that received federal aid. Today, it also outlaws discrimination based on sexual orientation and gender identity. On April 30, 1964, probably anticipating its passage, the Loudoun Hospital's Board of Trustees agreed to comply with the Civil Rights Act and to make "no distinction on the grounds of race, color or national origin," thus ending fifty-two years of segregated wards. However, the hospital then came under investigation for continued discrimination the following year, in part because "black physicians were denied staff privileges, or the nursing school was not open to all races."[25]

In a continued act of resistance, on January 31, 1958, the Virginia General Assembly repealed the state's compulsory school attendance law. Then in April it allowed county boards of supervisors to adopt compulsory school laws on the recommendation of the local school board, but the law also obligated local governments to excuse any student whose parents conscientiously objected to attending a particular school.[26]

Citizens for Segregation Make Link to Communism

Political support for Senator Byrd could be quite personal, as seen in a coarse letter to Oscar Emerick from a group of self-described white citizens of Leesburg. The letter is not only interesting because of its crude language but because it asserts that the people wanting integration were working with the communists.

> Mr. O. L. Emerick
>
> Dear Sir. We are writing to tell you we all hope and Pray that all you men will have enough get up and Pride and self-Respect, about all of you that you will Keep the negroes out of our wonderful schools . . . put your foot down and just say "you men are working with the communists" . . .
>
> Undated (about 1956–57) letter to Oscar Emerick from "A group of Friends to the white race" in Leesburg.[27]

Emerick on Segregation

With much of the legal profession and many politicians as well as Virginia's superintendent of public instruction, Dowell Jennings Howard, in favor of massive resistance at its constitutional convention, where was

Loudoun's head of education, considered by some as the most influential man in the county? Emerick had worked hard through his career to build a reputation as a progressive in education by the time he retired in 1957. As early as 1927 he had advanced night schools for adults and had introduced many other modern administrative measures as part of a long-term plan to accredit the then nine white high schools and to improve schooling in general.[28] He also pushed for consolidated elementary schools and new construction, sometimes with resistance from the board of supervisors. Those were classic bureaucratic struggles reminiscent of the differences in spending priorities between that body and the school board discussed by the very first superintendents. The debate was also often testy, with Emerick leading public debates in PTA meetings.[29] However, despite telling the school board in the past that the dual system was unfair and approving the construction of Banneker and Carver, modern elementary schools, and Douglass High School, as well as other important decisions that improved Black education, the bulk of Emerick's decisions were about helping whites.[30] The quality of education for Blacks under Emerick was inferior. Emerick had worried that maintaining racial inequality would cause a court takeover because the Loudoun system failed the *Plessy v. Ferguson* principle of separate but equal. However, nothing in his many progressive administrative policies indicates that he really grasped that inequality was an inherent characteristic of segregation. In fact, Emerick vehemently opposed integration and went on record in public forums supporting Senator Byrd and massive resistance.

As most county superintendents must have done, Emerick kept careful notes on court cases and political events related to integration, and many of his files survived. One file was written about the upcoming constitutional convention referendum and, in Emerick's opinion, if the vote were negative "so much encouragement will be given to those who want mixed schools forthwith that we shall find chaos and a serious blow will have been dealt to education. The main intent of the members of the Gray Commission is that no child be required to attend an integrated school."[31] He clearly understood the stakes for whites and, despite the consequences for Blacks, sided with segregation.

Emerick also gave a written statement on December 19, 1955, to the *Blue Ridge Herald* recognizing that the US Supreme Court had ordered Prince Edward County to integrate its public school with "deliberate speed." This was "Brown II," which decreed that the dismantling of separate school systems for Black and white students should proceed with "all deliberate speed." The problem was that the phrase was not defined. This gave ammunition for segregationists like Emerick to look for a loophole, to further resist. As Emerick put it,

> this becomes indirectly a notice to all Virginia School Boards to act accordingly. . . . There is a tendency on the part of supporters of integration to resort to reckless speed and thus to do incalculable damage to education. Also, we can have no way of knowing the exact definition of "deliberate speed" that is in the minds of the members of the US Supreme Court who have boldly reversed the former decision of the same court (different members), who said that segregation or integration was within the constitutional power of the State legislature to settle. Consequently, we need some means in Virginia to control the speed with which integration may be accomplished and as a safeguard we need this control before schools open in September 1956. The proposed amendment to section 141 of the Constitution is the only real and positive authority the voters can give to the General Assembly to provide that no parent shall be required to send his child to an integrated school and yet receive an education at public expense. . . .
>
> I am strongly in favor of the amendment to the constitution. I believe however, that the best way to get the most for our dollars in Loudoun is through continued segregation on a voluntary basis but that the people of the county should join in equalizing physical facilities for both races in certain areas.[32]

A similar statement was provided by the chair of the school board and the Loudoun County Bar Association, the State Board of Education, and superintendents of schools elsewhere in Virginia.[33] However, Loren Pope, a former Loudoun County PTA president, said the Gray Commission recommendations were futile.[34]

Having made his position clear to the public, Emerick then wrote directly to Senator Harry Byrd on January 1, 1956, responding to the senator's public statement of December 18 regarding the upcoming referendum. Emerick said he wished to "commend you for your very clear, very reasonable and commendable statement on the subject."[35] Finally, in response to attempts to integrate schools in Loudoun after *Brown* and somewhat contradicting his own guidance to the school board in the past, Emerick said to principals, "The courts do not administer the schools. The school system of Loudoun County is still subject to the direction of the General Assembly and of the State Board of Education. We have not authority in Loudoun to operate mixed schools."[36] However, Emerick did not support closing the schools, as would happen in Prince Edward County in September 1959 or as Powhatan County also threatened to do in 1962.[37] His love of education made that a bridge too far. Instead, like other superintendents around the state, he kept Loudoun public schools open. Then, in 1957, with failing eyesight and growing poor health hindering him, Emerick retired, marking the end of an era.

Emerick's public statements against integration, which were voluntary, although perhaps required to retain his professional standing, are a permanent stain on his reputation. It should be noted that in Loudoun Emerick faced extreme pressure to close the school, not only from Senator Byrd and Governor Stanley but also from the Loudoun political establishment. In 1956 the county board of supervisors passed a resolution submitted by Loudoun's commonwealth attorney and president of the Defenders of State Sovereignty demanding that no funding be given to integrated schools.[38]

The Role of the Curriculum

The curriculum was also a problem. In keeping with attitudes advanced by Jefferson and others described in earlier chapters, the official Virginia history textbook from the 1950s into the 1970s taught Blacks a perverted story of their forebearers' legacy, ignoring the tragedy and immorality of enslavement and conveying a false image of a race incapable of responsibility or social advancement. In 1965 James Baldwin, reflecting his personal revulsion with that idea, made an important point about Black history as it had been taught him in his home in Harlem, New York— essentially that Europe and whites saved the Blacks, who had no history of their own. This is a consistent thread through the various chapters of public education in the South and in Loudoun. But as Baldwin eloquently taught, this false history was also a pernicious part of education in the North.[39]

While "history" remained trapped in white supremacy, by the 1950s LCPS did provide Blacks with more classes and opportunities. Douglass High School even had a French Club. College scholarships were made available through partnerships like the Middleburg Community Center. In addition, in July 1950 the center formed the Marshall Street Community Center for Blacks. Then, in 1954, the center supported a partnership with George Washington University to enhance reading competency by Blacks and whites. In 1956 the center even issued college scholarships to Blacks in Loudoun and Fauquier Counties.

Transportation: A Continuing Issue

During the same era, transportation for Black schools was increasing, and Black students could become bus drivers. Records are incomplete, but the EWP team would like to record for posterity the drivers, without whom many students would not have reached school.[40] By 1950 consolidation of Black schools was well under way, and segregated buses were used to transport students to the larger schools of the relevant race all over Loudoun County. However, some students still walked, went by horseback, or carpooled. Records for the 1951–53 school years show an increase in buses to Black schools—Douglass High, Banneker, Carver, and Conklin—but there were three times as many buses serving white students. By 1953 there were ten school buses serving three Black elementary schools and one Black high school; there were thirty buses serving forty-four white elementary and three white high schools (three of those buses were privately owned). This ratio continued through 1956. In addition, by the mid-1950s student bus drivers were common for both races.

I attended Loudoun County Schools from 1955 through 1967. . . . I rode a bus with only white students on it to Aldie from my home on Watson Road (Route 860). . . . As a young boy, it always seemed strange to me that the kids of the Black family that lived across Watson Road from us rode a bus to Douglass Elementary in Leesburg, while I rode a different bus to

Aldie. My bus driver was an adult, though high school students did drive some of the buses at this time. The driver kept the bus at his home. He may have been a farmer that supplemented his income by driving a school bus. This was not an unusual arrangement in the county. . . . The county didn't erect shelters for students. Some days my dad would drive my older brother and me to Aldie Elementary on his way to work in Leesburg.

—Wynne Saffer, on a typical white student's experience, interview by Nathan Bailey, September 21, 2020

My family didn't own a car and the very fact that I was riding was a thrill in itself. . . . We'd pick up Black students living in tenant housing on farms in the area as the bus route went from Hillsboro to Woodgrove to Round Hill and finally to Purcellville and Carver Elementary. There were places along the primarily dirt road route where the road was very narrow. Mr. Reid would have to steer the bus over to the side . . . on the grass to let oncoming traffic go by. A cherry tree grew where Route 719 comes out in Round Hill near Thompson's. In the spring the tree would be full of ripe cherries, and we'd hope that Mr. Reid would let us off long enough to get a few. After 1959 my family moved to Purcellville. At Carver I'd transfer to bus #16 driven by Reverend Sulva Warner. From there, the bus made its way to Douglass High in Leesburg. Reverend Warner would pick up more students between Purcellville and Leesburg, with the bus being about 80 percent full by the time we reached Douglass.

—Mary Carey (née Timbers), interview by Nathan Bailey, November 7, 2020

By 1962, under the LCPS school transfer plan for Black students, Loudoun County High School and Loudoun Valley High School became the first individual schools to integrate, accepting one and three Black enrollees, respectively. Those within walking distance continued to walk, but some of the students rode buses. According to Loudoun Valley High Black student bus driver Mackley Lucas (1964–66), although the school was integrated, "there were never any white students on my bus. In fact, buses with Black drivers still didn't carry white students, though some buses with white drivers carried Black students." By 1968 integration in Loudoun County was well under way, including LCPS bus transportation.

Table 7.1
Loudoun County Bus Drivers Serving Black Schools

Driver	Bus	Served (when known)	Academic Years
LeRoy Allen	35	Conklin	1950–54
Norman K. Brooks	16	Douglass*	1952–54
Alexander W. Brown	32	Banneker	1950–54
James Bryant		Douglass HS	1950s and 1960s
Edward Caesar		Douglass HS	1950s and 1960s
George R. Carpenter	24	Douglass	1952–53
Ruth Smith Chinn	36	Douglass	1966
Charles P. Clark	33	Carver	1950–54
Roger Lee Cook		Douglass HS	1967–68
Sterling Cook	30	Douglass HS and Elementary	1964–66
Samuel Eugene Corbin, substitute		Douglass HS	1966–67, 67–68
Drue Gaskins		Douglass	ca. 1961
Walter Gaskins	16	Douglass	1951–52
Earl Hampton		Douglass	
Harold Hampton		Douglass HS	1950s and 1960s
Curtis Hatcher		Douglass HS	
Carlton Howard		Douglass HS	
Charles Jackson	5	Douglass HS	1967–68
George Long		Douglass HS	1966
Dennis Lucas, substitute		Douglass	1965
Robert F. McGruder Jr.	40	Douglass	1952–54
Glandwood D. Moore	26	Douglass	1950–54
Roscoe B. Newman			1953–54
Ester Nickens		Douglass HS	1967–68
Leonard Page	16	Douglass	1950–51
Joseph Preston Peterson, substitute		Douglass HS	1967–69
Alfred Pollard		Douglass HS	1967–68
William Pollard		Douglass HS	1966
Mutt Ramey		Douglass HS	1950s and 1960s
Richard Randolph			
Henry G. Reid	30	Douglass	1950–54
Lawrence Reid		Douglass	1966
Stephen Scott		Douglass	1966
Pearl Marie Simms		Douglass HS	1967–69
Luther F. Smith	36	Douglass	1950–54
Orland Ray Stewart	34	Carver	1950–54
Haywood Thomas		Douglass HS	
James Robert Thomas		Douglass HS	1967–69
Charles Thornton	24	Douglass	1950–52
Howard Timbers		Douglass HS and Loudoun Valley HS	1967–68

Table 7.1 (continued)

Driver	Bus	Served (when known)	Academic Years
Willis O. Trammel		Douglass HS	1967–69
Paul Vincent		Douglass HS	1966
Sulva Warner Sr.		Carver	
John Wilkins		Douglass HS	1950s and 1960s
Amos Wiley	39	Lincoln	1951–52
Calvin Wilson		Douglass HS	1950s and 1960s

Sources: Driver list is derived from EWP: 12.2 Bus Drivers; and Douglass HS Yearbook for 1966. Other sources of names and dates are Gert Evans interview, June 30, 2021; Mary Randolph interview, May 15, 2021; Howard Timber interview, May 15, 2021; and Sylvania Warner Preston, daughter of Sulva Warner Sr., interview May 15, 2020.

* LCPS records are not always clear on the use of the term Douglass, which could be Douglass High School, Douglass Elementary, or both.

Black student bus drivers: *Back row, left to right,* William Pollard, Sterling Cook, Paul Vincent, Lawrence Reid; *front row, left to right,* Mrs. Boyd, James Long, Stephen Scott. The photo indicated that Mrs. Boyd was not a driver, but interviews and some listings indicate otherwise. Gert Evans, the project docent, remembered her well, as did former driver Sterling Cook, also in the photo. She was also listed in the 1964–65 yearbook.
From 1965–66 Douglass High School Yearbook

Driver O. Ray Stewart at Carver in the 1950s.
EWP: 12.2 Yr. 1950s Orland Ray Stewart at Carver

Petitions Continued as a Grassroots Tool for Blacks

In the 1951–68 period no petitions were found in the files for the 1960s, but that probably reflects the political environment of massive resistance as well as the retirement of Oscar Emerick in 1957. Of the petitions that were dated (many were not), the EWP team found seven for Blacks and four for whites.[41] The white petitions focused on reappointing teachers at Aldie High School, extending the bus service in Mercer, and finding a new site for the Middleburg High School.

Ashburn and Willisville "colored" schools both complained about a lack of coal to heat their buildings, most famously in Willisville during the winter of 1955, explaining to Oscar Emerick that dirt did not burn. Conklin wanted to keep its bus driver but also replace a teacher who the community felt was not up to par, and the County-Wide League partnered with the Loudoun County Teachers Association to request repairs at Douglass High School, then just ten years old. This last petition in

1951 repeated complaints from 1948 and 1950 about conditions at Douglass that the Black community feared placed the school's accreditation at risk.[42]

- Crowding meant that several classes had to be held simultaneously in the auditorium, causing confusion.
- Despite its very varied goals, home economics was taught in a single classroom. As a result, students jointly studied the topics of "cooking, sewing, theory, home budgeting, childcare and development, and improving and beautifying the home."
- Thirty pupils were required to use the library at one time, which was designed for only twelve.
- The stage was also used as a classroom and did not have "a proper lighting system, blackboards, proper ventilation or anything that lends itself to a classroom atmosphere."
- The student body was expected to grow, so six new rooms were recommended to be added, especially for the tenth grade in the next term, and for two foreign language classes to be set up in 1952–53. They also needed a gymnasium and cafeteria, but additional classrooms were requested on an emergency basis.
- The commercial studies classroom only had twelve typewriters, and a lot of other equipment was needed, including worktables, sewing machines, desks, and chairs.

The Big Refusal—Loudoun Black Community Rejects Extortion

Despite what must have seemed an inevitable defeat in the federal courts, pushback by the government in Loudoun persisted, perhaps the most vivid example occurring January 23, 1956, when a joint meeting of the Loudoun Board of Supervisors and the Loudoun School Board recognized that the Black community needed significant improvements to their schools but said they would not comply with Black requests unless that community acquiesced to segregation.[43] This was part of Loudoun's broader attack on the *Brown* decision and perhaps was understood as appropriate for those looking through Emerick's lens of giving physical parity to ameliorate tensions.

Some consideration should be given to crowding at Hillsboro and to space for Negro children along the Fairfax boundary line; and that there seems to be no other means of financing the buildings except through a voted Bond Issue and that the estimated cost of the proposed buildings and additions including equipment is $700,000.00. However, the two boards feel that no steps should be taken in reference to construction of the proposed buildings and additions until and unless reasonable assurance shall have been given by the parents of colored children of the county that they will conform to our considerate opinion that their education can be promoted better by their continued school attendance on a segregated basis.

Sch. Ed. For — H. Marsh, F. Johnson, Y. Senn, J. Ashton, F. Marshall.

Not Voting — D. Myers.

Bd. Supers. For — E. Kirkpatrick, M. P. Frazier, S. Phillips, J. Fletcher, J. T. Hurst.

Not Voting — J. E. Arnold.

Decision by joint School Board/Board of Supervisors Jan 23, 1956. Not voting in the School Board was Douglass Myers, Chair and J. E. Arnold (Board of Supervisors). *EWP: 9.4 Yr. 1956. Segregationist Construction Strategy Revealed; probably taken by James Edward Arnold of Lovettsville*

To their great credit, the members of the County-Wide League, the Bull Run Elementary PTA, Banneker PTA, and the Loudoun County Branch of the NAACP met in joint session and agreed to "reject the proposal contained in the aforesaid resolution and urge all other Negroes of Loudoun County to do likewise; and direct that this resolution be signed by the presidents of our respective organizations and copies be forwarded to the School Board and the Board of Supervisors of Loudoun County."[44] The letter was signed by John W. Wanzer, president of the County-Wide League; Geneva Stewart, president of the Bull Run Elementary PTA; Shirley Wanzer, president of the Banneker PTA; and William McKinley Jackson (a.k.a. McK Jackson), president of the Loudoun County Branch of the NAACP.

Wanzer and the others might have made a "deal with the devil" to gain the new buildings and repairs, and so on right away. After all, the Black community desperately needed them. There is no question about the deplorable conditions. But instead of wavering under the weight of the government's pressure for a temporary victory, local leaders chose the more difficult high road of serving the long-term interests of every generation—the current students and all those to follow. It was a monumental decision, a risk, and real leadership. It was also the natural conclusion of nearly a century of struggle for equal education.

"Massive Resistance" Crumbles

The first steps in the desegregation of Virginia public schools came in 1950 at the university level with Gregory Swanson's enrollment at the University of Virginia School of Law. He became the first Black to attend a white public university in Virginia. After being rejected, he filed a complaint in US District Court with the aid of the NAACP. The court ruled in favor of Swanson's admission on the grounds that he was a qualified applicant and that UVA was the only institution in the state at which Swanson could pursue a graduate degree in law.[45] The same year, Black students were admitted to Virginia Tech and the College of William & Mary for programs not available at Virginia State College.

The walls of "massive resistance" begin to crumble with *Cooper v. Aaron* in 1958. Desegregation began in Virginia elementary and high schools in 1959 as courts ordered the admittance of a few Black students into a formerly all-white school. In response to slow desegregation, the public school system set up a plan by which Black students could only attend after applying to white schools. Black students like Louis Jett (today a respected local historian) who sought to transfer had to go through a complex selection process, and most applicants were rejected. Usually, as was the case in Loudoun, only the brightest Black students were allowed to cross the color line. Loudoun County did not approve a transfer until 1962, when four applicants were approved, one for Loudoun County High School and three for Loudoun Valley High School. After a lawsuit by rejected applicants, the acceptance rate was increased, and Loudoun Valley High had twenty-three Black students in its 1963 class.[46] Still, Loudoun would be the last county in Virginia to fully integrate.

The resistance to integration continued despite the courts' decisions, and as late as 1965 fewer than 12,000 of the approximately 235,000 Black students in Virginia went to desegregated schools."[47] The May 1968 Supreme Court decision in *Charles C. Green et al. v. County School Board of New Kent County, Virginia, et al.* ended these so-called freedom of choice plans and shifted the burden of integration from Black students directly onto school boards. The decision marked the beginning of full school integration. The political landscape was also changing. Linwood Holton Jr., who won election in 1969 as the first Republican governor of Virginia in the twentieth century, was opposed to segregation. In September 1970 he escorted his own daughter, Anne Holton, to a mostly Black Richmond public school. Later she would become first lady of Virginia as the wife of Democratic governor, now US senator, Tim Kaine.

By the 1968–69 academic year, with the help of the 1963 and 1968 court rulings, the 1964 Civil Rights Act, and other decisions by the US Office of Education and Department of Justice, the so-called dual system of schools ended. The Virginia State Advisory Committee to the United States Commission on Civil Rights had been blunt in its assessment of the commonwealth's mockery of the rights of its Black citizens. A frequent model for desegregation occurred in Albemarle County and in Charlottesville when the school boards closed Black high schools and assigned students to a formerly white high school. This is what happened in Loudoun. Douglass High School closed in 1968, with students going to the Loudoun County High School in Leesburg and Loudoun Valley High School in Purcellville. The building continued to serve in other educational capacities, including as a middle school, a special education and alternative school serving special needs students, and a community center, eventually evolving into a monument to civil rights.[48]

Conclusion

Throughout this book, the EWP team has attempted to authentically relate the Black education experience in Loudoun County, Virginia, from the end of the Civil War through the end of segregation in 1968, placing it into the larger Virginia and national story. Much of the narrative comes from numerous original documents from the period that share the exploits of normal people, mostly forgotten to history, who moved a community forward through the strength of their will and with incredible courage and grace. There are politicians, teachers, blacksmiths, parents, and students who all played important roles. It is a truly American

Ethel Ray Smith
Photo by Larry Roeder

story, filled with accomplishments as well as the horrors of the Black Codes, the KKK, Jim Crow, lynchings, and massacres.

Several themes recur throughout the collection of documents and across much of America during that period. The researchers and volunteers of the Edwin Washington Project were struck by the courage, sacrifice, and persistence of Loudoun's Blacks all the way back to enslavement and then Reconstruction. In the face of challenges, their focus on the value of education and their understanding of the power of organizing for action is inspiring. When the team discovered Ethel Smith's letter to the school superintendent asking for coal or wood to take care of her young students in the middle of a cold winter, everyone was hooked, especially after interviewing Mrs. Smith. The courage of that young Black teacher to argue eloquently and powerfully for her kids called to us across the years, and the team immediately felt connected. They wanted to tell her story, and—like Edwin Washington—she inspired all the subsequent work. Superintendent Edgar Hatrick asked that accounts in this book not only tell the truth about the past but also be relevant to any struggling minority today. That is what history can do—tell the stories and remind today's audience and tomorrow's that anyone can be strong, even if they are afraid, if they have purpose. When we learned more stories, including those of John Wanzer, Edythe Harris, Charles Houston, Edwin Brown, and so many others, a clear pattern emerged from the teenager Edwin Washington onward of a courageous and persistent community of people who were willing to sacrifice and organize to give their children an opportunity for a better life.

The EWP team has been honored to tell these stories and has felt a special obligation to share the uncomfortable and painful details not only because that was the mandate but because the stories are real and they are America. But they cannot stand alone. Prejudice is often based on ignorance and creates the fear of which Robert Penn Warren spoke. Unfortunately, the consequences of ignorance or unwillingness to seek truth can create a climate of violence with reverberations of a dark past, cultural ignorance, and hate that harm today's society. Dialogue is needed—a willingness to ask all sides what they fear and what they want before making assumptions. For example, rather than vilifying the Black Lives Matter movement or any civil rights movement like those supporting Muslims or the LGBTQ community, it would be better to have an honest dialogue and look for common values.

Edwin Washington, John Walker, Edythe Harris, Ethel Smith, and others may have had doubts. John Walker, for example, and his fellow Black educators managed a peaceful march through Leesburg even as Blacks were violently dying elsewhere in America. However, they overcame those fears and self-doubts and contributed to society in a positive way. Their actions echo through history to inspire a new generation of ordinary citizens to take a stand and contribute. We must have the courage to do the hard work that remains. Today Loudoun County is led by the first Black chair of the board of supervisors, Phyllis Randall, in the history of Virginia. At the same time, the KKK is leaving hate literature on driveways, and some citizens are upset because the school board, unlike during the days of segregation, is fostering racial, religious, and cultural understanding, as suggested by Justinian in the introduction, giving everyone their fair due. That is part of the social compact of any civilized society.

Notes

1. Henry Adams, *John Randolph*, American Statesmen, (Cambridge: Riverside Press, 1916).

2. EWP: 6.6 Yr. 1918–1931 Airmont W Grade 1–7.

3. EWP: 2.5.B Yr. 1931, September, Airmont Opposition to Colored Using School Room.

4. Hannah Natanson, "A Lost History, Recovered: Faded Records Tell the Story of School Segregation in Virginia," *Washington Post*, February 20, 2020, p. 1. See also EWP: 2.5A Yr. 1956 Ashburn Coal Request.

5. See the section on sanitation in chapter 4.

6. EWP: 2.5.A Yr. 1951, May, Toilets, and the NAACP.

7. EWP: 2.5.A Yr. 1951 NAACP on Toilets.

8. Charles Hamilton Houston, "NAACP Changes Course. Now All Suits Attack Segregation as Illegal," *Richmond Afro-American*, March 22, 1947, p. 4.

9. "Interposition Forces Likely to Act Swiftly," *Richmond Times-Dispatch*, January 10, 1956.

10. Marlyn Aycock, "New Court Curb Plan Outlined," *Richmond Times-Dispatch*, January 25, 1960, pp. 1 and 4.

11. EWP: 6.3.3 Yr. 1939/40 Term Report for Lincoln Colored.

12. *Cooper v. Aaron*, 358 US 1 (1958) PP, 358 US 16–17.

13. United States Commission on Civil Rights, *1961 United States Commission on Civil Rights Report*. Washington, DC: Government Printing Office, 1961), 66.

14. The Lost Cause is a false historical narrative stating that the Confederate cause was just and heroic, that slavery was moral, and that the enslaved were happy.

15. EWP 1.4.2 Yr 1955 11-11 Gray Commission Report, "Public Education Report of the Commission to the Governor of Virginia, Senate Document No. 1: Commonwealth of Virginia" (Richmond: Division of Purchase and Printing, 1955).

16. *Journal of the Constitutional Convention of the Commonwealth of Virginia to Revise and Amend Sec. 141 of the Constitution of Virginia* (Richmond: Commonwealth of Virginia Division of Purchase, 1956), preface.

17. Editorial, the *Loudoun Times-Mirror*, January 5, 1956.

18. Frank Raflo, *Within the Iron Gates: A Collection of Stories about Loudoun as Remembered after Reading the Loudoun Times-Mirror for the Years 1925–1975* (Leesburg, VA: Loudoun Times-Mirror, 1988), 381.

19. Raflo, 381.

20. EWP: 1.4.3 Yr. 1955 "Phillips Favors Gray Commission," *Blue Ridge Herald*, November 24, 1955.

21. "Voters Approve Convention by 2 to 1 in Heavy Balloting," *Richmond Times-Dispatch*, January 10, 1956, pp. 1 and 6.

22. EWP: 1.4.3 Yr. 1955, December 29, Baptist Pastors Oppose Amendment.

23. EWP: 1.4.4 Yr. 1956, December 29, Power of Placement Now in Pupil Placement Board, telegram to Oscar Emerick, Under provisions of Chapter 70, Acts of Assembly, Extra Session of 1956, effective December 29, 1956. See also EWP: 1.4.4 Yr. 1963 5-2 Legal Challenge to Loudoun Pupil Placement Board.

24. "Voters Approve Convention by 2 to 1 in Heavy Balloting."

25. Loudoun Hospital Archives, M-107 Box 1, Folder 1, pp. 72 and 76, Balch Library.

26. United States Commission on Civil Rights, *Civil Rights U.S.A.: Public Schools, Southern States* (Washington, DC: Government Printing Office, 1962), 167; and Va. Code (Supp. 1962), sec 22-275.4.

27. Signed with initials. Grammar errors kept. EWP: 1.4.4 Yr. Unk Letter from Friends of the White Race to Emerick. *Samuel Eugene Corbin v. County School Board of Loudoun County et. al*, Defendants. Civ. A. No. 2737. United States District Court, E.D. Virginia, May 16, 1963, Order August 29, 1967.

28. EWP: 3.1.3 Personal Files of Oscar Emerick on High Schools.

29. "County School Chief Blasts Loudoun Board," *Times-Herald* (Washington, DC), August 9, 1953, p. 15.

30. On the unfairness of the dual system, see EWP: 1.1.1 Yr. 1944 Emerick on Resource Equality.

31. EWP: 1.4.4 Yr. Notes on Gray Commission, Supreme Court and Amendment.

32. EWP: 1.4.3 Yr. 1955, December 19, Emerick on Segregation.

33. EWP: 1.4.3 Yr. 1955, December 13, State Board of Education on Constitutional Convention; and EWP: 1.4.3 Yr. 1955, December 14, State Superintendent's Advisory Committee.

34. EWP: 1.4.3 Yr. 1955, December 22, Former PTA President Sees Amendment as Futile.

35. EWP: 1.4.3 Yr. 1956, January 1, Emerick to Senator Byrd Supports Amendment.

36. EWP: 1.4.1 Yr. 1956, September 4, Emerick Denies Authority of Supreme Court.

37. "Powhatan Negroes File US Appeal," *Richmond Times-Dispatch*, August 18, 1962, p. 4.

38. "Loudoun County Acts to Prevent Integrated Schools," in *The Progress-Index*, Petersburg, Virginia, August 7, 1956, p. 9. Records of the local branch of this body are held in the archives of the Balch Library, Leesburg, Virginia. See also Eugene Scheel, "Timeline of Important Events in African American History in Loudoun County, Virginia," *History of Loudoun County Virginia*, accessed May 20, 2021, https://www.loudounhistory.org/history/african-american-chronology/.

39. Debate between James Baldwin and William F. Buckley Jr., Cambridge University, February 18, 1965, available on YouTube, https://www.youtube.com/watch?v=oFeoS41xe7w.

40. The Edwin Washington Project is developing a series of films on transportation to compare and contrast white and Black transport opportunities and to extol the virtues of the drivers, who were sometimes students.

41. Black Petitions are found in the Edwin Washington Project in EWP 2.5.A. White Petitions are found in the Edwin Washington Project in EWP 2.5.B.

42. EWP: 2.5.A Yr. 1951 CWL on Douglass HS Repairs.

43. EWP: 9.4 Yr. 1956, January 23, Segregationist Construction Strategy.

44. EWP: 1.4.4 Yr. 1956, January 28, County-Wide League Rejects Segregation Decision.

45. Gregory H. Swanson Award, University of Virginia School of Law, accessed June 30, 2021, www.law.virginia.edu/students/gregory-h-swanson-award.

46. Eugene Scheel, opinion column, by Eugene Scheel, the *Washington Post*, May 21, 2000, https://www.washingtonpost.com/archive/local/2000/05/21/eugene-scheel/f72cadff-f4cd-4246-816b-3176c0f13a50/. Scheel is perhaps Loudoun County's most famous historian and cartographer.

47. "*Brown* and Massive Resistance," in *Encyclopedia Virginia*, accessed May 16, 2021, https://encyclopediavirginia.org/.

48. Teckla Cox and Richard Calderon, August 30, 1991, "National Register of Historic Places Registration Form: Douglass High School," VLR (Virginia Landmarks Register) Listing Date 10/09/1991, NRHP (National Register of Historic Places) Listing Date 9/24/1992, NRHP Reference Number 92001274, https://www.dhr.virginia.gov/VLR_to_transfer/PDFNoms/253-0070_Douglass_High_School_1992_Final_Nomination.pdf.

EPILOGUE

The struggle for equality and an end to prejudice in Loudoun and elsewhere in Virginia did not conclude with the demise of segregation. The struggles continue. Nevertheless, many positive things have happened that offer hope. This epilogue is designed to study and comment on a few of those positive things, keeping in mind prejudice is still an evil that permeates society.

Student Protests in 1963, by Gert Evans

Gert Evans is the docent of the Edwin Washington Project and is one of its most prolific volunteers. She is also the historian for the Loudoun Douglass High School Alumni Association, a member of the Black History Committee of the Friends of the Balch Library, and one of Loudoun County's most respected artists.

During the summer of 1963 I participated with my brother and other teens from Leesburg and Purcellville, Virginia, in protest marches. There were probably ten or more who joined in on the marches. My brother had tried to sit downstairs at the Tally-Ho Theater instead of the segregated balcony area. The next day he was making protest signs. After persuading other teens in the neighborhood, everyone decided it was the right thing to do. We proceeded to walk the mile to the theater, although the teens became scared and turned around and went back home. My brother turned around and told me if I didn't follow him, he would never speak to me again. After hearing those words, I decided to follow him and the two of us went to the theater and protested alone. Cars slowed and people looked

Gert Evans with a rendering
of Douglass High School.
Photo by Larry Roeder

at us. I have never been more scared in my life. A half hour later a teen
that lived up the street saw us and picked up a sign and marched with us.

After that night, the teens came together to protest and after about a
week the barriers came down and we were allowed to sit downstairs. It
was the best time of my life! We were making a difference and we didn't
know what would happen. My good friend Barry and I went to the movies
for the first time and saw *West Side Story*. I was terrified and really didn't
enjoy sitting downstairs. I felt out of place. That's what segregation does;
it makes you feel out of place.

After the Tally-Ho Theater integration, the teens immediately proceeded to try to integrate the Leesburg Firemen's Swimming Pool. With
fifty cents in hand and our bathing suits [on], about eight of us went to
gain access. That day I lagged and didn't get to the counter. I couldn't swim
and, if allowed in, what was I going to do? That day we immediately began our protests near the entrance of the swimming pool for a couple of
weeks. When the carnival came to town, the firemen's largest fundraiser,

Blacks were asked to boycott the carnival. The teens protested during the day and were allowed to have backyard parties during the evenings. Picketing (protesting) in the day and partying at night! The NAACP was working behind the scenes at this time and supported our efforts. Our protest efforts failed, but in 1965 teens were again refused entry to the pool, so a federal lawsuit was filed by the teens and their parents. The firemen were ordered to allow Blacks to swim, but instead they decided to close the pool to everyone. In 1968 the pool and land were sold, and the pool was filled in with dirt and garbage by my uncle's refuse company.

That fall, most of my friends had transferred to either Loudoun County High or Loudoun Valley in Purcellville. My brother and some of the others enrolled at Loudoun County with Helen Ramey, the first Black female student, who attended the previous year. I decided to stay at the all-black Douglass High School in Leesburg.

My Story, by Louis Jett

Louis Jett is one of the founding members of the Black History Committee of the Friends of the Balch Library, a former secretary of that body, a respected historian on local matters, and a frequent speaker at Edwin Washington events and at the Carver Center, the former Carver Colored School. Louis was also immensely helpful supporting the Conklin study, an examination of the former village of Conklin and its segregated school, which led to the Edwin Washington Project. Louis has also been a guide on Black history bus tours.

For over twenty years Douglass had been the only high school in Loudoun County that Blacks could attend. At times there were as many as four county high schools for whites while there was only Douglass for Blacks. By the time I started at Douglass, Loudoun Valley High School (LVHS) had already started to integrate. I became close friends with a young lady while attending Douglass. She wanted to transfer to LVHS. It was closer to her home in Purcellville and would only require taking one bus. There were ten to fifteen Blacks attending LVHS at that time. She asked if I would transfer with her. It made sense to me, attending a school closer to my home. "Why not?" I thought; plus, I was a little sweet on this young lady. I

Louis Jett as a
tour guide.
*Photo by
Larry Roeder*

agreed to transfer with her, but there was a process. Your academic record had to be good enough to qualify for a transfer to a white school. I was still maintaining a B/B+ average at Douglass. You would also have to petition the state to transfer to LVHS. I sent my petition to transfer along with my transcript (which I'd gotten from Leesburg) to the state capital in Richmond. The approval came by mail. I would soon start attending LVHS.

In 1965 I began ninth grade at LVHS, and the environment was a bit of a shock. I regretted my choice after the first day. There was very much de facto segregation in Virginia at the time. I'd never been in such close proximity to so many white people before. Most of them had never had a Black person in school with them. We were certainly the minority at the school. I would be the only Black student in some of my classes. While my white teachers remained pretty much neutral, overall the white students were unwelcoming. They would roll their eyes and mutter things under their breaths. I heard the word "nigger" whispered in class on many occasions. There were one or two Black teachers at LVHS while I was there, but that did little to ease my anxiety. Though physical violence was rare, on the whole it was a hostile environment. My grades began to suffer.

VARSITY WRESTLING TEAM: Kneeling: [John] Cream-
er, David Lee, Kenneth Mawyer, Mike Bradshaw, Gran
Goodnow, Brian Luppi, John Tipton, Paul Chinn, Walter
Bell, David Norris, Whit Goodnow, Jimmy Campbell.

Standing: Louis Jett, Robert Rector, Hugh Grubb, Fred
Price, Mark Page, Mark Brownell, David Culbert, Ed
Nix, Stanley Newman, John Janney, Bobby Mansfield,
John Norris.

Loudoun Valley High School 1969 Wresting Team, featuring Louis Jett.
Personal collection of Louis Jett

Though still enthusiastic about sports, I decided not to try out for football, basketball, or baseball. All the team coaches were white and there
were only a few Black students on those teams. The white players were
not above using the word "nigger" at practice or during games. I wouldn't
have lasted a week before being thrown off a team for fighting. I also didn't
feel those coaches, while not outright racist, were very welcoming. On the
other hand, the wrestling team was one-third Black. Unlike the coaches
for the other sports, the wrestling coach [Evan Moler] was welcoming and
encouraging. Mr. Moler was also my biology teacher. In wrestling practices and meets, Black and white boys might have to wrestle against one
another. Though some whites refused to wrestle Blacks and left the team,
those that did stay on the team had no problem getting on the mat with a
Black wrestler. Wrestling became my only extracurricular activity while
I was at LVHS.

Norman and Betty Camp's Story

One of the project's best friends before he passed away in 2018 was Norman Cleszester Camp III, PhD. He was head of the chemistry department at Douglass High School and taught science, chemistry, biology,

Norman Camp
EWP: 4.5 Colored Teacher Cards;
photographer unknown

and math between 1956 and 1961, alongside his wonderful wife, Betty Stancil Camp, who instructed in English, history, civics, and physical education between 1956 and 1960.[1] Norman left Douglass to work on a grant through the National Science Foundation. Later he was also dean of arts and sciences at Denmark Technical College in South Carolina.[2] For both Betty and Norman, Douglass was their first job. While in Loudoun, they lived in an apartment at Round Hill.

As Emerick's study from 1927 showed, Blacks had the rules stacked against them, resulting in low salaries and benefits.[3] This made their accomplishments even more remarkable. When Camp left Loudoun to help America succeed in space, he and his family drove west to his new assignment at Arizona State, frequently being refused entry into hotels because of their race, despite bring in the middle of a bitter winter, and despite his wife being pregnant. In other words, and lest it be forgotten, prejudice was not just in the schools. It was everywhere. According to Norman, they were only allowed to stay in a motel in St. Louis, Missouri, after the manager agreed because he was allowing Hispanics to stay, so a "colored person could as well."

Betty Camp
EWP: 4.5 Colored Teacher Cards;
photographer unknown

The Idea of the County-Wide Leagues of Black PTAs

Loudoun's County-Wide League, active from 1938 until at least 1958, focused on (a) moving students out of the Loudoun County Training Center, which was considered a death trap by some; (b) gaining an accredited high school building for Blacks, eventually Douglass High School; (c) moving children out of the dilapidated Grant School in Middleburg, also considered a death trap; (d) expanding Douglass High School, due to overcrowding; and (e) rejecting an effort by the Loudoun County Board of Supervisors and the school board to impose permanent segregation in return for providing improved buildings. The league also spawned great future leaders, like John Tolbert, who was a chef and bus driver and later a councilman on the Leesburg Town Council. Tolbert worked extremely hard to achieve an accredited Black high school (Douglass) on the Gibbons property on Route 7 at the eastern edge of Leesburg. Interestingly, Tolbert felt that Emerick was mostly on the side of the Black community, but as Tolbert told the editor of the , when Emerick went to the school board, "Their answers were always the same. 'We hear you, but we can't do anything now; we just haven't got the money.'"[4]

It is worth noting that the league was but one of a number around Virginia inspired by the NOS and Jeanes teachers to stimulate Black grassroots activity. The Edwin Washington Project found no one in Loudoun who was aware that such bodies existed elsewhere, and people in other counties with a County-Wide League that the team contacted were similarly unaware of the companion organizations. Because this is an important, nearly forgotten aspect of Black history, the team plans to study the others.

A good example of such leagues still exists as the County-Wide League of Botetourt County, three hours to the south of Loudoun and near Roanoke. Like the Loudoun league, it was formed in the late 1930s with a history like Loudoun's, making it not only a good candidate for comparison but also a way of understanding the core mission of such bodies. In Botetourt, Blacks went to one-room schools in each village, even to churches, as in Loudoun. The league then argued for better quarters, and eventually the one-roomers were consolidated into an old garage called Academy Hill in Fincastle.[5] It had no indoor plumbing, the playground was gravel, and although a cafeteria did exist, it did not always have enough food. A better structure was needed, so in 1959 Central Academy was built on land owned by a Black man named Mr. Fairfax. Black children were sent there for all grades up to twelfth.

The Botetourt-based league continued to play a major role in local education into the 1960s, purchasing curtains, supplies for the gymnasium, and books. In one memorable incident, the cafeteria ran out of food, which meant that to feed the children the cafeteria workers took funds out of their own pockets. Responding to the emergency, the Botetourt County-Wide League raised funds to keep the cafeteria operating. The league disbanded in 1966 with integration, and the school was renamed by the white school board as the Botetourt Intermediate School, which operated from 1966 to 1996. Then the county decided that two intermediate schools should feed the high school and renamed the intermediate school William Clark after the famous white explorer. That led to new political action by the Black community, which reassembled their County-Wide League and lobbied for five years, until 2001, when the school was again renamed Central Academy. But the new league did not stop operating. They continue to this day to raise money to support local students regardless of race.[6]

2020: An Apology

The use of apologies is now an accepted form of political reconciliation around the world, a way for politicians and systems to atone for past conflicts. Of course, an apology is often not enough by itself. Concrete actions are also required, but apologies are especially important as a first step.

In 2020 the Loudoun County Public Schools (the system and the school board) apologized for the segregated past and were joined unanimously by the Loudoun County Board of Supervisors. More should be done to build bridges between white and nonwhite populations and people of all cultures and religions; however, the Edwin Washington Society is proud to have been part of this effort, joining the Minority Student Achievement Advisory Committee, the Loudoun Douglass High School Alumni Association, the Black History Committee—Friends of Thomas Balch Library, the Loudoun Branch of the NAACP, the Loudoun Freedom Center, and the Loudoun Diversity Council.

STATEMENT OF APOLOGY

September 25, 2020

To the Black Community of Loudoun County:

We, the Loudoun County School Board, the Administration of Loudoun County Public Schools, and the Loudoun County Board of Supervisors sincerely apologize for the operation of segregated schools in Loudoun County and for the negative impact, damage and disadvantages to Black students and families that were caused by decisions made by the Loudoun County School Board, LCPS Administration, and the Loudoun County Board of Supervisors. More specifically, the additional effort required, and resources provided by the Black community to obtain an equal education created hardships to which other community members were not subjected. Black people were denied rights and equal treatment.

The following timeline provides context for a long-overdue apology to the Black community of Loudoun County:

1954: The US Supreme Court declared via *Brown v. Board of Education* that segregation in public schools is unconstitutional and that public schools should integrate "with all deliberate speed."

1956: As documented in the minutes of meetings of the Loudoun County Board of Supervisors, the Board of Supervisors voted on January 3 to support the proposed amendment to Section 141 of the Virginia State Constitution which ultimately allowed the use of public funds to be used for nonsectarian schools. This would have the effect of providing funding for white students to attend private schools and avoid attending integrated public schools.

On January 23, 1956, the Board of Supervisors and Loudoun County School Board met jointly and discussed, among other topics, additions to both Douglass Elementary School and Douglass High School. The two Boards felt that no steps should be taken in construction of these additions unless reasonable assurance was given by the parents of Black children of the County that they would conform to the opinion that their education could be promoted better by their continued school attendance on a segregated basis.

On August 6, 1956, the Board of Supervisors passed a resolution to stop funding public schools if the federal government forced integration. *The Board of Supervisors later rescinded this action on August 6, 1962.*

On September 4, 1956, the Board of Supervisors unanimously voted to request that Virginia Delegate Phillips and Virginia Senator Button support the Governor's plan that was designed to ensure racial segregation, including giving the Governor the power to close any schools facing a federal desegregation order.

1963: A US federal court ordered Loudoun County to comply with *Brown v. Board of Education* and to approve all applications from Black children to attend formerly all-white schools.

1967: A US federal court ordered Loudoun County to establish geographic attendance zones regardless of race to fully integrate all schools by the 1968–69 school year.

In addition to the blatant disregard and disrespect of Black people and their education during the era of segregation, such as inequitable school calendars, teacher salaries, facilities, transportation, as well as instructional materials, supplies and equipment, there are many examples and instances in which systemic racism, inequitable treatment, and disproportionality began and have persisted since. For example:

- The County-Wide League consisted of members of the Black community that worked hard to coordinate efforts, raise money then purchase land for $4,000 in 1939 for a high school, the Douglass School. The fact that the Black community had to not only sell the land to the School Board for $1 in 1940, but also had to again raise money to provide furniture and books because the School Board would not, was inexcusable. These actions taken by the School Board were symbolic of a lack of respect for the Black community's effort and its needs.
- There was significant resistance by the School Board and Superintendent to integrate our schools during the era of Massive Resistance and several other inequities persisted as a result, such as:
  - inequities in teacher salaries, recruitment, on-going professional learning, as well as administrative leadership development for principals and staff.
  - inequities in recruitment for college and advanced placement preparation for students.
  - a lack of diversity among applied and admitted students to the Academies of Loudoun.
  - disproportionate discipline of Black students.
  - school names and a school mascot named after or potentially named after Confederate figures and plantations.
  - the facilitation of lessons and activities that do not reflect cultural responsiveness and instead reinforce subservient gender and racial roles.
  - failure to teach students about the Black Post–Civil War communities that existed into the mid-century.

LCPS is appreciative of the organizations listed below who are deeply committed to the well-being, equity, and advancement of Black people in Loudoun County and who contributed to this letter by providing

LCPS feedback on specific topics that could not go unaddressed. Thank you to the Minority Student Achievement Advisory Committee, the Loudoun Douglass High School Alumni Association, the Black History Committee—Friends of Thomas Balch Library, and the Edwin Washington Project for your insight and contribution. We thank the aforementioned organizations and the Loudoun Branch of the NAACP, the Loudoun Freedom Center, Loudoun Diversity Council, Excellent Options, and other organizations whose continued advocacy has led to this apology and an intentional focus on racial equity in LCPS.

As one organization shared, LCPS must continually assess the status of racial equity in the school system and correct its past transgressions as it pertains to race. Although we recognize that we have yet to fully correct or eradicate matters of racial inequality, we hope that issuing this apology with genuine remorse is a valuable step followed by additional actions, including demonstrable policy changes as outlined in both the Comprehensive Equity Plan and the Action Plan to Combat Systemic Racism. We must pursue a bold, yet methodical, path of continuous improvement driven by a strong sense of urgency.

Last Thoughts

The mass murder by a white youth in May 2022 of ten Black people in Buffalo, New York, provides a chilling and appropriate backdrop for a final thought in *Dirt Don't Burn*. The book's examination of centuries of white subjugation of minorities should make it easy to see a direct line of dots between enslavement in the colonial period, the deportation of some Blacks to Africa up to the end of the Civil War, and the treatment of Blacks during Reconstruction as well as the denial of civil rights during segregation. In fact, segregation itself was a purposeful subjugation of an entire race. Some practices essentially treated Blacks as less than human. Some of this was based on fear, a false impression that there was some conspiracy to "replace whites" with minorities, Jews, Blacks, or something else. This fear is a natural offspring of ignorance—an ignorance that can only be cured through fact-based, balanced education. It is also essential not to react to hate with more hate or violence but instead with empathy and education. This last point is a great lesson we have all learned from the Black community of Loudoun County.

Fortunately, and repeatedly, ordinary Black citizens in Loudoun County and elsewhere in the nation have pushed back. That is why we honor heroes such as Edwin Washington, John C. Walker, Edythe Harris, and Ethel Smith for their courageous efforts in education. We continue to see echoes of their courage today in organizations such as the Black History Committee of the Friends of the Balch Library, the Douglass Commemorative Committee, and the Loudoun Chapter of the NAACP.

Purposeful subjugation restricts the normal evolution of minorities, creating an intentional societal imbalance that has tarnished America's own development as a beacon of hope to a troubled world. To deny that the system has unfairly placed generations after generations of Blacks and other minorities at an economic and political disadvantage to whites is simply a denial of the facts. Similarly, the tearing down of overt symbols of subjugation is not about erasing history, as some political leaders have said. It is about restoring truth to the national story. Some statues should remain as educational exhibits about troubled times, with explanatory signs. Just as clearly, many in the public space must be removed.

Although the terrible periods of slavery and Jim Crow described in this book are thankfully in the past, the echoes of those periods of subjugation remain. Even today we see reminders of the continuing racism in individual acts and in policies that perpetuate inequity. The most visible acts of hatred, such as the killing of George Floyd in Minneapolis in 2020 or the slaughter in Buffalo in 2022, serve as horrible reminders of the need to continue to battle against hate.

Recent criticisms by certain elected officials of how race history is taught in schools is also troubling, sometimes described as inappropriately making children feel uncomfortable or guilty about their family's or community's past. Teaching history is never about assigning blame to the children of today. Instead, it exposes certain truths that must be studied and understood if we are to deter future hate speech, racial violence, and other acts that seek to subjugate any race, religion, or "minority." The title of the book comes from an incident when neither coal nor wood was provided to heat a classroom in winter. Education, even about a painful past, is the fuel that will heat the minds of children, helping them avoid the dark, cold domain of hate.

Notes

1. EWP: 4.5 Colored Teacher Cards.

2. Dr. Camp and Larry Roeder became friends toward the end of the educator's life. Betty and the EWP team are still in contact. Betty was also helpful with this section of the epilogue. As a result, one of the rooms in the revamped Douglass High School building is now named after both of the Camps.

3. See chapter 5; and EWP: 3.1 Yr. 1927 Emerick Study on school conditions.

4. Frank Raflo, *Within the Iron Gates: A Collection of Stories about Loudoun as Remembered after Reading the Loudoun Times-Mirror for the Years 1925–1975* (Leesburg, VA: Loudoun Times-Mirror, 1988), 348.

5. Curtis Brown, president of the Botetourt County-Wide League, interview by Larry Roeder, July 17, 2021. The interview included a visit to the old structure, which is now a residential building but still has retained its original car garage architecture.

6. Curtis Brown, president of the Botetourt County-Wide League, interview by Larry Roeder, March 1, 2020. Brown attended Central Academy from 1959 to 1966. The league can be found at www.facebook.com/countywideleague/.

ACKNOWLEDGMENTS

The book is the work product of the Edwin Washington Project, the flagship of a 501(c)(3) known as the Edwin Washington Society, formerly Diversity Fairs of Virginia. The unstinting devotion of more than thirty volunteers and donors made a very difficult project possible. However, we must also acknowledge that our research could not have happened without the assistance of the faculty and staff of Loudoun County Public Schools, especially Superintendents Dr. Edgar B. Hatrick III and Dr. Eric Williams as well as senior staff officers Wayde Byard and Donna Kroiz. They expressed a deep desire to bring out the truth about the past and allowed us to study thousands of nearly lost historical records dating back to Reconstruction. Mr. Hatrick inspired us to also place what the local Black community achieved into the larger context of the commonwealth, the nation, and the world.

In 2019 the Project was recognized by Loudoun Cares as the best volunteer organization in the county. In addition, we must acknowledge the Virginia Senate and House of Delegates, which in 2016 jointly lauded preserving this history, thanks to lobbying by Virginia senator, then delegate John Bell. Many other government officials have also been very helpful, especially Leesburg mayor Kelly Burk and Leesburg town councilmember Neil Steinberg (also project photographer), as well as State Delegate David Reid, State Senator Jennifer Barton Boysko, school board member Jeff Morse, and the entire Loudoun County School Board.

In addition, we wish to thank Stephen Price and Christopher Brown, both eminent attorneys, for their review of our legal opinions; the members of the Dean, Emerick and Schumate families and the Country School Association of America; the editors of the *Bulletin of Loudoun County History*, which is the oldest history journal in the county; the members of the Black History Committee of the Friends of the Balch Library; the Douglass High School Commemorative Committee; the Loudoun County Branch of the NAACP; and the Loudoun County Genealogy Group on Facebook as well as the faculty and staff of Atlanta University, the Balch Library, the Archives of the Circuit Court of Loudoun County, George C. Marshall International Center, George Mason University, Hampton University, Howard University, the Josephine School Museum, Laurel Grove School, Loudoun School for the Gifted, Lovettsville Historical Society & Museum, Swarthmore University, Virginia Military Institute, Virginia State University, the members of the Loudoun County Preservation and Conservation Coalition, and, finally, the Prosperity Baptist Church, which is where the research began. The pastor of that church, Carlos Lawson, is also a director of our society and the society pastor. And while a book is the product of authors and researchers, too often we forget the value of professional editing. We thank Patricia Bower of Diligent Editorial for her excellent editing.

Since 2014 one local historian and mapmaker has been of consistent help, himself having researched the county's history for decades. Eugene Scheel inspires others to excellence and has been recognized by President Bill Clinton, the government of Loudoun County and the town of Leesburg for his scholarly work as well as by the Virginia Historical Society. Scheel is the author of nine books on Virginia history and over fifty historical maps. He also provides Loudoun County school instructors "history in the field courses."

We are also especially grateful to the citizens and organizations of Loudoun, many of whom granted us interviews about their experiences and those of their ancestors, both white and Black. This book is their story. We want to recognize the following individuals who conducted research, provided insights and artifacts, and performed volunteer services critical to the writing of the book. Our hope is that we have forgotten no one because our success is their success, the common effort of many people acting as a team in order to reveal truth and its relevance to today's world.

Lisa Prosser Aktug, contributor
Anthony Arciero, Board of Directors and director of EWP

Kelly Arford-Horne, archaeologist

Guthrie Ashton, contributor

Nathan Bailey, Society secretary and transportation historian

Belinda Blue, contributor

Donna Bohanon, chair of the Black History Committee, Balch Library

Emily Branch, statistical analysis

Christopher Brown, civil rights and constitutional law

Gladys Burke, advertising

Katie Bushman, statistical analysis

Norman and Betty Camp, contributors on Douglass High School

Robert B. Carter, contributor on Oscar Emerick

Myron Curtis, adviser on student volunteers

Alvin Dodson, contributor on Douglass High School

Patricia, Esther, and Nellie Dean, experts on evangelist Jennie Dean
    and Conklin Village

Nancy Emerick, contributor on Oscar Emerick

Gertrude Evans, project docent, senior transcriber, liaison to the
    Loudoun Douglass High School Alumni Association

Julie Goforth, Board of Directors, web design, and digital preservation

Maddy Gold, chief cartographer

Kerri Gonzalez, expert on Foxcroft School

Laura Di Biasi, Hannah Heidelmeyer, Raoul Oprisch, and Niklas
    Ritter, German exchange students

Delores Grigsby, petitions research

Leah Smith, Peyton Moriarty, Kamran Fareedi, Liam Moriarty, and
    Shailee Sran, Loudoun County School for the Gifted

Sofi Conway, Katie Knipmeyer, Loudoun County School for the
    Gifted on Teachers' salaries and the Ashburn Colored School

Kent Hardcastle, expert on management

Delores Nash-Hicks, expert on Rustburg

Randy Ihara, Board of Directors and expert on labor rights

Louis Jett, local historian and expert on Carver school

Lori Hinterleiter Kimball, local historian

Mallika Lakshmminarayan, statistical analysis

Carlos Lawson, Board of Directors, society pastor, expert on Conklin
    Village

Ryan MacMichael, contributor

Doug Miller, Board of Directors, alumni

David Prebich, expert on petitions and property research

Stephen Price, constitutional and contract law

Virginia Pierce, Amanda West, Freddie West, Joy West, Joe Jackson, Prosperity Baptist Church volunteers

Mary Randolph, contributor

Kathy Reid, contributor and researcher on religion

Jim Roberts, expert on the Training Center in Leesburg

Claude and Wynne Saffer, local historians

Hari Sharma, Board of Directors and treasurer

Eugene Scheel, cartographer and historian

Barbara Evans Scott, contributor

Sherri Jones Simmons, Board of Directors alumni, expert on Douglass High School building

Ethel Smith, Loudoun teacher, contributor, and inspiration for the title of this book

Matthew Smith, LCPS expert on geospatial analysis and cartography

Edward Spannaus, Lovettsville Historical Society

Luvinia Bowles Taylor, contributor

Phyllis Cook-Taylor, contributor

Mary Carey (née Timbers), contributor

Phyllis Walker Ford, Laurel Grove School, Fairfax

Dorothy Washington, contributor

INDEX

Note: Information in figures and tables is indicated by page numbers in italics. Entries for Virginia schools are followed by (B) or (W) to indicate if the school served Black or white students, respectively.

Memorial to the Unknown, 41. *See also* Grant Colored School (B)

Middleburg Community Center, 218

Middleburg High School (W), *102t*, 138n23, 222

Middleburg PTA (B), 163

Middleburg School (B), 68. *See also* Grant Colored School (B)

middle-class jobs, 61, 105

Middleton, John, 121

Mills v. Board of Education of Anne Arundel County, 168

Milltown School (W), *102t*

Mitchell, Arthur, 177

Mobberly, John, 61

Moler, Evan, 237

Monroe, James, 30, 33

Moody, P.M., 41

Moton, Robert Russa, 81, 82, 85–6

Mountain Gap Colored School (B), 99, 136, 150, 154, 182, 207

Mountain Gap White School (W), 68

Mount Hope School (W), 132

Mount Pleasant Colored School (B), 163

Mount Zion Methodist Church, 117

Mt. Gilead District School Board, 184

Mt. Hermon High School (B), 89

Murray, Bushrod, 126, 128, 182

NAACP (National Association for the Advancement of Colored People): and County-Wide League, 173, 175, 178, 183; Houston and, 170, 183–84, 187–9; in Loudoun, 3, 136, 143–44, 167, 181, 207, 224, 241, 244–45; Massive Resistance, 205, 209, 225, 235; teachers' salaries, 123, 167–9

National Science Foundation, 238

Negro Extension Service, 126

Negro Health Week, 13, 98

Negro Organization Society (NOS): Alexander and, 172–3; County-Wide League and, 174–5, 240; established, 85–6; health & sanitation, 8, 13–14, 16, 96, 99–100, 207; schools, 112, 123, 143

Niagara Movement, 1

nine-month academic year, 167, 170

Nokes (B), 99

Noland, Charlotte, 174

nonsectarian schools, 242

normal schools: 9, 43, 62, 73, 132, 167. *See also* Hampton Institute/University; Richmond Colored Normal School (B); Snow Hill Normal and Industrial Institute; Virginia State University

Norris, Mary B., 128

Norther Virginia Tuberculosis Association, 148

Norton, Elizabeth M., 166

NOS. *See* Negro Organization Society

Notes on the State of Virginia (Thomas Jefferson), 3, 10

Nottoway County, VA, 74

nullification, 210–11. See also *Brown v. Board of Education*

Nuremberg Trials, 7, 29

nurses: policies/West Law, 100, 128; in schools, 15, 92, 103–4, 129, 130, 149; training denied to, 96, 151, 214. *See also* health care

nutrition: Armed Forces physicals, 155; food preparation, 18; in schools, 100, 104, 129, 135, 152–4. *See also* school lunches

Oakdale Quaker School (B), *30f,* 33, 47, 68

Oat Lands School (W), *102t*

Oglesby, Ernest J., 203

ABOUT THE AUTHORS

Larry Roeder, CEO of the Edwin Washington Society and the book's principal author, has seen prejudice throughout Europe, Africa, Asia, and the Middle East as he has lived and worked around the world. The Edwin Washington Society advocates for social and racial diversity. Roeder graduated from Culver-Stockton College with honors in history, focusing on the Palestine Question, and has co-chaired a college Black history committee. He also studied at the Foreign Service Institute and acquired a master's degree in Library and Information Science from the Catholic University of America, focusing on preservation and information management. His career included army intelligence, disaster management and economic affairs at the US Department of State, foreign affairs at Springer Publishing, and the UN affairs director for a British nonprofit with the mission of protecting livestock in poor nations. In addition, Roeder conducted extensive political/cultural research and analysis in order to conduct diplomatic missions with labor union activists in Albania, Bedouin tribes in the Sinai, rebels in South Sudan, and members of the African National Congress in South Africa. He was once the chair for research on the Black History Committee of the Friends of the Balch Library in Leesburg, Loudoun County, and the chair for diversity in the local chapter of a political party. Loudoun County Public Schools asked Roeder to take on the Edwin Washington mission after he completed a similar study for the Prosperity Baptist Church, a traditionally Black chapel in Conklin Village. The superintendent, Edgar B. Hatrick III, asked Roeder to study the entire county, although he stipulated Roeder and his friends were to cover costs, and he recommended that the history of the impact of segregation on Loudoun's Black population be placed into the state, national, and international context.

Barry Harrelson, a retired intelligence officer, is an editor with the Edwin Washington Society, a nonprofit that advocates for social and racial diversity with a focus on the history of school segregation in Loudoun County, Virginia. He is also a copy editor for the *Bulletin of Loudoun County History*. A longtime resident of the Capitol Hill neighborhood of Washington, DC, Harrelson is cofounder of Sustainable Waterfronts, a nonprofit that produces films dealing with all aspects of the Washington waterfront for educational purposes. He is coproducer of a forty-minute film, *A Bridge Across History: Capitol Hill and the Washington DC Waterfront*, released in 2021. During his thirty-five years with the Central Intelligence Agency and the National Geospatial-Intelligence Agency, he was a librarian, political analyst, manager of leadership analysis branches, and an instructor for writing courses. On assignment to the CIA's Center for Studies of Intelligence, he served as lead project officer for historical review programs including the JFK assassination and Nazi war crimes records. At National Geospatial-Intelligence Agency he managed map, photo, and reference libraries. Mr. Harrelson holds a bachelor's degree in history from the University of South Carolina and a master's degree in Library and Information Science from Catholic University of America.